The Debt Boomerang

How Third World Debt Harms Us All

Susan George

Pluto Press
with the Transnational Institute (TNI)

First published 1992 by Pluto Press
345 Archway Road, London N6 5AA
22883 Quicksilver Drive,
Sterling, VA 20166–2012, USA

in association with the Transnational Institute
Paulus Potterstraat 20, 1071 DA Amsterdam

02 01 00 99
 7 6 5 4

Distributed in the Netherlands by the
Transnational Institute

British Library Cataloguing in Publication Data
George, Susan
    The debt boomerang. How third world debt harms us all.
    I. Title
    336.3

    ISBN 0 7453 0593 8 cased
    ISBN 0 7453 0594 6 paperback

Produced for the publisher by
Chase Production Services, Chadlington
Typeset in Stone by Stanford DTP Services, Northampton
Printed and bound in the EC

The Debt Boomerang is a project of the Transnational Institute, Amsterdam, undertaken in cooperation with the Institute for Policy Studies, Washington DC.

Research and documentation were supplied by Peter Andreas, Humberto Campodonico, John Cavanagh, John Denham, Cameron Duncan, Claudio Jedlicki, David Pedersen, Dan Smith, Indra Wahab and Susan George.

About the Transnational Institute (TNI)

The Transnational Institute was founded in 1973–4. Its brief is to 'address the fundamental disparities between the rich and poor peoples and nations of the world, investigate their causes and develop alternatives for their remedy'. TNI is decentralised, with headquarters in Amsterdam and Fellows living and working in many countries on several continents. TNI Fellows aspire to be 'public scholars' or 'scholar-activists', carrying out research of the highest calibre and presenting it in formats accessible and relevant to a broad audience. TNI Fellows participate in a variety of public or media events and popular movements. Because Institute Fellows do not take a purely academic approach to their subjects, TNI is not just another research institute but an important intellectual resource for people throughout the world who seek positive social and political change.

Funding for the Institute's work has come from a wide range of sources including private foundations, European public development cooperation agencies, churches, non-governmental organisations, trade unions and individual donors. TNI Directors and Fellows do not receive salaries but rather grants to encourage intellectual work they could not otherwise undertake. Larger projects often call upon scholar-associates outside the Fellowship itself. Fellows meetings – designed as festivals of ideas – bring TNI Fellows and guests together twice yearly in the Amsterdam centre, where conferences and symposia on a variety of topics are also held throughout the year.

As of mid-1991, the Director of TNI is Dan Smith (UK citizen and resident); Susan George (US citizen, French resident) and Pedro Vilanova (Spanish citizen and resident) serve as Associate Directors. The Executive Secretary, resident in Amsterdam, is Laurian Zwart.

For further information concerning the Institute's activities and programme, please contact Laurian Zwart, Executive Secretary, TNI, Paulus Potterstraat 20, 1071 DA, Amsterdam, Netherlands; tel. (31-20) 662 66 08 or fax (31-20) 675 71 76.

Contents

Abbreviations	viii
Highlights	ix
Acknowledgements	x
Introduction	xiii
The First Boomerang: The Environment	1
The Second Boomerang: Drugs	34
The Third Boomerang: How Northern Taxpayers are Bailing out the Banks	63
The Fourth Boomerang: Lost Jobs and Markets	93
The Fifth Boomerang: Immigration	110
The Sixth Boomerang: Conflict and War	136
Conclusion	168
Notes and References	175
Index	191

Abbreviations

CGCED	Caribbean Groups for Cooperation in Economic Development
COSV	Comitato de Coordinamento delle Organizzazioni per il Servicio Voluntario
DEA	Drug Enforcement Administration
HIC	Highly Indebted Country
ICERC	Interagency Exposure Review Committee
ILO	International Labour Organisation
IPCC	Intergovernmental Panel on Climatic Change
GATT	General Agreement on Tariffs and Trade
LDC	Less Developed Country
MILIC	Moderately Indebted Low-Income Country
MIMIC	Moderately Indebted Middle-Income Country
NATO	North Atlantic Treaty Organisation
NIC	Newly Industrialised Country
NIDA	National Institute of Drug Abuse (USA)
ODA	Overseas Development Aid
OECD	Organisation for Economic Cooperation and Development
OFPRA	French Office for the Protection of Refugees and Stateless Persons
OPEC	Organisation of Petroleum Exporting Countries
SILIC	Severely Indebted Low-Income Country
SIMIC	Severely Indebted Middle-Income Country
SOPEMI	OECD Permanent Observation System of Migrations
UNEP	United Nations Environmental Programme
USAID	United States Agency for International Development

Highlights

The Debt Boomerang shows how:

• **Deforestation** in the South – a major contributor to global warming – is directly linked to the debt crisis. A country's debt burden strongly correlates with both the pace and the extent of its tropical forest destruction. Bio-diversity, the source of our future foods and medicines, is disappearing along with the forests.

• **Cocaine** will continue to flood Northern markets – with all its attendant social problems – so long as deeply indebted Latin American countries are dependent on drug dollars for survival and while tens of thousands of people displaced by the International Monetary Fund's economic austerity programmes cannot find a livelihood in the legal economy.

• **You are paying** enormous disguised subsidies to commercial banks, which have taken at least US$73 billion from the public purse since 1987, while receiving huge payments from the third world. Yet the debtors have received almost no relief and in 1991 were 61 per cent more in debt than they were in 1982.

• **Jobs** have been lost in Northern industries by the hundreds of thousands, and farms have failed because the debtor countries can no longer purchase Northern products and must send every spare dollar to the banks.

• **Immigration**, legal or illegal, can only swell so long as millions seek to escape the dire economic consequences of austerity in their own countries. Solving the debt crisis is the vital initial step to making their lives worth living at home.

• **Conflict and war**, with the ever-present danger of spillovers into our own daily lives, are the constant companions of debt, now doubtless the single largest contributing factor to global instability.

The Debt Boomerang also points the way towards the future we must build. Northern citizens can work together, and with their counterparts in the South, to force governments and international agencies to end the havoc wreaked everywhere by the debt crisis. It belongs at the top of the political agenda.

Acknowledgements

The Transnational Institute gratefully acknowledges the support of FINNIDA, the Finnish International Development Agency, whose grant has made *The Debt Boomerang* project possible.* We wish to express our deep gratitude to Mikko Pyhälä, formerly of FINNIDA, now with the United Nations Environment Programme in Nairobi, for his overall interest in the Institute's work and his particular commitment to this project; thanks also to Ms Anu Pärnänen-Landtman, Programme Officer at FINNIDA. The Finnish grant also supports other institute activities including the work of several third world TNI Fellows.

We are much indebted to the Comitato di Coordinamento delle Organizzazioni per il Servicio Volontario (COSV) of Milan and Rome* and to the General Directorate for Development Cooperation of the Italian Ministry of Foreign Affairs* for providing us with the means to complement our research and to undertake and strengthen outreach activities centred on the conclusions and recommendations of this book. Thanks to the generosity of COSV and Italy's Development Cooperation programme, TNI can seek endorsements, organise events and generally press for the adoption of these recommendations. TNI wishes to thank especially Cinzia Giudici and Cristiana Cometto of COSV who share the Institute's view that scholarship should serve to advance the debate on North–South issues.

We would also like to thank the Max and Anna Levinson Foundation* whose support has provided us with the welcome and unprecedented opportunity to undertake outreach activities in the United States as well.

Finally, we can never adequately express – much less repay – our debt to the Rubin Foundation (New York).* Its founder, the late Samuel Rubin, was a guiding force in the establishment of TNI in 1973. Since that time, the Foundation has consistently renewed its general support for our work.

* The views presented in this book do not necessarily reflect those of the project's donors, all of whom have respected TNI's intellectual freedom and independence.

We hope that these donors, and other TNI supporters who help to finance the whole range of the Institute's activities, will find their confidence justified by *The Debt Boomerang* project. We hope in particular that through this book and its associated campaign, TNI may contribute to genuine change in official debt policy, benefiting the vast majority of citizens in both the North and the South.

From the *Notebooks* of Leonardo da Vinci:

That shall be brought forth out of the dark and obscure caves, which will put the whole human race in great anxiety, peril and death. To many that seek them, after many sorrows they will give delight, and to those who are not in their company, death with want and misfortune. This will lead to the commission of endless crimes; this will increase and persuade bad men to assassinations, robberies and enslavement, and by reason of it each will be suspicious of his partner. This will deprive cities of their happy condition; this will take away the lives of many; this will make men torment one another ... For this the vast forests will be devastated of their trees; for this endless animals will lose their lives.

The Prophecies, 'Of metals'

Introduction

This book examines six major 'Debt Connections'; six ways in which the third world 'Debt Boomerang' strikes the North as it flies back from the South:

- Environmental Destruction
- Drugs
- Costs to Taxpayers
- Lost Jobs and Markets
- Immigration Pressures
- Heightened Conflict and War

The Debt Boomerang presents the findings of a research project undertaken by the Transnational Institute (TNI), Amsterdam, working in close collaboration with its sister institution, the Institute for Policy Studies (IPS) in Washington DC. We who have contributed to this book are not newcomers to third world debt issues. For the better part of a decade, TNI/IPS Fellows and associates have carried out research, written books, articles and study guides; contributed to network television films and classroom videos; spoken, in person and on radio, to audiences on six continents, and participated in countless conferences and colloquia on the debt crisis.

Indeed, considering our means, we may well have devoted proportionally more human resources to this issue than any comparable group of people, even including the official debt managers of the World Bank and the International Monetary Fund. Although justifiably proud of our work, it has to be said that we are also frustrated and worried. Too little has changed. For a decade, human misery and ecological devastation have worsened throughout the indebted world with each passing year, exacerbating North–South tensions.

If the goals of official debt managers were to squeeze the debtors dry, to transfer enormous resources from South to North and to wage undeclared war on the poor continents and their people, then their policies have been an unqualified success. If, however, their strategies were intended – as these institutions always claim – to promote development beneficial to all members of society, to preserve

xiii

the planet's unique environment and gradually to reduce the debt burden itself, then their failure is easily demonstrated.

One obvious aspect of this failure, or success, depending on one's point of view, is financial. From the onset of the debt crisis in 1982 through 1990 (as of this writing the last year for which complete figures are available) each and every month, for 108 months, debtor countries of the South remitted to their creditors in the North an average six billion five hundred million dollars (US$6,500,000,000) in interest payments alone. If payments of principal are included in the tally, then each of the 108 months from January 1982 through December 1990 witnessed payments from debtors to creditors averaging twelve billion four hundred and fifty million dollars ($12,450,000,000).

What happened to this money, remitted to private banks, state creditors and international public institutions, thanks to the toil and tears of hundreds of millions? Theoretically, the third world's interest payments alone could have provided every man, woman and child in North America and Europe with over US$1000 or 500 pounds sterling during this nine year period.* Practically speaking, of course, ordinary citizens in the North obtained no such advantages, in spite of the unprecedented financial haemorrhage flowing from the less developed to the wealthy countries. On the contrary, these Northern citizens paid, as we intend to show, huge and varied penalties to compensate for the foolish lending policies of their own banks and governments.

Another aspect of the success/failure story has been the opportunity debt has provided to intervene in the management of dozens of debtors' economies. The International Monetary Fund and the World Bank, acting on behalf of the creditor countries which are their major stockholders, have undertaken this task. Their job is simple: to make sure the debt is serviced. Thus a chief goal of their economic management must be the accumulation of enough hard currency to ensure levels of payments like those just cited. Since the average citizen

---

* Almost all debt figures in this study are taken directly or derived from OECD, *Financing and External Debt of Developing Countries: 1989 or 1990 Survey*, Organisation for Economic Cooperation and Development, Paris, 1990 or 1991. We generally use this source in preference to the World Bank's *Debt Tables* because OECD figures include short-term debt – for many countries a fairly large proportion of total borrowings – whereas the World Bank's do not. The above calculations are based on total interest payments of US$706 billion for the nine calendar years from 1982–90, divided by 108 months or by 600 million Northern citizens. If payments of principal (amortisation) of long-term debt are included, total payback from South to North for the same period was $1,345,300,000,000. In that case, each of these 600 million Northern citizens would have theoretically received an average $2242.

of a low-income debtor country is 55 times poorer, and the average citizen of a middle-income debtor country is 9 times poorer than the average citizen of an OECD creditor country, this process has been justifiably likened to extracting blood from a stone.*

To accumulate hard currency one must increase exports and reduce government outlays: we will not elaborate here on the specific measures which are supposed to allow governments to 'earn more and spend less'. The problem for the debtor country is that it must remit most or all of its debt service before it is free to engage in any other pursuits. Most debtor governments have for years cooperated, and forced their peoples to cooperate, with the draconian policies of the IMF and the World Bank. Much good it has done them.** A decade has passed since the third world debt crisis first erupted, yet in spite of harsh measures faithfully applied, this crisis is today more intractable than ever.

At the behest of the Bank and the Fund, debtor countries have deprived their people – particularly the poorest among them – of basic necessities in order to provide the private banks and the public agencies of the rich countries with the equivalent of six Marshall Plans. This unprecedented financial assistance to the rich from the poor may be startling but it is nonetheless arithmetically true.

According to the OECD, between 1982 and 1990, total resource flows to developing countries amounted to $927 billion. This sum includes the OECD categories of Official Development Finance, Export Credits and Private Flows – in other words, all official bilateral and multilateral aid, grants by private charities, trade credits plus direct private investment and bank loans. Much of this inflow was not in the form of grants but was rather new debt, on which dividends or interest will naturally come due in the future.

During the same 1982–90 period, developing countries remitted *in debt service alone* $1345 billion (interest and principal) to the creditor countries. For a true picture of resource flows, one would have to add many other South-to-North outflows such as royalties, dividends, repatriated profits, underpaid raw materials and the like. The income–outflow difference between $1345 and $927 billion is thus a much understated $418 billion in the rich countries' favour. For purposes of comparison, the US Marshall Plan transferred $14

---

* According to World Bank statistics, the average GNP per capita (1988 dollars) for Low Income countries is $320, for Middle Income Countries $1930, for OECD countries $17,470.
** For greater detail on these measures and their human costs, see Susan George, *A Fate Worse than Debt*, Penguin (UK and Commonwealth) and Grove Press (US) 1988.

billion 1948 dollars to war-ravaged Europe, about $70 billion in 1991 dollars. Thus in the eight years from 1982–90 the poor have financed six Marshall Plans for the rich through debt service alone.

Have these extraordinary outflows at least served to reduce the absolute size of the debt burden? Unfortunately not: in spite of total debt service, including amortisation, of more than 1.3 trillion dollars from 1982–90; the debtor countries as a group began the 1990s *fully 61 per cent more in debt than they were in 1982*. Sub-Saharan Africa's debt increased by 113 per cent during this period; the debt burden of the very poorest – the so-called 'LLDCs' or 'least developed' countries – was up by 110 per cent.

Clearly, the economic policies imposed on debtors by the major multilateral agencies – policies packaged under the general heading of 'structural adjustment' – have cured nothing at all. They have, rather, caused untold human suffering and widespread environmental destruction while simultaneously emptying debtor countries of their resources; rendering them each year less able to service their debts, let alone invest in economic and human recovery. The World Bank and the IMF structural adjustors have now had a generous period to impose their plans and cannot complain that their measures have not been given enough time to work. Had these public debt-management officials been corporate executives, with so little to show for themselves, their shareholders would have doubtless sacked them long ago for incompetence. Had they been politicians, they would have been trounced at election time and sent back to where they came from.

Corporate managers and local or national public office-holders can be dismissed for poor performance. No such accountability applies to the international bureaucrats acting on behalf of the creditor governments. The international debt managers need never submit to the judgement of their victims. They answer only to their own equally unaccountable superiors, and, at the top of the bureaucratic tree, to a Board of Governors reflecting the majority voting strength of the richest creditor countries. These lavishly compensated international civil 'servants' are consequently still to be found in Washington and throughout the third world, living exceedingly well.*

---

* In early 1991, the author was seated on an airplane next to a supervisor of an international construction firm. An old Africa hand, he was on his way to the desperately poor African country Guinea (life expectancy 43 years; illiteracy 72 per cent, according to World Bank figures). There his company was constructing the country's largest swimming pool to enhance the charms of the villa occupied by the World Bank mission chief. According to this informant, the Bank – that is, you, me and the Bank's bondholders – was footing the bill. As of 1 August 1991, salaries for the heads of the World Bank and the IMF were raised to $285,000 per annum. The pay ceiling for their top staff is $190,000.

The international debt managers, whose requirements include higher levels of exports and radical cutbacks in government spending, do not feel the effects of the massive unemployment, depressed wages and drastically reduced public services which quite naturally follow. The social dislocation they have encouraged has not even bought economic health – the debt managers would be hard pressed to point to a single third world success story. Economically, socially and ecologically speaking, 'structural adjustment' has been a disaster, but the Fund and the Bank are undeterred.

Their perseverance can be at least partly explained by the unequivocal encouragement they have received from certain quarters. The ultimate verdict on IMF and World Bank activities depends entirely on who serves on the jury. For corporations operating in debtor countries – both local and transnational – structural adjustment has reduced both wages and the power of unions, thus enhancing corporate profitability. For many international banks, debt service payments at unusually high interest rates in the early 1980s helped to fuel several years of record earnings. From the corporate or banking perspective, the World Bank and the IMF pass the test with flying colours.

Nor have third world elites much cause for complaint. They have weathered the 'lost decade of the 1980s' with relative ease and have sometimes profited handsomely from it. They too benefit from plummeting wages and their money is often in safe havens outside their own countries, in US dollars or Swiss francs. Each time the IMF requires a devaluation of the national currency to encourage exports, those whose holdings are in foreign currencies automatically become richer at home. And although public services may deteriorate or close down, rich people can afford private ones. Thus it is not surprising that third world governments have failed to unite and to demand debt reduction. Each debtor country sits down alone to negotiate, across the table from a united creditor front.

The debtors' lack of unity ensures the draining of their economies and a continuing South-to-North resource flow on a scale far outstripping any the colonial period could command. The debtor governments have from time to time made mild remonstrances and called for debt relief but have never collectively confronted the creditors. Even if they suddenly tried to do so, the historic opportunity they might once have seized has passed: the banks are far less vulnerable to pressure than they were until 1987.

As a reward for docility, the creditors have allowed most debtor country elites to maintain their links to the world financial system, providing them with at least a trickle of fresh money and offering them frequent opportunities to purchase local assets at bargain prices through so-called 'debt-for-equity swaps' or privatisation programmes. Third world debt should not, therefore, be seen as a straightforwardly 'national' problem. Different social classes in debtor countries have vastly divergent interests and are unequally affected. Although debt has visited unprecedented pain on the vast majority of third world people, the crisis is not necessarily a crisis for everyone.

While the topmost layers of third world societies remain largely insulated from debt distress, ordinary people in the South sacrifice to pay back loans they never asked for, or which they even fought against, and from which they derived no gain. Knowledge of their plight is by now fairly widespread in the developed, creditor countries, thanks to the efforts of thousands of concerned people patiently explaining the human and ecological consequences of the debt crisis in the third world.

Yet despite the best efforts of such people, pressures exerted by dozens of non-governmental organisations in both North and South have so far failed to alter basic debt-management policies. Although the Fund and the Bank now claim they seek to 'mitigate the social costs of adjustment', official response to the crisis advances at a calculated snail's pace, inching from one feeble and ineffective 'Plan' to the next, while leaving the status quo essentially untouched.

Until now, those in the North, including many TNI/IPS Fellows, who have tried to change the debt management strategies of their governments, the World Bank and the IMF, have rightly based their arguments on ethical and humanitarian grounds. The social and ecological disaster debt has brought upon people in the South, particularly the poorer among them, provides ample justification for this approach.

The impact of third world debt fallout in the North is much less well known – doubtless because the consequences of debt are far more serious and life-threatening in the South than in the North. Nonetheless, we believe it is vital to show how such a seemingly distant phenomenon in fact harms nearly everyone in the North. We view *The Debt Boomerang* as one way to bridge the information gap; to demonstrate that ordinary citizens of debtor and creditor countries have every interest in joining forces to demand an entirely new approach to third world debt. Although people in the South are far more grievously affected by debt than those in the North, in both cases, a tiny minority benefits while the overwhelming majority pays.

Rarely in human affairs can one show a linear, one-to-one causal link between events; the consequences of the debt crisis are no exception. Thus nowhere do we claim that third world debt is the *only* cause of, say, increased illegal drug exports to the United States and Europe or of accelerated deforestation hastening the greenhouse effect. We do, on the other hand, try to show that debt is, at the very least, an aggravating factor in these negative trends. Thus we stress feedbacks more than linear connections and tend to see debt and its multiple consequences as mutually reinforcing. For example, debt-burdened Latin American governments become hooked on dollars from their coca producing regions. This severely dampens their incentive to encourage legal crops. Increased drug exports, in turn, escalate the costs of law enforcement and contribute to social breakdown in the North.

These harmful effects did not, so to speak, suddenly spring fully armed from the head, or the belly, of the World Bank. They result from a conscious set of policies aimed at promoting a particular kind of development. During the late 1960s and throughout the 1970s, borrowing financed an expensive, capital-intensive, energy-intensive, unsustainable development model favourable only to third world elites, Northern banks and transnational corporations. This model marginalised the majority which could not hope to partake of the fruits of a spurious 'growth' based on human exploitation and natural resource depletion.

Not surprisingly, massive overborrowing (encouraged by the creditors, welcomed by the borrower governments) coupled with high interest rates led to the debt crisis. This crisis in turn provided official debt managers in the 1980s and 1990s with a perfect lever, immediately used, to entrench the very development model which had caused the original problem. Relying on unbridled free market forces and export-led growth, they have devastated the unprotected – poorer, more vulnerable groups and the environment.

They are still doing it, and, quite simply, they have to be stopped.

We hope this book may show that while any standard of human decency or any ethical imperative demands a change in debt management, *so does enlightened self-interest.* Everyone outside the narrowest of elite circles has a stake in positive change. Perhaps if enough people in the North realise that the third world debt crisis is their crisis as well, they will insist on radically different policies. They will speak out and will seek to join with similar forces in the South.

We also hope that this book may help to promote a particular kind of change. Readers have a right to know at the outset that ours is a political, social and economic agenda. TNI seeks to promote, through its scholarship, an alternative approach to debt. It further seeks to discredit a development model which has proven itself to be beyond reform and which, unchecked, will lead to future disasters as it has led to the present one.

We believe that genuine development must be based on three principles:

- popular participation in decision-making at every level
- social equity
- ecological prudence

Later on in these pages these principles will become more explicit. If *The Debt Boomerang* is successful, it will help to point the way towards this goal; it will become one tool for building bridges in the North between environmentalists, trade unionists, people concerned about drugs, activists for immigrants' rights, members of third world solidarity groups or non-governmental organisations (NGOs) and that broadest category of all – taxpayers. We hope that each of these constituencies will see the need to work together for alternative policies and, simultaneously, the need to work effectively with their counterparts in the South. All of us would benefit from a new approach to debt and development based on shared principles and shared interests.

Throughout the book we outline the necessary elements of an alternative debt strategy. We also make recommendations which we believe could lead to a development strategy based on, and guaranteed to uphold, the vital triad of popular participation, social equity, environmental prudence – in other words a model taking into account the real needs of people everywhere.

In 1991, the world witnessed a major war – some called it the first North–South war. Certainly it was partly about control over resources, about political control via debt, about the rights of all peoples to a homeland. Because of oil, because of the Israel-Palestine deadlock or the largest national minority of all without a country – the Kurds – the Middle East has never been typical of what we, following the conventional verbal shorthand, call the third world. Here, we will comment only in passing on the Gulf War, even though its effects may be felt for years to come. It is, however, well within our subject to note that Saddam Hussein saw the invasion of Kuwait as one way of wiping out his colossal debts owed both to that country and to the allies; and that George Bush granted massive debt forgiveness to an allied Arab nation like Egypt as a reward for staying on his side.

So long as the policies of the rich North represent a mixture of crude carrot-and-stick manoeuvres, coupled with basic contempt for the

South, its problems and its peoples, we can expect more lethal North–South tensions, more powerful boomerangs hurtling back at us, a further forced retreat of the rich countries into Fortress America and Fortress Europe. Or we can decide that it is time – high time – we began to live together on this improbable planet as *homo sapiens* a good deal more *sapiens*.

We need first to understand that we will be, in the end, far better off without demanding the South's annual pound of flesh. Then we need to recognise that this 'South' is rapidly approaching four-fifths of humanity which, in a positive or negative way, will necessarily make its presence felt. Finally, we must accept that none of us, from North or South, can do without the planet. If we learn none of these things, then the planet can, and may yet, decide to do without us.

* * *

Research and documentation for the *The Debt Boomerang* were undertaken by a team. The names of the scholars involved are to be found following the title page and at the heads of the chapters to which they contributed. I have, however, entirely reworked the material they supplied and have frequently added to it; thus final responsibility for the contents of this book is mine alone. People on the team should not be blamed for the uses to which I have put their work or for the conclusions I may have drawn from it: they may not agree with me. Dan Smith's chapter on conflict is the exception: he supplied a finished draft; I made only editorial or stylistic changes.

S.G.

The First Boomerang:
The Environment

Research and Documentation by John Cavanagh and Susan George

Civilisation exists by geological consent, subject to change without notice.
Will and Ariel Durant, *What is Civilisation?*

If the Amazon is the lungs of the world, then the debt is its pneumonia.
Luis Ignacio da Silva ('Lula', Brazilian labour leader
and presidential candidate)

Debt Sets the Stage for Disaster

Over the past quarter century, vast swathes of ecological devastation have been cut across the southern hemisphere. The damage began in earnest in the late 1960s; the 1970s saw it compounded, in the 1980s it went out of control. The destruction of tropical forests in particular is now common knowledge; everyone has seen the pictures, reminiscent of nuclear holocaust, showing huge stands of burnt, bulldozed and broken trees.

Nor are forests the only ecological victims of the crisis. Especially during the past decade, throughout the third world, deserts are spreading in rural areas, and pollution in urban ones; among the several disastrous consequences are food shortages and widespread illness. The term 'environmental refugee' has lately been added to the terrible lexicon of the human condition. Like the Joads of Steinbeck's *Grapes of Wrath* fleeing the Dust Bowl in the 1930s, millions of third world people now seek to escape, but for them there is no California at the end of the road.

Is third world debt the cause of these phenomena? Not exclusively, perhaps not even directly, but the pressure of debt is a major contributing factor to them and weighs on the entire earth, not just on its southern hemisphere. We have found the positive correlations between high levels of indebtedness and environmental degradation, especially deforestation, overwhelmingly strong. Structural

1

adjustment programmes designed by the International Monetary Fund and the World Bank have placed further stress on already fragile ecosystems. ▮

We will not claim that wiping out debt could, of itself, halt this damage – for that to happen we must first change radically the whole present 'mal-development' model. We do argue that debt has been and remains a central factor in the overall crisis of the third world and particularly in its ecological crisis. Both the accumulation of the debt and the structural adjustment policies that are supposed to lead to its reimbursement and to economic growth are, in turn, central to the mal-development model – one which can only lead to further environmental havoc.

Without the cascades of easy money in the 1970s and early 1980s, much ecological damage could have been averted. Heavy borrowing in the 1970s financed huge, ecologically harmful projects such as mega-dams, nuclear power plants, smelters designed to be fuelled with forest-derived charcoal, huge industrial and agricultural estates and so on. When the bills came due, as they did especially after the debt crisis exploded in 1982, ever-greater quantities of environmental resources had to be cashed in to pay them.*

The IMF's structural adjustment programmes are designed to ensure the restoration of a positive 'Balance of Payments' (a 'positive' BOP registers an excess of export earnings over import outlays) so that a country's debts to Northern governments, commercial banks and multilateral institutions can be paid. The first goal of adjustment, more popularly known as austerity, is thus to accumulate hard currency for the purpose of reimbursement. Only when debt service obligations can be substantially met does the IMF consider the debtor country free to pursue other objectives. The debtor has no choice but to heed the Fund's advice, since without its 'seal of approval', no other source will provide loans, not even short-term trade credits.

Structural adjustment is best summed up in four words: earn more, spend less. While such advice might be valid if it were given to only a few countries at once, dozens of debtors are now attempting to earn more by exporting whatever they have at hand; particularly natural resources including minerals, tropical crops, timber, meat and fish. With so many jostling for a share of limited world markets, prices plummet, forcing governments to seek ever-higher levels of exports in a desperate attempt to keep their hard currency revenues stable. The 'export-led growth' model, on which the Fund and the World

* For numerous examples, see Susan George, *A Fate Worse than Debt,* Chapter 10, 'Debt and the Environment: Financing Ecocide'.

Bank insist, is a purely extractive one involving more
than the management – much less the conservation –

Soils are exhausted to grow cash crops. Senegal, f
borrowed heavily to install refining capacity for a millio
groundnuts. But its soils are so depleted by groundnut production
that today it can produce nowhere near that amount. Still, the cost
of the industrial plant must be reimbursed – through exports of
groundnuts. Other export crops like off-season fruits and vegetables
often require large doses of chemical pesticides and fertilisers which
poison the soil in the South, cling to the produce and ultimately
return to the tables of the North, rounding out the familiar 'circle
of poison'.

Export orientation encourages not only industrial-scale agriculture
but also the granting of huge timber and mining concessions, geared
to short-term profit with no thought for conserving natural resources.
Such concentration of wealth and advantage in few hands leads
directly to disregard for the environment, as it leads to poverty and
marginalisation for the majority. And poverty, too, poses a grave threat
to ecological balance. In country after country undergoing structural
adjustment, poor people have become poorer still. The survival
strategies they are forced to adopt place further pressures on the
severely limited, fragile resource bases left at their disposal.

When export crops take priority and monopolise the best land,
wealthier landowners tend to buy out or evict smallholders who then
move into teeming cities. Or they may try to cultivate nutrient-
poor forest soils, or move to steep and easily eroded hillsides, stripping
them of their cover as they try to scratch out a living. Poor rural and
urban people also cut down trees to make charcoal, to sell as firewood,
to clear a little extra space for growing food or raising animals.
Increasingly, in a number of countries, they participate in the illegal
drug economy (the subject of the next chapter) which also ravages
the environment.

There is no point in asking the poor to take the long view: the long
view is a luxury they cannot afford. However, given enough space
and a fair chance, people have shown time and again that they
know how to use their environment prudently.

As the debtor countries' heritage is put on the block, forests are
felled to provide furniture, window frames or chopsticks. Sometimes
they are simply levelled for pasture so that beef cattle may safely graze
until they are turned into fast-food restaurant hamburgers. Fish
stocks are devastated, coral reefs are dynamited to make them yield
up an increasingly meagre catch. Meanwhile, as part of 'spend less'

cutbacks, third world environmental ministries and resource conservation programmes, underfunded to begin with, are invariably among the first casualties of austerity. When, for example, debt service requires 44 per cent of all government spending, as it does in the Philippines, it is not surprising that ecological protection and sustainable resource management should be low priorities. Governments can concentrate only on short-term objectives.

As Robert Repetto of the World Resources Institute put it in a *Scientific American* article,

> Data ... indicate that both the logging and the conversion [of forest to pasture or agricultural uses] are largely the result of government policies. Many of those policies are driven by the severe economic pressures afflicting debt-burdened underdeveloped countries. Those pressures in turn are exacerbated by certain practices of developed countries and their national and international financial institutions.[1]

Those who suffer most from these policies are of course the local people whose immediate livelihoods depend on their own ecological backyard.

When forests are destroyed, people living there are deprived of survival resources. Farmlands are covered with mud, which torrential rains sweep down from denuded hillsides, and rivers silt up. When coral reefs are destroyed, millions of fisherfolk go hungry. When lands lose fertility because of the pesticides and fertilisers that accompany intensive cash crop production, future farming generations are impoverished. Yet if these are the immediate concerns for the South, debt-encouraged devastation also affects people in North America and Europe.

- Deforestation accounts directly for at least a sixth of greenhouse gas emissions leading to unpredictable climate change including global warming. Compounding this impact, the animals grazing on recently cleared forest land themselves contribute substantial amounts of greenhouse gases to the atmosphere.
- Deforestation is also the chief cause of species destruction among animals and plants. This loss of biological diversity – a tragedy for the South – also robs Northern agriculture of vital genes which could contribute to future food production and medicinal cures.

Turning up the Heat

Warnings – and clichés – about 'small planets' and 'common futures' to the contrary, Northern policymakers have behaved up to now as if the earth could be sliced in half like a grapefruit, leaving most of the South to its fate. Most of them do not seem to understand that the one-third of greenhouse gases that are generated in the South affect both halves. The atmosphere cannot be conveniently bisected. Perhaps the most frightening aspect of the debt-environment connection on the North, as we see it, is the massive deforestation now occurring in the southern hemisphere and its contribution to the greenhouse effect, leading to a rise in temperatures and other climatic changes such as altered rainfall patterns, more severe storms, etc.[2] Outside the White House, few doubt the reality of global warming.*

The 300 scientists who took part in the unprecedented Intergovernmental Panel on Climate Change (IPCC), convened by the United Nations General Assembly, displayed a unanimity rare in scientific circles when in May 1990 they issued a report stressing the need for 'immediate reductions in emissions (of greenhouse gases) from human activities of over 60 per cent to stabilise their concentrations at today's levels'.[3]

Note that even in the unlikely event of such drastic reductions occurring, this would merely 'stabilise' present concentrations of greenhouse gases. The IPCC Report makes clear that this might not be enough to avoid extremely unpleasant surprises. In particular, the climatologists point to the likelihood of 'positive feedbacks' – natural phenomena which can be awakened as warming occurs and which then further amplify that warming. 'It appears likely that, as climate warms, the feedbacks will lead to an overall increase rather than decrease in natural greenhouse gas abundances. For this reason, climate change is likely to be greater than the estimates we have given', say the IPCC scientists.[4]

---

* President Bush, asked to comment on the scientific consensus that the world faces potentially disastrous global warming linked to the greenhouse effect, replied, 'That's not what my scientists are telling me.' Whereas the world's best-known climatologists, including the top man at NASA, believe that global warming is a clear and present danger, poor George relies on advice from the George C. Marshall Institute, a privately-funded (by whom?) foundation in Washington DC. John Gribbin, writing in the *New Scientist*, makes well-deserved hash of the Marshall Institute's position and of its ill-informed yet pretentious 'scientific experts' who have been on the road spreading their gospel. See 'An Assault on the Climate Consensus', in *New Scientist*, 15 December 1990.

Some plausible climate models hypothesise that several mutually reinforcing positive feedbacks could combine to cause a runaway greenhouse effect (for example, if the oceans warmed enough to release the billions of tonnes of carbon dioxide they store). The science of complex ecological interactions is young and its practitioners are the first to admit how little they know. As one of them says,

> Feedbacks between atmosphere and biosphere are non-linear, sensitive to initial conditions and capable of enormous amplifications. Complex feedbacks in the Earth System can produce unexpected and potent responses ... Without crying wolf, it is worthy of our concern as a society that biogeochemical and ecological feedbacks may result in more rapid environmental change than is predicted by purely physical models.[5]

If 'enormous amplifications' do befall us, then *homo sapiens sapiens* could simply go the way of the dinosaur. Already, six of the warmest years since record-keeping began occurred in the 1980s.

Most people are familiar with the effects global warming would – or will – have on the planet; this is not the place to describe its impact in any detail. Suffice it to say that even without spectacular changes, any significant temperature increase would place unprecedented stresses on natural and social systems, precipitating major dislocations of agriculture, industry, and coastal areas while posing grave threats to species survival, human health, geopolitical stability, and so on.

Although greenhouse gases have always been produced through natural processes, their recent rapid build-up is due to 'anthropogenic', or human-generated, greenhouse emissions. Roughly two-thirds of these emissions can be traced to the activities of the 25 relatively rich per cent of the planet's population that lives in the rich, Northern countries, including Eastern Europe and the USSR. Their contributions to global warming are deadly serious and demand immediate and drastic reduction – but they are not the subject of this chapter. Deforestation in the South – linked to debt, as we shall show – warms the greenhouse as well. As tropical forest expert Norman Myers explains,

> Deforestation leads to the release of large amounts of biomass carbon into the global atmosphere where it combines to form carbon dioxide – the gas that is accounting for almost half of the greenhouse effect. It also releases significant quantities of two other potent greenhouse gases, methane and nitrous oxide.[6]

These three gases all occur naturally in the atmosphere – it is their heightened and rapidly increasing concentration that worries scientists. Carbon dioxide (CO_2) is the chief greenhouse culprit, accounting for about half the total effect. Its atmospheric concentration is 25 per cent higher than a century and a half ago, and rising fast. Concentration of nitrous oxide (N_2O) is 19 per cent higher, methane fully 100 per cent higher than in the pre-industrial era. The notorious CFCs – chlorofluorocarbons – do not occur naturally in the atmosphere. They are joining the trio of CO_2, N_2O and methane, to 'let sunlight in but trap the resulting heat'.[7]

The speed with which tropical deforestation is intensifying concentrations of greenhouse gases is without precedent. The best calculations of CO_2 emissions caused by deforestation in 1979 ranged from 1.3 to 1.9 billion tonnes ('gigatonnes') with the 'mean working figure' of 1.6 billion tonnes. A decade later, estimates ranged from 2.0 to 2.8 gigatonnes. Thus the lowest estimate at the end of the 1980s was higher than the highest one at the end of the 1970s. The 1989 'mean working figure' of 2.4 billion tonnes, compared to the same figure of a decade earlier, marks an increase of 50 per cent in deforestation-related CO_2 emissions. Although CO_2 constitutes half of all greenhouse gases, 'molecule for molecule, methane is 25 times more effective as a greenhouse gas than is carbon dioxide' and 'deforestation-derived methane can be roughly reckoned ... to be worth about 4 per cent of the total (greenhouse) effect.' Little is known about the exact quantities of N_2O that escape into the atmosphere because of deforestation. However, given that this gas is '200 times more effective than carbon dioxide as a greenhouse gas', it would seem urgent that its release should be in any event sharply curbed.[8]

Myers own scientific summation of the case is as follows:

Tropical forests [he actually means the destruction of these forests] are now contributing 30 per cent of the buildup of carbon dioxide in the global atmosphere ... When we add other greenhouse gases emitted by tropical deforestation, namely methane and nitrous oxide, the overall contribution of tropical deforestation to global warming can be estimated to be around 18 to 19 per cent, possibly more.[9]

Thus forest destruction in the third world is reponsible for up to one-fifth of impending global climate change, and the rate of greenhouse emissions resulting from deforestation has gone up by something like 50 per cent in only ten years. Some analysts have claimed that this heightened rate of gas release has nothing to do with the financial obligations of forested countries and is merely the result of population growth. Myers, however, points out that 'while tropical forest countries' populations have expanded by amounts ranging from 15 to 36 per cent during the 1980s, deforestation has expanded by 90 per cent.'

Certainly increased human pressures take their toll on tropical forests, but this is not so much the result of 'population growth' as of marginalisation of huge numbers of poor people in debtor countries who no longer have a chance of finding a decent livelihood. Myers points in particular to the impact of those he calls 'shifted cultivators'. The 'shifted', as opposed to the 'shifting' cultivator (one who practises traditional 'slash-and-burn' farming, moving from plot to plot, year by year) is a victim of 'development'. Increasingly, he or she is a victim of the debt crisis as well and is often a person who has been shunted off land so that it can be put under export crops.[10]

Clearly, forces beyond population pressures were at work during the 1980s, the decade of the debt crisis. We believe that debt accelerates the deadly forces driving deforestation in several obvious or subtle ways:

- Pressures to increase export earnings stimulate increased exploitation of timber.
- The same pressures lead to the expansion of pasture land (and hence to the clearing of forests) for beef exports.
- Debt increases poverty and marginalisation, which in turn increases the exodus of poor people into forests in the hope of finding a means of subsistance.
- Mangrove forests in coastal areas are also destroyed to make way for ponds to raise shrimp and prawns for export.

Let the Figures Speak for Themselves

What evidence can one offer to show that debt and deforestation are indeed linked? Let us stress once more that we are not trying to establish a crude, one-to-one causality. The numbers do, however, show several extremely disturbing correlations. In particular, they show that:

- Third world countries where significant stands of tropical forests remain also have significant debt burdens, either in absolute terms or relative to the size of their economies and to their capacity to pay.

- Third world countries that deforested the most or the fastest in the 1980s were also, on the whole, the largest debtors.
- In a number of smaller countries with less significant forest reserves, the fastest deforesters were also the most heavily indebted.
- Countries with the highest 'debt service ratios' or subject to the highest levels of IMF 'conditionality' also tend to be the largest and fastest deforesters.

The correlations may be even stronger than they first appear. Although we can measure debt with near-total accuracy, even the best figures on deforestation are subject to caution and may easily be underestimated. In its extensive survey of deforestation, the World Resources Institute stated in 1990:

> Recent studies covering several key countries suggest that deforestation in the tropics may be much worse than was previously thought ... Until recently, the most authoritative estimate of annual deforestation in the tropics was 11.4 million hectares (per year) based on a 1980 FAO assessment ... Several recent studies show that deforestation is much higher in Brazil, Costa Rica, India, Myanmar (formerly Burma), the Philippines and Viet Nam. Forest clearing also increased sharply in Cameroon, Indonesia and Thailand ... If these new studies are accurate, the world is losing up to 20.4 million hectares (51 million acres) of tropical forest annually – 79 per cent over FAO's 1980 estimate.[11]

We will now examine several debt/deforestation correlations in turn.

In Table 1.1, the first column gives the list of the world's top debtors in descending order. Their total debt as of 1989, in billions of US$, follows in parentheses. Israel and Egypt, which have received huge US loans, often for military purposes, are excluded from this debtor list, as are Eastern European countries and Turkey.

In this first column, countries listed in italics do not have significant forest reserves on a world scale and thus do not appear on Myers' list of the countries that contain 97.5 per cent of total remaining tropical forests. Some, however, like Chile and Bangladesh, are destroying their forests in ways which are highly destabilising to the local environment. Myers treats 'Central America' as a single entity, so for purposes of consistency we have done the same, but have excluded Panama, which is a special case.

The second column gives the list of the countries which were the largest deforesters in the 1980s, also in descending order and according to the two best available sources: first the World Resources Institute, then Myers.

The third column gives the percentage of original forest cover already destroyed in the *second* country listed opposite it in the second column. These figures are calculated from Myers. In the world as a whole, 43 per cent of the original forest cover has already disappeared, most of it in the decade of the 1980s.

Table 1.1

Rank Debt Country/US$ billions	Rank Deforestation 1980s acc. WRI/Myers	Percentage of Original Forest Already Destroyed
1. Brazil (112.5)	1. Brazil*/Brazil*	23
2. Mexico (112)	2. India*/Indonesia*	30
3. *Argentina* (65)	3. Indonesia*/Myanmar	51
4. India (60)	4. Colombia*/Mexico*	58
5. Indonesia (53)	5. Myanmar/Colombia*	63
6. *China* (45)	6. Mexico*/Thailand*	83
7. *South Korea* (44)	7. Côte d'Ivoire*/Malaysia*	48
8. Nigeria (31)	8. Sudan*/India*	90
9. Venezuela (30)	9. Central America*/Nigeria*	61
10. Philippines (29)	10. Nigeria*/Zaire*	20
11. *Algeria* (28)	11. Thailand*/Papua New Guinea	15
12. Thailand (24)	12. Zaire/Vietnam	77
13. *Chile* (22)	13. Ecuador*/Peru*	26
14. Peru (20.7)	14. Peru*/Central America*	82
15. *Morocco* (20.5)	15. Malaysia*/Ecuador*	42
16. Cen. America (20)	16. Venezuela*/Philippines*	80
17. Malaysia (19.5)	17. Paraguay/Côte d'Ivoire*	90
18. *Pakistan* (18)	18. Philippines*/Cameroon	25
19. Colombia (16.5)	19. Cameroon/Venezuela*	16
20. Côte d'Ivoire (14.5)	20. Vietnam*/Madagascar	61
21. Ecuador (12.5)	21. Madagascar/Bolivia	22
22. Vietnam (11.6)		
23. *Bangladesh* (10.7)		
24. Sudan (10)		

* Member of the 'over $10 billion' debtor club

Of the 24 largest debtors, 8 never had, or no longer have forest reserves significant on a world scale. Of the 16 remaining major debtors ($10 billion or more) *all are to be found on the list of major deforesters*. The correlation is particularly strong for mega-debtors such as Brazil, India, Indonesia, Mexico, Nigeria (among the top 8 debtors) all of which rank among the top 10 deforesters according to both the World Resources Institute and Myers.

To reinforce the argument, let us look at the debt-deforestation connection from another angle, this time listing by order of rank the top 15 debtors, excluding those countries given in italics in Table 1.1 which do not have significant forest reserves. After the name of the country, in parentheses, is a reminder of its absolute deforestation rank according to WRI/Myers (cf. second column of Table 1.1). The next column shows the rate of change – the acceleration or deceleration of deforestation – between the late 1970s and 1989; that is, prior to the onset of the debt crisis and after its full impact was felt.[12]

Table 1.2

Debtor Country (Deforestation Rank)	Change in the Rate of Deforestation late 1970s–1989(%)
Brazil (1/1)	+ 245
Mexico (6/4)	+ 15
India (2/8)	+ 54
Indonesia (3/2)	+ 82
Nigeria (10/9)	+ 29
Venezuela (16/19)	+ 36
Philippines (18/16)	- 41
Thailand (11/6)	+ 76
Peru (14/13)	+ 21
Central America	- 28
Malaysia (15/7)	+ 65
Colombia (4/5)	+ 41
Côte d'Ivoire (7/–)	- 34
Ecuador (13/5)	+ 36
Vietnam (20/12)	+ 94

Negative rates in the Philippines, Central America and Côte d'Ivoire could be interpreted as showing how little forest there is actually left to destroy, since, as shown in Table 1.3, these three countries have already lost 80 per cent, 82 per cent and 90 per cent respectively of their original forest cover. Most debtors have, however, increased the rates of exploitation of their forests by at least one third since the late 1970s. The rates of increase for such major debtors as Indonesia and especially Brazil – 82 and 245 per cent – are especially alarming because so much of the planet's remaining forest lies within their boundaries.

Immediate pressures to cash in natural resources are also reflected in the alarming pace at which deforestation is taking place in several major debtor countries. In spite of extremely high proportions of original forest already obliterated, these countries appear undeterred from destroying the remainder at astonishing rates. Rates given in the third column are for 1989. Some examples:[13]

Table 1.3

Country	Orig. Forest Already Destroyed 1989 (%)	Current Defor/year (1989)(%)
Côte d'Ivoire	90	15.6
Nigeria	61	14.3
Thailand	83	8.4
Madagascar	61	8.3
Vietnam	77	5.8
Philippines	80	5.4
Mexico	58	4.2
Central America	82	3.7
India	90	2.4

Worldwide, as noted earlier, 43 per cent of original forest in the developing countries has already been irredeemably lost. In the light of the destruction of this original cover in countries like India, Côte d'Ivoire or the Philippines – 80 to 90 per cent – 43 per cent seems almost 'moderate'. If their current pace of destruction is maintained, the countries listed above will be theoretically denuded of all forests within 6 to 40 years (although in fact much sooner because of 'positive feedbacks' through which destruction accelerates further destruction by changing rainfall patterns, encouraging species out-migration and the like).

The most extreme case on the above list, Côte d'Ivoire, has a per capita debt of $1200 and a per capita GNP of $770 – a debt to GNP ratio of 156 per cent – a measure of its need to earn hard cash by any available means. Dense tropical forests once covered half its territory – they have now been reduced to 5 per cent. Having already cashed in nine-tenths of its once abundant forest resources, the country seems bent on razing the rest – partly to pay for such twentieth century *folies* as the replica of Saint Peter's, larger than its original Vatican model, in Yamasoukro, the home village of Président Félix Houphouët-Boigny. Less than 15 per cent of the country's population is Catholic anyway, but all of its people will pay for the end of nature in their country. Unlike most African countries but like the other major African deforester Nigeria, Côte d'Ivoire owes a high proportion of its debt to private banks.

The top 13 countries with the most substantial forest reserves (150,000 km^2 or more) are, in descending order, Brazil, Zaire, Indonesia, Peru, Papua New Guinea, Venezuela, Colombia, Myanmar,

Gabon, Mexico, India, Cameroon and Malaysia. Between them, the first three contain roughly half the planet's remaining forested area. Fortunately, not all these countries are destroying their reserves at the same rates as Côte d'Ivoire or Nigeria. But Brazil's apparently 'reasonable' rate of 2.3 per cent per year in fact means 50,000 km^2 of forests cut, burnt or bulldozed yearly – as much as the total annual destruction perpetrated by the next ten countries on the list: Zaire, Indonesia, Peru, Papua New Guinea, Venezuela, Colombia, Myanmar, Gabon, Mexico and India – taken together! Of total forest clearance in Brazil – the top debtor and the top deforester – 69 per cent has occurred since 1980.[14]

Of the 23 major deforesters cited by WRI and/or Myers (see Table 1.1), six – Bolivia, Cameroon, Madagascar, Myanmar, Papua New Guinea and Paraguay, are smaller countries and do not appear on the list of major debtors. Their indebtedness and the consequent pressures on them to destroy their forests can thus be better expressed in terms of debt per capita as compared to Gross National Product per capita (Table 1.4). This can be seen as a rough measure of their capacity to pay.[15]

Table 1.4

Country	Debt per capita US$	GNP per capita US$	DEBTpc/GNPpc (%)
Bolivia	770	570	135
Cameroon	430	1010	42
Madagascar	335	190	176
Myanmar (Burma)	150	200	75
Papua New Guinea	650	700	93
Paraguay	625	900	69

Of the six, only Cameroon, and perhaps Paraguay, have a fairly comfortable margin of difference between the per capita debt burden and per capita national product. Myanmar and Papua New Guinea have only a $50 per capita margin of product over debt; while Bolivia and especially Madagascar have significantly more debt obligations per citizen than national wherewithal to pay them.

Some smaller debtor countries are playing a large role on the deforestation scene. Papua New Guinea has been called 'a Southeast Asian Amazon'. Its lush forests are particularly vulnerable now since the country has recently lost significant mineral revenues, and Japanese and American logging corporations are putting heavy pressure on the government to grant new timber concessions as they exhaust the forest reserves of neighbouring countries like Thailand, Malaysia and the Philippines.[16]

Bolivia is better known for its soaring mountains than its forests yet it has – or had – 50 million hectares (125 million acres) of Amazonian forests compared to Brazil's 300 million. According to the forestry project officer for Conservation International, Bolivia's forest depletion rate is one of the 'worst in South America', only marginally lower than Brazil's. Every year about 200,000 hectares (500,000 acres) are estimated to be lost to timber extraction, cattle ranching and 'shifted cultivators'. They have become a large and growing population in Bolivia since 1985 when the IMF and the Bolivian government instituted one of the toughest austerity programmes ever enforced in Latin America. The nationalised tin mines were closed down and thousands of miners suddenly lost their work. As we will see in the following chapter, many of them switched to growing coca, the raw material of cocaine. Furthermore, fully 40 per cent of Bolivia's remaining forest has been legally conceded to timber companies that log them for export.[17]

Exports and EFFs

Some experts stress that the best indicator of the real hardships imposed by debt is the so-called 'debt service ratio' (DSR) which expresses debt service payments as a proportion of a country's export earnings. The DSR shows at a glance how much of a country's economy is, so to speak, 'sterile' because:

- The exported goods are *ipso facto* not enjoyed by the citizens of the exporting country and the human, material and financial resources required to produce them are also therefore largely of benefit to foreigners.
- Much of whatever income the export goods do procure cannot be reinvested or used to purchase vital imports because it must be immediately redirected towards foreign creditors.

Thus the higher the ratio of debt service payments to exports of goods and services, the stronger the pressures to increase one's export earnings even more, simply to have some hard currency left over for investment or for imports. Many large deforesters have unusually high DSRs. The following ratios include not just exports of raw materials or manufactures, but also those of services, including worker remittances. Some debtor countries like the Philippines have been significant exporters of labour. Major deforesters with especially high debt service ratios are shown in Table 1.5, in descending order.[18]

Table 1.5 Debt Service Ratios of Major Deforesters

Country	DSR
Madagascar	64
Côte d'Ivoire	61
Mexico	53
Myanmar	52
Bolivia	46
Brazil	44
Colombia	41
Indonesia	39
Venezuela	37
Philippines	35
Nigeria	35
Papua New Guinea	33
Sudan	32
Ecuador	32
Cameroon	32
India	29

Note: Central American countries Nicaragua (92) Guatemala (63) and Honduras (42) also figure high – indeed for Nicaragua highest – on the DSR list.

A final indicator suggesting a strong relationship between debt and deforestation is the number of debtor/deforester countries which have been recipients of International Monetary Fund loans accompanied by strict conditions. The IMF offers two kinds of loans to troubled debtors: 'Stand-by Arrangements' and 'Extended Fund Facilities'. The latter are lent over three-year periods and are the most rigorous in terms of the 'conditionality' attached to them. As already noted, IMF conditions always require that countries make every effort to increase their exports in order to restore a positive balance of payments (or excess of export revenues over imports expenditures). Natural resources like forests are not exempt from such requirements.

Between 1980 and 1990, the IMF granted 28 Extended Fund Facilities (EFF) to 25 debtors. By comparison, over this same 10 year period, the IMF approved 198 somewhat less rigorous Stand-by

Arrangements for several dozen countries. On the list of recipients of high-conditionality EFFs are 12 major deforesters: Brazil, Côte d'Ivoire, Gabon, India, Mexico, Peru, Philippines, Sudan, Venezuela, Zaire, plus Central American countries Costa Rica and Honduras.[19]

Who Let the Greenhouse Gases Escape?

We find all the above strong correlations convincing, but whether or not one accepts that third world debt is at least partly responsible for the increased scope and pace of deforestation in the highly indebted countries, there is no doubt that deforestation itself is contributing more today to the greenhouse effect than it did a decade ago, before the debt crisis emerged. (This, of course, is another way of saying that, for whatever reason, rates of forest destruction are markedly accelerating.) Forests also act as 'sinks' for absorbing CO_2, so the fewer trees, the less carbon can be removed from the atmosphere. And as we know, cutting or burning of timber emits the familiar greenhouse trio: carbon dioxide, methane and nitrous oxide whose presence in the atmosphere increased significantly between 1979 and 1989.

Can one fairly say that these dangerous greenhouse gases are, so to speak, debt-driven?

The example of Brazil, largest deforester and largest debtor, is instructive. Although it did not begin with the advent of the debt crisis, the great soybean exodus in Brazil is one example of a policy resulting in the expulsion of vast numbers of smallholders from good southern land which large growers then planted to soya.

Like thousands of other landless Brazilians, many of these displaced farmers, along with additional thousands of city dwellers attempting to escape their poverty, ended up in Amazonia, hacking down trees. Some of the 'shifted' may also be people displaced to make way for huge dams of the sort favoured by the World Bank, whose energy projects have already forced at least 1.5 million rural people to leave their homes. How did all of them get so deep into the forest? Usually via roads financed by loans from the World Bank and other practitioners of the mal-development model.

The Bank joined forces with the Brazilian military government in an attempt to deal with the sheer numbers of people streaming into the cities and to entice them to settle in the Amazonian states instead, where they were promised a better future and title to land. From 1982, the year the debt crisis came to a head, the Bank financed the paved highway allowing settler penetration as well as the partial takeover of the forest by timber, mining and cattle ranching companies, whose contributions to ecological ruin we will shortly note.

The results were not long in coming: 'Since [1985], NASA space surveys show that the area of deforestation has doubled [in the State of Rondonia] approximately every two years.' The neighbouring state of Mato Grosso once contained over 300,000 square miles of virgin forest. By 1987, virtually all of it was gone, and that same year, 'satellite photographs showed 6,000 forest fires burning across the entire Amazon basin – every one of them started deliberately by land clearers. Many of the fires were burning close to the [World Bank-financed) Highway BR-364.'[20]

Whether the destroyers of the forest are 'refugee-cultivators', cattle raisers or logging companies, their activities have other deleterious effects. Recall that each molecule of methane is 25 times more effective than one of carbon dioxide. One way methane gets into the atmosphere is through biomass burning, which contributes at least 8 per cent of all methane releases. The actual emissions of both CO_2 and of methane as a result of fires, mostly of forests, are not known precisely, but as Paul Crutzen, an atmospheric chemist at the Max Planck Institute explains, '[fires related to] agricultural practices and land-use conversion have a very large impact on the overall chemistry of the atmosphere. That is something that has come as a surprise.' Crutzen notes that chemists used to believe biomass fires contributed about 2.5 billion tonnes of carbon to the atmosphere annually, but they have now had to revise this figure upwards to 3 or 4 billion tonnes. These gigatonnes are in addition to those caused by deforestation itself.[21]

In the world as a whole, Myers estimates that there are now some 300 million shifted cultivators, setting fires, pressing deeper and deeper into forests each year, as they progressively exhaust their fragile, denuded soils. 'Behind them come still more waves of shifted cultivators, allowing the forest no chance to re-establish itself.'[22]

Even if one argues, as Myers does, that his estimated 300 million 'shifted cultivators', not debt itself, are the chief agents of forest destruction, and thus prime causes of increased greenhouse emissions, Myers is the first to recognise that this cultivator 'is no more to be held responsible for felling the forest than a soldier is to be blamed for fighting a war'.[23] These landless, last-resort, slashing and burning forest dwellers would not be where they are had they any alternative. 'Shifted' people, as the term suggests, are almost always displaced against their will – whether by export crops, loss of a job, poverty, or any other force beyond their control. The debt crisis should be seen here as a 'push' factor.

Shifted people have the misfortune to live in countries that have for years applied a debt-driven development model (designed by the World Bank and its emulators), paying virtually no attention to equitable land tenure, aid to small, food-producing farmers, credit for the poor, education for women, child survival/family-planning programmes and the like; much less sustainable environmental policies. So long as cash-strapped governments are strangled by debt, they cannot possibly change the present model and institute such programmes, even assuming they would like to.

The Brazilian Environment Minister under President Collor, José Lutzenberger, was one of his country's best known environmental activists before joining the government. He sees the major cause of Amazonian destruction not in the thousands of poor and powerless forest migrants but rather in the actions of the rich and powerful, including transnational corporations and individuals whose way into the forest has often literally been paved by the World Bank which planned and financed the first roads to penetrate the Amazonian forest. A short list of corporate devastators would include Anderson Clayton, Goodyear, Volkswagen, Nixdorf Computer, Liquigas, Nestlé, Borden, and Kennecott Copper. Their projects are various: 'cattle ranches, paper mills, single-species monocultures of exotic trees for pulp, immense rice plantations, sugarcane plantations for the Gasohol programme, timber mills and mining operations'.[24]

These ecologically destructive schemes are not even 'economic' in the sense of any normal business calculation. Rather, they have been financed with tax rebates and write-offs and can thus accept 'scandalously low' rates of productivity. Cattle raising is especially wasteful: according to Lutzenberger, an Amazonian ranch is lucky to get 50kg of meat (and no milk) to the hectare, compared with 600kg of meat and an average 5000 litres of milk on modest European organic farms using no purchased animal feed. Yet in Brazilian Amazonia, close to the Bank's roads, according to Robert Repetto of the World Resources Institute there are 'more than 600 cattle ranches averaging more than 20,000 hectares (50,000 acres) each ... typically losing more than half of its invested capital within 15 years'.[25]

These pastured animals also put extra methane into the atmosphere – about 15 per cent of the total of this greenhouse gas. The phenomenon can be scientifically described as 'enteric fermentation in ruminant digestive tracts'. The layperson would more likely speak of animals belching and farting. Mammals, including people, need anaerobic bacteria to help them digest their food. 'Ruminants such as cattle and sheep are especially dependent on bacteria to digest the cellulose in their diets and they emit large amounts of the gas.' Of all ruminants, cattle are the most numerous and the biggest methane emitters (sheep are a close second; termites are also major producers of methane – and the more felled timber, the more they proliferate). Of the world's roughly 1.2 billion cattle, about 70 per cent live in developing countries. If the 'debt connection' seems tenuous here, recall how significantly beef cattle raising for export increased in Brazil throughout the decade of the 1980s. Destroying forest to create cattle ranches contributes doubly to the greenhouse effect, delivering a one-two punch to the atmosphere.[26]

Typically, these animals, part of the transnational 'hamburger connection', are not intended to help feed local people since the government's chief concern is exports. Lutzenberger claims, however, that the forest, left intact, could 'produce at least ten times as much food in the form of tropical fruit, game and fish. Every single adult Brazil nut tree left standing can produce hundreds of kilos of precious food ... ' And ironically, the forest, properly used, could not only feed millions of presently undernourished or starving Brazilians but produce far more revenue for Brazil, sustainably, year after year, than it does through present once-and-for-all extraction.

Several economically viable forest products other than timber have already been identified – from edible oils to cosmetics to ice cream flavours. Such products could provide thousands of jobs and be processed on the spot, using, for example, *babassu* palm kernel shells for energy. A few factories in Brazil are already fueled with *babassu* charcoal and no longer cut wood from the coastal mangrove forests.[27] To date the World Bank and the IMF have shown little interest in helping Amazonian debtor countries invest in sustainable economic use of their forests – one way they could be preserved.

Japan imports about two-thirds of all Southeast Asian timber exports. Little of the final value remains in the producer countries: they receive only the price of the raw logs while sawing and processing usually take place in Japan. The Japanese construction boom absorbs much of the imported wood, but a new phenomenon contributing to Japanese timber use are *waribashi* – disposable wooden chopsticks. *Waribashi* may represent a trivial proportion (though still some 200,000 cubic metres of logs) of the country's total imports but are highly symbolic of the 'Japanese lifestyle based on mass consumption and waste', as a member of the Japanese Committee on Asian Tropical Forests puts it. Chopsticks used to be kept and washed after each meal. Every year more than 20 billion pairs of *waribashi* are used once and thrown away.[28]

Just as deforestation has a measurable impact on climate and temperature, so does it also contribute to the destruction of the ozone layer. Atmospheric concentration of methane is growing at a rate of more than 1 per cent a year, twice as fast as that of carbon dioxide. Because its atoms react in complex ways with those of other gases in the stratosphere, methane is also one of the prime culprits in the creation of ozone holes.[29] The destruction of the ozone layer and the reality of the greenhouse effect are no longer in doubt. The relevant questions begin not with 'If' but with 'How soon?' and 'How much?'. These phenomena are not what scientists call 'linear', increasing steadily at the same rate and producing a smooth, regular, predictable curve. The same can be said for the loss of the animals and plants on which we depend.

Bio-Diversity

'Nothing is nothing.' (Australian Aboriginal saying)

The decimation of the vegetable and the animal domains – the flora and the fauna – does not always get the same star billing as the greenhouse effect when deforestation is discussed. Yet the 'mass extinction' of the late twentieth century is comparable only to the one which did away with the dinosaurs 65 million years ago. If present rates of tropical forest destruction continue, reputable sources estimate that worldwide, some 15 to 20 per cent of all species will have disappeared before the year 2000. But how many is that? Such percentages tell us nothing about the actual numbers of species we will lose, for the excellent reason that no one knows how many species there are. The catalogue of earth's bounty has never come even close to completion and, at the rate we are going, never will.

We are not even sure how many species we *have* catalogued – estimates range from 1.3 to 1.8 million (including both plants and animals). Compare this with the estimates of probable numbers of insect species alone (admittedly the most numerous life form) ranging from 5 to 80 million, of which only about 875,000 have been identified and catalogued! Ten to 40 per cent of living plants probably still await discovery and Linnaean naming. In 'normal' geological periods, a few species disappear every million years or so; we are losing several every day.[30]

Species are highly interdependent; they sustain each other and they require specific amounts of space to do so successfully. When large enough parts of their habitat are destroyed, so, eventually, is the whole. Scientists working in the Amazon know that 'isolated patches of primary forest of 10, 100 or even of 1000 hectares (2500 acres) cannot sustain themselves.' Many ecologists have established the reality of the 'island effect' which causes veritable species 'population crashes'. Rainfall patterns change: rain makes trees, trees make rain – get rid of one and you lose the other. Nutrients are lost, food sources dry up, animals leave, general 'ecosystem decay' sets in. To make matters worse, the greenhouse effect and the island effect reinforce each other.

As temperatures warm, many plant and animal species will not be able to migrate fast enough to keep up with the changes in ecological conditions. One biologist compares such forced animal and vegetable species' migrations to 'having to cross Los Angeles to reach the promised land'. In a greenhouse world, a species shake-out would ensure that 'the only sure winners are pests and opportunists: rats, crows, flies, mosquitoes, weeds. Their ranges are so cosmopolitan that they will hang on ... Parasites are good at solving problems, and because they reproduce so quickly, they always win.'[31]

Because of the positive feedbacks between the greenhouse and the island effects, projected plant extinctions for the year 2000 in Latin American rainforests alone range from a best-case 15 per cent to a worst case two-thirds.[32] In other words, just creating parks and 'bio-reserves' won't do the trick. Nor, clearly, will zoos, herbariums or botanical gardens. Establishing single species tree plantations on previously forested land and calling it 'reforestation' is a tragic lie, one of which the World Bank has been frequently guilty in its so-called 'Social Forestry' projects; consisting of large stands of eucalyptus which restore none of the characteristics of the original forest nor the millions of species that once inhabited it.

Why should we care? Aside from the philosophical, ethical and biological arguments – abundance and diversity of life are good in themselves – there are a great many more mundane reasons why we should care very much indeed.

Compounds derived from a variety of tropical plants have been shown, experimentally, to be extremely promising for use in human medicine or agriculture. Alkaloids derived from one tropical plant can suppress the rise of glucose in the blood – of obvious interest to diabetics. When cultured tumour (cancerous) cells from mice were treated with an extract of another tropical plant before being injected into healthy mice, 'the cells were less likely to form tumours in the lungs than the untreated cells'. Even putting alkaloids from this plant in the mice's drinking water inhibited the ability of cancer cells to invade their lungs. This is possibly because the alkaloid does not act on the cancer itself but rather enhances the entire immune system, which would have enormous implications for diseases like AIDS.

Other tropical plant derivatives could provide 'natural, and therefore biodegradable, chemicals which deter insects from feeding without killing them indiscriminately. [They] could be ideal agents for protecting crops.' One recent discovery, extracted from a plant that grows in Australia's tropical state of Queensland and also in South America, seems to inhibit the enzymes of crop pests but to have no effect on humans.

As this scientist concludes,

People have previously considered most plants that supply us with sugar-shaped alkaloids to be of little use. These species do not figure prominently in lists of economically important species. This anomaly may give us cause to reflect that wild plants enabled us to evolve into what we are today, and that we still need all of them.[33]

Many tropical plants are already providing large economic benefits to the industrial countries (which, it should be mentioned in passing, rarely compensate the countries where the plants grow). Already, a plant like the Madagascar periwinkle provides alkaloids that have a high success rate in treating childhood leukemia and Hodgkin's disease. Sales of the drugs derived are worth about $160 million a year. The major pharmaceuticals firms recognise the value of tropical plants and are attempting to collect as many as they can while there is still time. The US National Cancer Institute has reportedly sponsored 'the world's single largest tropical plant collecting effort by recruiting ethno-botanists to document the traditional medicinal uses of plants and other species'.[34]

Tropical forests are the great unexplored botanical frontiers: we simply have no idea what future foods and medicines they may contain. Twenty-five acres of forest in Indonesia contain more species of trees than the whole of North America. A single ecological research station in Costa Rica counts twice as many plants and animals as California. Costa Rica's Minister of Energy and Natural Resources calls his country a 'biological superpower'. But he adds, wistfully, 'In the twenty-first century, the tropical forests will be like cathedrals because there will be so few of them left.'[35]

Costa Rica may well have more biological diversity per square foot than any place on earth and it has an excellent conservation programme as well. That is the good news. The bad news is that Costa Rica's foreign debt is $4.7 billion; a debt burden of nearly $1650 for every citizen of the country.[36] It has a high debt service ratio as well with 25 per cent of its export revenues devoted to reimbursement.

According to the World Resources Institute, the country has been throughout the 1980s one of the world's fastest deforesters. 'At current rates, Costa Rica will run out of forest in less than ten years [i.e. by the year 2000], except for land in parks and other protected reserves.'[37] And as we know, because of the 'island effect', not even the so-called 'protected' land can be considered secure.

Between 1982 and 1988, Costa Rica came up with $2.9 billion in debt service payments – a staggering figure when one realises that there are, after all, only 2.9 million Costa Ricans. In spite of these herculean efforts, the country's debt burden grew during that same period by over 50 per cent – from $3.1 billion in 1982 to $4.7 billion in 1988. To perform the annual servicing feat on the basis of an ever-expanding base of debt means exporting one's forests as fast as possible.[38]

Costa Rica also happens to be a cradle of bio-diversity, at the heart of one of the 'Vavilov centres', named for the Russian botanist who was a victim of his country's revolution but not before he had identified the world's chief gene-rich areas. The Central American Vavilov centre has given the world the original germplasm for corn, beans, tomatoes, cassava, avocado, squash, gourds, sweet pepper, upland cotton, sisal and cacao. As all plant breeders know, the seed varieties farmers buy are only a step or two ahead of their predators. To keep that lead, ensure resistance to disease and pests, and continue to increase yields, a constant supply of fresh genetic material is essential. The 'natural' varieties to provide crop-saving genes are fast disappearing, yet the US Department of Agriculture has estimated that improved genetic material contributes a billion dollars a year in increased crop productivity to the American economy.[39]

In a general way, as Professor Jack Kloppenburg reminds us,

> Inter- and intra-hemispheric transfers of germplasm have created a world in which domestic agricultures are often based on genetic materials with origins well beyond domestic borders. Any assessment of the political economy of plant genetic resources must take into account this 'genetic geography'.

The farming systems of entire continents – Australia and North America – depend almost 100 per cent on genetic materials they cannot themselves supply. Much the same is true of Europe. 'Ironically, the agricultures of what are regarded as ... the principal breadbaskets of the world are almost completely based on plant genetic materials derived from other regions.'[40]

The financially rich North is gene-impoverished and depends on the indebted, poor, but gene-rich South for an incalculable proportion of its food and medicines! The World Commission on Environment and Development (a.k.a. the Brundtland Commission) notes that half of all medical prescriptions dispensed in the North have their origins in wild organisms.

Clearly we have a stake in preserving the forests and the bio-diversity they shelter. But as we wage this battle, we must also recall that so far, the profits derived from exploiting forest resources have gone to a small number of giant food and pharmaceutical firms in the North. Because people in the South have little buying power, their food and medicinal needs are neglected. A just resolution to the debt crisis should be accompanied by a conscious effort to build up indigenous research and development capacities so that the benefits of forest resources can serve all the planet's inhabitants.

Sometimes the only way to convey the full scope of modern disasters is to resort to ancient images. The Greeks recognised three Fates: 'Clotho, the Spinner, who spun the thread of life; Lachesis, the Disposer of Lots, who assigned to each man his destiny; Atropos, she who could not be turned, who carried "the abhorrèd shears" and cut the thread at death.'[41] Those who do not understand the aboriginal saying 'Nothing is nothing'; those who believe we can 'afford' to lose numberless species would do well to heed these words of Jonathan Weiner's:

> the loss of a single species ... alters the ability of the biosphere to weave the web of life, on the ground, in the air, and in the water. We are riding a Fate, an Atropos, that cuts the thread of life. How many threads can we cut before we cut the one thread upon which our own lives depend?[42]

The Trans-Border Boomerang

Of general significance but of special concern to Americans is the debt connection linking Mexico to the southwestern United States. Mexico is the world's second largest debtor and earned the dubious honour of precipitating what came to be called the international debt crisis when, in August 1982, the government announced that it could no longer meet its payments. However, crisis or no crisis, between 1982 and 1988 Mexico somehow managed to scrape together and pay its creditors more than $100 billion in debt service – an amount exceeding the total debt it owed in 1982!

The cost for the majority of the Mexican people was enormous – their standards of living dropped back to the level of the 1960s and they suffered massive unemployment, hunger, deep cuts in social services – the usual sequence of events under IMF-sponsored structural adjustment. Mexico's reward for these massive efforts was to be 18 per cent more in debt than at the beginning of the decade, owing not $95 billion as it had in 1982 but a total of $112 billion. The highly touted Brady Plan scarcely made a dent in the mass of Mexico's debt – the negotiations were complex and the financial results hard to compute, but most experts think the Plan reduced the Mexican debt only by about 8 per cent in 1990–1. Interest payments averaging a billion dollars a month can still be expected to fall due regularly.[43]

So the country is desperate for cash. Like many other debtors, Mexico exports raw materials and foodstuffs but it has also made a great effort to encourage export manufactures and has given every incentive to entice foreign firms to set up shop within its borders. This policy has been eminently successful: today, just across the border from the United States, nearly 1800 factories employing half a million workers have been built.[44] Most are North American, but the Germans and the Japanese have begun to install plants as well, and other countries are testing the waters. This is the *maquiladora* zone, for so-called 'in-bond' production which encourages cross-border sharing of production with almost no customs restrictions in either direction.

There are few environmental regulations in this zone either, and virtually none that Mexico can now afford to enforce. Ann Bourland, whose job with the Mexican state of Sonora is to help attract foreign companies, says that 'the red tape and the expense' of American environmental law is a powerful motivation for firms to come to Mexico.

> In order to stay in the United States, a lot of these companies would have to invest in very expensive equipment to treat these chemicals and solvents and wastes. I've had a couple of companies come down solely for that reason.

The *maquiladora* area is now such an ecological disaster zone that the US embassy in Mexico has estimated it would cost $9 billion to clean up the border environment.[45]

Even in the unlikely event of such an investment, the area would probably not stay clean for long. New companies, creating more pollution, would soon follow and the older ones would have scant reason to change their behaviour. Besides the lack of environmental standards, they have another powerful incentive for settling in the *maquiladora* zone. The International Monetary Fund, following the dictates of the export-led growth model, and on grounds of making Mexican exports more competitive, has demanded so many devaluations of the Mexican peso that workers are now paid below-subsistence wages. For example, in February 1990, a 48-hour week at the La Reynosa Zenith television plant netted workers the equivalent of US$26.16 at the then going dollar–peso exchange rate – just under 55 cents an hour. Testimony from workers like these stresses their exposure to dangerous chemicals and fumes, lack of protective clothing or other safeguards and serious health problems directly related to workplace conditions.

These companies, if they think about it, must be glad of Mexico's debt burden which helps to keep their own operating restrictions at a minimum and wages at rock-bottom, thus ensuring them millions of dollars in savings and much higher profits than they could obtain in their home countries. US trade unions are understandably less pleased with this situation since

> tens of thousands of American workers have lost their jobs and tens of thousands more have seen employment opportunities vanish, as US companies transferred production to Mexico to take advantage of the poverty of Mexican workers and the absence of any effective regulations on corporate behavior

as a trade union economist stated before a US Congressional committee.[46] Since about three-quarters of Mexico's debt is owed to US banks, the financial Establishment is also doubtless grateful for the debt management policies applied by the Fund and a compliant Mexican government, allowing the accumulation of a transferable surplus in dollars.

For ordinary people, however, crowded and unsanitary living conditions, social degradation and rampant environmental destruction have combined to make the *maquiladora* zone a reasonable facsimile of hell on earth. United States immigration policies can keep at least some of the social problems at bay, but ecological havoc recognises no boundaries, as is becoming increasingly clear in the US states bordering on Mexico.

Tijuana, just the other side of the California border from San Diego, has grown from a sleepy, middle-sized town to a city of more than one million inhabitants, with an annual employment growth rate of 7 per cent. The combined metropolitan area of Tijuana-San Diego has swelled to 3.5 million people. More people means more sewage. Already, discharge of untreated sewage from Tijuana into the Pacific Ocean has forced the closure of California beaches on several occasions. In the coming decade, existing facilities are likely to be completely swamped whereas the area will have to deal with 140 million gallons (about 560 million litres) of raw sewage daily. Since there seems no hope of sufficient investment in treatment plants, much of this untreated waste will doubtless find its way to the Pacific as well.

Water sources vital to both sides of the border are dwindling and becoming salinised. Sixty million yearly border crossings in cars, trucks and buses foul the atmosphere. The *maquiladoras* themselves generate huge quantities of toxic wastes, many of which end up in California via the New River which flows northward. The Salton Sea, California's largest lake, in the Imperial Valley 'contains 100 industrial chemicals traceable to factories in Mexico, whereas the New River itself 'contains every disease known in the Western Hemisphere' according to a US Environmental Protection Agency official quoted in the *San Francisco Examiner*. 'Toxins emitted into the air in Tijuana blow into California each night, just as Los Angeles smog heads toward Mexico in the morning.'[47]

US states separated from Mexico by the Rio Grande are doing no better. Juarez, on the Texas border, has undergone the same chaotic growth as Tijuana and 'there is no sewage treatment system for its growing population, so waste used in the plants goes into a canal that is used for irrigating crops.' Thus the 'risks from bacterial and industrial contaminants may be to the workers in the fields and consumers in both Mexico and the United States who eat foods grown in these areas.' Falcon Lake in Texas receives so much waste from Nuevo Laredo (Mexico) that it has become 'one of the largest sewage ponds in the United States' according to a Texas official. The same person notes that, 'As *maquiladoras* increase in number and production, we will get toxic waste in the river [Rio Grande] which we can't treat out and which is detrimental to the human system.' Not surprisingly, studies of 33 US counties that take their drinking water from the Rio Grande have already shown significantly higher rates of liver and bladder cancer than the US national average.[48]

Land, sea and air are polluted by the activities and the waste products of 1800 *maquiladora* plants. Authorities in both countries are confronted with insoluble public health problems and millions of Mexican and US citizens are threatened with their consequences. The stage is now set for a major human and environmental disaster. Toxic substances, dangerous chemicals and flammable materials are trucked daily back and forth across the border or left lying about on factory property without proper storage facilities. The whole border region is a Bhopal waiting to happen.

The World Bank and the IMF call for export-led growth, structural adjustment based on competition and the supremacy of the private sector. The US government extends this logic in its call for ever-freer trade. One's economic doctrine – 'doctrine' is intended here in its religious sense – is governed by one's vision of the desirable society. Massive transfers of productive capacity to Mexico under the *maquiladora* programme do indeed make US or other transnational enterprise more competitive and they doubtless bring some economic benefits to Mexican financial, technical and political elites as well.

The logic of this doctrine also means that minimum wage and child labour laws do not apply, that health and safety regulations need not be observed, that workers' compensation and unemployment insurance need not be paid, that the environment can be pillaged and degraded at will. The Bank and the Fund are fond of quoting the 'doctrine of comparative advantage', but as the trade union economist cited above points out, 'Mexico's single comparative advantage is the poverty of its citizens and their willingness to work for subsistence wages ... No matter how productive, US workers cannot compete with labour costs of less than $1.00 an hour.'[49]

Such is the magic of the marketplace.

Where Must We Go from Here?

If we hope to stop the flight of the environmental boomerang, profound change in present debt management policy is the necessary – although not sufficient – condition. We believe debt relief should be combined with measures preventing a return to the same destructive policies that set the infernal machine going in the first place. The most urgent task is to break with the terrible logic of the twentieth-century 'development' model – energy- and resource-intensive, as exploitative of people as it is of their environment.

While it is true that too much money – as in the debt-driven maldevelopment model – leads to environmental disaster, so does too little. This is why the burden of debt must be lightened and the crisis used creatively to institute a healthy and prudent development model of benefit to all natural beings – vegetable, animal and human.

In particular, if we hope to stop the destruction of tropical forests, the human element is crucial. The forests cannot be saved without also saving the people who live in them, whether older inhabitants or new arrivals. People have from time immemorial learned to practise lifestyles that respect the forest while still providing them with a generous livelihood. One hopeful development in forest management is the policy of the Colombian government. In a farsighted move, Colombia has given more than 18 million hectares (45 million acres) of the Colombian Amazon over to the collective care of Indians belonging to some 50 ethnic groups. Between Indian lands and national parks, Colombia now protects an area of the Amazon forest nearly as large as Britain.

Indians make excellent forest managers because their whole way of life is based on a complex economic, but also religious and profoundly ecological system of giving to and receiving from the forest. In the words of Peter Bunyard,

> The traditional economy of the Indians is almost the exact opposite of a market economy in which a person's status increases with his wealth and possessions. In the Indian community, a person who accumulates is evidently one who lacks social relations with others and has no one with whom to share.[50]

Thus the Indians pity anyone with too many possessions. But it must be noted that their forest management systems work partly because each person has plenty of space – sometimes as much as a hectare or more per person may be required to sustain non-destructive forest livelihoods. In countries such as Brazil or Indonesia, hundreds of thousands more have joined the original forest dwellers and they cannot be shunted aside for the simple reason that under current circumstances there is no 'aside' where they can be shunted. Some, of course, like the rubber tappers of Brazil (whose leader was Chico Mendes) are seeking to earn their living by working sustainably with forest resources. We stress that any solution must take *all* people dependent on the forest into account and must develop *with them* the necessary means to preserve their common habitat. A strategy proceeding as if the forest were somehow empty, as if the people living there had no needs and no ideas of their own, will necessarily fail.

Even assuming substantial debt relief, it could not do the whole job by itself. Land reform, credit to the poor and other remedial social policies would be the best additional antidotes to ecological destruction. We do not intend to propose a 'master-plan' for saving third world forests. Many such plans have been elaborated, including the World Bank-FAO Tropical Forestry Action Plan (TFAP), which has been so widely and justifiably criticised that, as of the beginning of 1991, it had been withdrawn and put back on the drawing board. If TFAP were to be fully applied, it would compound, not prevent, forest destruction.[51]

Another, more beneficent plan to reduce the greenhouse effect and restore forest livelihoods recommends 'reforesting the earth' by planting 130 million hectares of forest in the southern hemisphere before the end of the millennium – a task which would require the planting of 18.4 billion trees annually; roughly 5 annually for every man, woman or child now living in the third world.[52] Such schemes are full of good intentions and convey much useful knowledge about the need for reforestation but tend to ignore the power relations, ownership questions, and sheer poverty that prevent the eminently sensible ideas they propose from being implemented.

Just as we do not want to propose a master plan, so we want to be 'ecumenical' in our views on debt reduction. Much debate, sometimes generating more heat than light, has taken place within the still tiny community of people in the North anxious to do something about third world debt. Some call for unconditional and total write-offs, on the grounds that the debt is illegitimate to begin with, that it has already been paid many times over, and that any conditions attached to its reduction would infringe upon national sovereignty and represent old colonialist practices dressed up in new clothes.

Others are less trusting in the benevolence of the third world State and in its spontaneous desire to give first call on resources to the poor majority. They also call for substantial write-offs – well over 50 per cent – but caution that countries should not through such measures be inadvertently cut off from all future sources of credit. They also want social and ecological conditions attached to debt relief, ensuring that it benefits the majority of each debtor country's population and contributes to saving their natural environment.

The present author has been firmly in the latter camp, but believes we must all recognise that the first task today in the North is to bring a great many more people into the debate; the second to recognise that no single solution is going to resolve the crisis. This book is written in the hope of increasing our numbers and our strength and, when we do, we will still need to combine many different approaches and seek many different kinds of solutions if we are to have an impact.* We must also stay in close touch with our counterparts in the South who are the debt crisis's first victims.

'Debt-for-nature swaps' haven't worked very well so far and have involved just a tiny portion of the debt, but this is no reason to scrap the idea. Swaps can, however, monopolise limited government resources for environmental protection, applying them to whatever piece of territory the donor finds attractive while not even stopping unsustainable extractive practices (as in the logging still going on in

---

* A fuller account of the debt debate, the need to reduce debt by more than 50 per cent to make any difference, and proposals for 'creative reimbursement' will be found in the last chapter of Susan George, *A Fate Worse than Debt.*

the Beni Bio-reserve, Bolivia). In some cases, donors of swap funds pick as a working partner in the debtor country a local organisation that turns out to be the most reactionary one among a range of possible choices.

Suddenly this local environmental organisation has wealth, responsibilities and prestige; whereas less 'conservationist', more socially oriented organisations go begging and find their influence reduced. Often the needs of the actual forest dwellers have not even been acknowledged. If debt-for-nature swaps are to be more effective, we have to pick better objectives and better partners in the South, and follow their lead.

Even if their worst pitfalls are avoided, swaps cannot make a real dent in the outstanding debt, nor can they save the environment by themselves. They will never absorb the necessary significant reductions – substantially more than 50 per cent – needed, and they will have somehow to be coupled with social and political change, whether through conditionality or through new programmes of cooperation involving fresh money and different kinds of partnerships in which the civil society in the debtor country has a genuine voice. It is, indeed, a tall order. But there is no way around it.

Equally urgent is the task of addressing the US administration's obsession with 'free trade', whether for the Western hemisphere through various regional agreements, or for the globe through GATT (General Agreement on Tariffs and Trade). In part, these negotiations are intended to sidetrack debt reduction proposals. They offer indebted country governments the carrot of increased investment and access to Northern markets in exchange for continued docility in playing the debt repayment game. 'Free trade' sounds, perhaps, fair and democratic but will inevitably place further strains on the environment and on working people everywhere. All countries must compete to offer the most attractive, least regulated conditions to transnational corporations. 'Free trade' is an invitation to multiply *maquiladoras*, based on lowest common denominators.

Groups in the North need to add to their debt and development agenda a demand that any trade agreements between nations of creditor North and indebted South be accompanied by binding and enforceable standards for wages, and for health, safety and environmental regulations. In a world without economic borders, as we will note particularly in the chapter on jobs and markets, downward pressure on these standards in one place means downward pressure everywhere.

If no action is taken now, the pace of ecological destruction can only accelerate. Delay will be costly, in every sense. If we finally wake up in, say, the year 2000 and decide that urgent steps are indeed necessary to save the forests and to break out of the greenhouse – always assuming this is still possible – it will cost us at least twice as much to obtain one half the effect we could obtain today with immediate measures. In this chapter we have naturally concentrated on greenhouse gas emissions from third world countries since they are the debtors under discussion. Debtor countries are not, however, primarily responsible for greenhouse gas emissions. The industrialised countries are the chief culprits; as such they should be held accountable for reducing emissions not only at home but in the third world as well. This they could do by compensating the debtors financially for preserving their forests and by helping them to adopt energy-efficient, renewable-energy-based development models.

As we write the conclusion to this chapter in May 1991, we have begun to grasp the monumental human, economic and environmental toll of the Gulf War. This is not the place to express political and strategic opinions on this war, but surely it is clear that Northern governments, particularly the United States, are collectively foolish to remain so dependent on petroleum-based energy systems for transport, industrial power, and domestic use. Haven't the multiple warnings since 1973 been enough? As the Palestinians are reportedly fond of saying, 'If Kuwait exported carrots, it is doubtful Bush would have been so concerned with international law.' Fair enough. But there is another warning implicit in this war and perhaps – dare one say? – a silver or at least an aluminium foil lining.

Humans – and their governments – tend to react to events, not processes – to Bhopals, to Chernobyls, to invasions but not to the long histories that made such disasters possible. Biologists know the experiment in which a frog is placed in a beaker of very hot water. Wisely, it jumps out. But if the frog is placed in a beaker of cold water which is then slowly heated to boiling point, it will remain there and, if no one intervenes, be boiled alive because nature has not equipped it to sense small gradations of temperature. Since public opinion does have its froglike attributes, we may end up thanking – after a fashion – Saddam Hussein for shaking us out of our complacency on energy policies.

Meanwhile, there's a lot of work to be undertaken. Although individual lifestyles in the developed countries can be held partly to blame for environmental destruction, we believe that it is above all the actions of the Northern creditor governments, and those of the international institutions they largely control, which drive the forces behind this destruction. They invented the initial 'development' model which has led to ecological disaster. They have used the leverage provided by the debt crisis to perpetuate this model. We have indeed met the enemy and he is not so much 'us' as the people and the institutions we have allowed to speak for and to represent us. Only informed and active citizens can call them to account.

The Second Boomerang: Drugs

Research and Documentation by Peter Andreas and Humberto Campodonico

Violent crime in the United States jumped 10 per cent in 1990, continuing a six-year surge fueled by more murders and a wave of drug-related incidents ... The Federal Bureau of Investigation said its preliminary statistics ... showed all offenses in the violent-crime category increasing sharply last year. Murder and aggravated assaults each soared 10 per cent, rape went up 9 per cent and robberies jumped 11 per cent ... The figures marked the sixth straight year the overall crime rate rose in a trend which experts attributed largely to more drug-related violence ...
> Reuters dispatch, *International Herald Tribune*, 29 April 1991

The drug trade is Latin America's only successful multinational.
> Alan García, former president of Peru

In 1989, a record number of Americans – 64 per cent – cited drugs as the number one problem of the United States – the highest proportion of people ever to agree on the priority of a single issue if we are to believe the pollsters.[1] In his first televised speech to the nation on 5 September 1989, President Bush declared 'war on drugs', or, more formally speaking, instituted the multi-billion dollar programme known as the National Drug Control Strategy. In September 1990, the president marked its first anniversary by assuring the American people that the drug war would remain the 'nation's top priority'.[2]

Americans have good reason to be alarmed and the president has arguably used their fears to justify his drug war. Although, for obvious reasons, any figures relating to the booming drug economy – whether they concern production, consumption or revenues – are impossible to certify and subject to caution, probably a minimum of 13 million US citizens use illegal drugs. The National Institute of Drug Abuse (NIDA) claims that drug use has been declining: there may once have been as many as 23 million users (defined as people who tried illegal drugs at least once) in 1985. That's the good news.

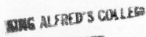

The bad news is that this decline has been registered among so-called 'casual users'. The number of hard-core addicts is, on the other hand, rising. NIDA estimates that the number of people using cocaine every day has risen by 37 per cent since 1985. According to NIDA, and contrary to received opinion, three-quarters of drug users are white; about 12 per cent are black, most of the rest are hispanic. Most consumers of illegal drugs are upper or middle class, educated people. NIDA estimates, ominously, that nearly 20 per cent of high school seniors consume drugs at least once a month.

Although drugs are overwhelmingly a 'mainstream' phenomenon, minority groups who live in deprived circumstances get most of the media attention. Presumably, upper and middle class users can afford to sustain their habit from their regular incomes. Not so the poor, the jobless and the young. In mid-1990, press reports, based on NIDA documentation, stated that 'robbery and murder rates are running at record levels and cocaine is being found in the urine of the majority of those arrested in the major cities.'

Most of the violence is related to turf wars between dealers, but the nearly 2.5 million heavy users, many addicted to crack, also send the statistics shooting up. They make the news stories about prostitution and AIDS, 'crack babies', homelessness and violent crime of all kinds. Drug-related criminal violence and social dislocation naturally get worse whenever the the price to pay for one's fix escalates. Like other prices, the price of cocaine fluctuates according to the laws of supply and demand, but tend to change more radically than those of legal goods. For example, between December 1989 and mid-1990, the New York wholesale street price reportedly rose by over 40 per cent.[3]

Minor drug offenders are swamping the US civil courts where drug-related cases increased by more than 300 per cent between 1980 and 1990. The chief federal district judge in Miami said, 'It's gotten to the point where we're very close to not having a civil court.' In some parts of the country, according to lawyers and judges, courts have become 'little more than processing plants for low-level drug offenders' with no time to spend on cases posing basic Constitutional issues. The promise of 'justice for all' is becoming a hollow one as mounting numbers of drug cases far outdistance the funds available for public defenders. Exhausted attorneys in Philadelphia confide that 'justice may become the biggest casualty of the drug war.' In 1988 alone, over 750,000 people were arrested for violating drug laws; the majority of them for simple possession. Drugs are the main reason that the US has the highest incarceration rate in the world. The number of prisoners doubled in the 1980s and in Washington

DC, for example, half of those jailed have been sentenced for drug-related offences.[4]

Nor is the drug phenomenon confined to the great metropolises – far from it. Whether they concern the upper class or the underclass, drugs are now a major problem in American towns whose very names used to be synonymous with an upstanding, righteous and sober – if rather boring – way of life. Peoria, Illinois, witnessed its drug-related crime triple from 126 to 418 cases in 1988. That same year, the president of the Chamber of Commerce of Guttenberg, Iowa, pleaded guilty to participating in a drug trafficking ring covering Iowa, Wisconsin and Colorado.[5]

There are plenty of explanations for the phenomenal growth of the drug economy in the United States since the beginning of the 1980s. Some of them are psychological and cultural, part of larger societal phenomena provoking alienation and despair; but it seems no accident that chronic unemployment in the legitimate economy accompanied the drug boom. The anxiety of joblessness may lead to a desire for escape through 'highs'; more concretely, the dearth of economic prospects elsewhere draws thousands of newcomers to the trade, especially in minority communities. Terry Williams, the author of *Cocaine Kids**, who knows this end of the drug industry intimately, explains,

> Many teenagers are drawn to work in the cocaine trade simply because they want jobs, fulltime or even as casual labour ... there is another strong motivating force and that is the desire to show family and friends that they can succeed at something ...

The United States of the 1980s proved fertile terrain in which both users and dealers flourished. Between 1979 and 1984, 11.5 million American workers lost their jobs because of plant closures and plant relocations (to places like the *maquiladora* zone in Mexico, as described in the previous chapter). Only 60 per cent of them found new work, and half of those who did were obliged to accept lower wages, often drastically lower. Three out of five new jobs created in the same 5-year period from 1979–84 paid less than US$7400 (£3700) a year; $616 or £308 monthly. By 1988, weekly earnings (adjusted for inflation) for US families were lower than at any time since 1960.

Rural areas were also hard hit: between 1983 and 1988, over 400,000 family farms went bankrupt. Massive farm losses meant rural businesses, services and communities dragged down with them.

* Addison-Wesley, 1991.

By 1988, the gap between rich and poor Americans had become a chasm. During the Reagan years, living standards for the bottom fifth of the US population fell by 9 per cent whereas the top fifth found itself better off by fully 19 per cent. Small wonder that even a heartland city like Omaha, Nebraska, could be described in 1988 as 'the perfect environment for selling crack'.[6]

The drug economy offers an alternative to the alienated, the marginalised, the unskilled and the newly jobless and may, temporarily, seem to solve many of their individual problems. The costs to society as a whole are, however, tremendous. For example, in addition to all the obvious crime-related losses visited on the larger community, the price of intensive care for 'crack babies' now costs the United States $2.5 billion a year. Each of the million 'drug-exposed' babies born between 1988 and 1991 will have required up to $100,000 just to make it through infancy. No estimates appear to have been attempted for the investments these children will require if they are to reach adulthood.

Drugs take their toll on the American education system as well, in sorry enough shape without this added burden. Across the United States, underfunded schools are discovering that they cannot both teach basic skills and cope with the ravages of the in-schoolhouse drug trade. Even first-graders are now recruited as lookouts and runners for pushers who sell and use drugs at school at all age levels.

Economists estimate that, all in all, illegal drugs cost American society $60 billion a year. The federal government's martial response to this spreading calamity, as the phrase 'war on drugs' suggests, is totally inadequate: predictably heavy on law enforcement, it stops well short of attacking root causes. More prisons are promised; more small-time dealers and users are being sent there, treatment and rehabilitation get short shrift. The deeper societal ills promoting drug use and abuse are virtually ignored.

The drug boomerang is also flying towards Europe. Europeans have a history of heroin use, with an Asian or Turkish provenance, as the 'drug of choice', but many signs indicate that with regard to cocaine, 'Europe is where the United States was 8 or 10 years ago', as the head of Spain's National Drug Programme said. European heroin addicts are overwhelmingly lower class, marginal people and a substantial proportion of them have AIDS as well; whereas cocaine is the 'yuppy' drug – usually, and erroneously, perceived as harmless and non-addictive. Crack, on the other hand, is just beginning to surface. Crack's appearance in a culture is more a matter of economics than anything else. When drug markets become saturated, crack is introduced to reach new consumers. A drugs trade expert quoted in the *New York Times* explains that Colombians have pumped a lot of cocaine into Europe because of sharply declining prices in the US. European prices have been sliding as well – they declined by about 50 per cent between 1987 and 1989, to $25,000–$30,000 the kilo. 'When it's down to $8000–$13,000 in a year or two, when it's that cheap, it's worth turning into crack', this expert explains.

Seizures of cocaine are one indicator of its prevalence. European police reported in November 1990 that cocaine seizures had risen sixfold since 1986 – from 1.5 tons to nearly 9 tons. Portugal and especially Spain, where Colombians move like fish in water, are the favoured entry points but the head of the London Metropolitan Police also admitted in 1989 that Britain is a 'prime and growing market' for international coke dealers. The single European market of 1992 and the opening up of Eastern Europe will be a boon to the traffickers. US narcotics officials of the Drug Enforcement Administration (DEA), extrapolating from various signs in Europe, think that cocaine consumption was about 90 tons in 1989, followed by a huge jump, to 160–180 tons in 1990. A DEA expert confirms the view of his Spanish colleague: 'The Europeans are where we [Americans] were ten years ago. They are facing a cocaine epidemic.' A Bogota newspaper, citing Colombia's security police and Interpol, even reported in August 1990 that Europe had already replaced the United States as the biggest market for the drug.[7]

Tracing the Debt–Drug Link

As a result of the steady demand for drugs in Europe and the United States, the supply side of the cocaine economy in the Andean countries of Bolivia, Colombia and Peru is flourishing. The roots of the drug problem tap deep into the subsoil of Northern societies, yet the United States looks southwards for solutions, seeking to cut off the supply 'at the source' by waging 'war on drugs'. Unfortunately, the North American anti-drug warriors are shooting themselves in the foot. US policy towards the debts of producer countries combined with International Monetary Fund austerity programmes absolutely ensure that the cocaine will continue to flow so long as the demand exists. So long as the US refuses to recognise the flagrant contradiction between its economic policy and its drug policy, no degree of 'warfare' will stop this flow.

Of all the 'boomerangs' we examine in this book, the Andean drug economy is perhaps the most clearly and directly linked to chronic indebtedness in the three Latin American drug-producing and trafficking countries. Coca has always been grown in the Andes for medicinal and ritual purposes. It also serves as a remedy against fatigue and hunger for an often exhausted and famished population.* Recently, however, production has skyrocketed. Most of the growing and primary processing of cocaine takes place in Bolivia and Peru. Once reduced to Basic Cocaine Paste, it is then generally airlifted to Colombia, whose celebrated 'drug barons' and their vassals handle final processing and marketing. Except for the fact that every stage of its production, transformation and distribution is illegal, the drug industry is run like any other efficient business, like any 'successful multinational' as the former Peruvian president put it.

We will look at the situation of each of the three debtor-drug industry countries in turn, then argue that the military and law enforcement approach of the US 'war on drugs' is both dangerously misguided and woefully inadequate. A lasting solution to the drug crisis will ultimately have to be found on the demand side, but an effective supply side strategy should concentrate not on warfare and 'eradication' but on severing the debt–drug link.

Genuine and legal alternatives must be provided to the millions in the producer countries who depend on drugs for a livelihood. The International Monetary Fund must cease to impose policies which today make it, with or without its knowledge and consent, an accessory before and after the fact to the crimes of the cocaine outlaws.

First, here are some basic debt figures for the three coca-countries:[8]

Table 2.1

	Debt 1982	Debt 1988	% Change	Cumulative Debt Service 1982–8 (US$ bn)	Service 1982–8 as % Debt 1982
	(US$ billion)				
BOLIVIA	3,591	5,273	+47	2,232	62
COLOMBIA	10,671	16,537	+55	14,233	133
PERU	12,608	20,680	+64	9,333	74

As is apparent in the third column of Table 2.1, all three countries are substantially deeper in debt now than they were at the beginning of the decade in spite of quite massive debt service payments. Except

* Indians have chewed the coca leaf from time immemorial, but this gives a 'high' several hundred times less potent than the processed, industrial variety of the drug.

for Colombia, which has been able to obtain some new loans, heavier indebtedness is mostly the result of unpaid arrears in interest being added to the principal. Bolivia and Peru are, by any standards, in desperate straights. As the last column in Table 2.2 shows, Bolivia, under strict IMF surveillance, devotes nearly half of its meagre export income – at least of its *legal* export income – to debt service. Even so, its indebtedness has risen by nearly half since 1982 and Bolivian debt per capita substantially exceeds its GNP per capita.

Table 2.2

	Debt per Capita 1987(US$)	GNP per Capita 1987 (US$)	Ratio Debt/GNP per Capita (%)	Debt Service Ratio 1988 (%)
BOLIVIA	764	580	131	46.5
COLOMBIA	533	1,240	43	40
PERU	984	1,470	67	17

As for Peru, the only reason its debt service ratio shows up on the above table at a reasonable 17 per cent of exports of goods and services is because the figure concerns 1988 when the country had declared a *de facto* moratorium on debt repayments. Peru's reimbursements to the IMF, for example, dropped from US$144 million in 1984 to just $1 million dollars in both 1987 and 1988. After Alan García became president, the IMF put Peru on its 'pariah' list, thus warning other possible credit sources that this government should be considered ineligible for loans. Peru remained beyond the financial pale for five years.

In complete contrast, Colombia, since 1982, has managed to pay its creditors an average of more than $2 billion a year in debt service. Even so, the country is 55 per cent more in debt than it was in 1982 and its annual service payments doubled between 1982 and 1988 (from $1456 to $2969 billion). Many experts argue that Colombia's drug-related revenue is the critical factor keeping the country's finances afloat, allowing it to sustain a heavy debt burden with less stress than that felt by other countries in Latin America.

Now we will look more closely at the debt–drug connections in each of these countries.

Bolivia

For most of its people, life in Bolivia is nasty, brutish and short. It is the poorest country in Latin America; it has the continent's lowest life expectancy – some 50 years – and highest child mortality rates;

malnutrition is chronic and 85 per cent of the rural population lives below the poverty line.[9]

The country's chief legal export is, or at least was, tin, but the bottom has dropped out of the tin market. It does not seem a coincidence that Bolivia also has the most cocaine-dependent economy in the region.

The Bolivian government itself estimates that half a million of its citizens are engaged in cultivating, processing and/or transporting coca and its derivatives. Since Bolivia's population is only 7 million people, with perhaps 2 million in the workforce (the official figure is 1.7 million), this means that one job out of every three or four is provided by drug-related activities.[10] According to Bolivia's former finance minister Flavio Machicado, the half million people directly engaged in the coca business generate through their earnings further economic activity creating at least another 300,000 jobs. 'I've said very clearly, every time I've had a chance, that there would be a social and economic catastrophe here ... If narcotics were to disappear overnight, we would have rampant unemployment. There would be open protest and violence', says Machicado.[11]

Coca is a hardy, fast-growing plant and with several harvests a year, Bolivia can produce between 100,000 to 150,000 metric tonnes of coca leaves on the 70,000 or so hectares (175,000 acres) cultivated. This is vastly more than enough to satisfy the needs of the Bolivian people. As in the rest of the Andes, a small part of the coca crop is perfectly legal: some of the leaves are chewed, some are used to make coca wines or *mate de coca* tea which is great for coping with Andean altitudes – the present author drank several litres of it in Peru to good effect. Such products are sold in shops and supermarkets. A huge spurt in demand from the United States and unprecedented economic crisis in Bolivia have, however, combined in recent years to unleash a prodigious expansion of coca production. In 1972–4, only about 9000 tons were produced annually, almost entirely for internal consumption, compared to the 100,000 to 150,000 tonnes grown in the early 1990s.[12]

In 1988, coca cultivators earned about $316 million on their crop – more than the total value of all the rest of Bolivia's agricultural production, worth about $300 million. More and more peasants are active in reducing the leaves to Basic Cocaine Paste (BCP). Even children can help boost family income by trampling the coca leaves in pits, akin to stamping the grapes in Mediterranean countries. All told, Bolivia can produce over 1 million kilos of valuable BCP. According to Peruvian economist Humberto Campodonico's calculations, 'the cultivation of the coca leaf and the preparation of the

BCP have become the main source generating foreign currency in Bolivia, above the value of *all legal exports* of the country ... at a minimum, some US$500 million a year is monetized.' (His emphasis)[13] An economic adviser to the Bolivian president puts the numbers even higher: 'Coca and cocaine production generated $1.5 billion (in 1987) which represents around 29 per cent of our GNP. Of this, $600 million stayed inside the country.'[14]

Everyone agrees that Bolivia now supplies roughly one third of the world's coca. How did the Bolivian economy itself become so addicted to cocaine?

Though we will not burden the reader with an explanation beginning in 1825, the year of Bolivian independence, it may still be useful to know that the country has chalked up more than 180 *coups d'état* since then. One of them occurred in 1964 and its history is worth relating. In the early 1950s, popular peasant and miner militias carried out a successful social revolution which had supposedly abolished the Bolivian armed forces. The United States, however, began contributing heavily from its Military Assistance Program to the rebuilding and the modernisation of the Bolivian military.

These North American efforts took over a decade to bear fruit, but in 1964 the Bolivian army overthrew the democratically elected civilian government. A succession of military regimes then proceeded to run – and to loot – the country for the following 18 years. The ruling officers also nurtured the drug trade on the side. As Bolivia specialist Kevin Healy, of the US (Congressionally funded) Inter-American Foundation says,

> It is ironic that the United States reconstructed a military estab-
> lishment during the 1950s and 1960s which, during the 1970s and
> 1980s was led by high-level officers who, under a militant anti-
> communist platform, pursued illegal drug trafficking to the United
> States.[15]

In 1980, an event widely known as 'the cocaine coup' brought to power yet another military man who, with his minister of the interior, was one of the leaders of the major national drug smuggling mafia.

The generals' fiscal management was creative to say the least, and favoured heavy borrowing as well. Successive military regimes took advantage of all the money on offer in the 1970s, which was a lot. As economist R.T. Naylor explains,

The state, controlled by the military, borrowed heavily and lent the proceeds to private Bolivian firms with which the military leaders were associated. If a project was successful, everyone came up smiling. If it was not, the state picked up the bill and everyone still came up smiling. In both cases most of the funds went to import consumer durables ... or were spent on arms purchases, or were diverted to [foreign] banks.*[16]

When General Banzer assumed power in 1971, Bolivia's debt was $700 million. By 1982 there was nothing much left to steal and the country was returned to civilian control. As the officers rode off into the sunset, their pockets full of dollars, they left a national debt which had been multiplied by more than five. Bolivia was now saddled with a debt of $3.6 billion, most of it government guaranteed, and had almost nothing to show for it. The burden the generals left behind was the result of consumption and fraud, not productive investment, so reimbursement posed predictably insoluble problems. Not least of these was the refusal of private commercial banks to have anything further to do with Bolivia.

The years from 1980–5 were extremely unpleasant ones for most Bolivians. The country's GNP dropped by one fifth, per capita consumption fell by one third, family incomes plunged 28 per cent. Unemployment doubled. Meanwhile, the country was using up to one third of its meagre export receipts to pay interest. If Bolivia had actually paid all sums theoretically due, it would have had to use the totality of its hard currency income for debt service alone.[17]

As if the internal shocks were not enough, the Bolivian economy was buffeted from outside as well. For decades, Bolivia's name was associated with tin. Like other countries dependent on one or two commodities, it was especially vulnerable to price fluctuations. 'Fluctuation' is not, however, the word to describe what happened to the tin market in 1985. The International Tin Council went bankrupt in late 1985, leaving its huge stocks of tin virtually worthless. It could easily cost a producer country six times more to mine a ton of tin than the market would pay for it. Bolivia's second income earner had been natural gas exports to Argentina, but Argentina had its own debt-induced cash crunch problems and wasn't buying.

* R.T. Naylor is also well worth reading on the links of the Bolivian military to former Gestapo official Klaus Barbie (eventually extradited and tried in France); to Reverend Sun Myung Moon's Unification Church; to the notorious right-wing P-2 'Masonic' lodge in Italy and right-wing Italian terrorists as well as other assorted international fascists.

The government's response to these various disasters was to print pesos. The ensuing inflation was 'one of the highest in world history' according to Harvard economist Jeffrey Sachs. From August 1984 to August 1985, prices rose by a breathtaking 30,000 per cent. 'During the final months of the hyperinflation, from May 1985 to August 1985, the inflation surged to an annualized rate of 60,000 per cent', writes Sachs.[18]

Such was the state of this sorry nation when Victor Paz Estenssoro took over in August 1985. He quickly implemented the toughest IMF-style austerity programme ever attempted in Latin America. Paz Estenssoro wasted no time. His structural adjustment plan, called the New Economic Policy (NEP), was decreed almost immediately after he took office. Formal agreement with the Fund was completed by mid-1986, followed by an agreement with other official creditors through the so-called Paris Club. Professor Jeffrey Sachs, the chief architect of the Bolivian NEP or 'stabilisation' plan, describes in some detail how a full range of drastic economic measures were instituted and how inflation was quickly brought to heel. Sachs does not, oddly enough, mention the single bright spot in a generally sombre tableau, the one factor many other experts credit with keeping the Bolivian economy afloat: coca.

Among the NEP measures were massive lay-offs in the public sector and the closure of the money-losing tin mines. Some 20,000 miners were sacked. Where were these people to go, if not to the coca economy? For Bolivian political scientist Eduardo Gamarra, this was obvious. He told a US Congressional committee in mid-1990:

> Ironically, the NEP encouraged peasants and laid-off workers to flock to the coca-growing regions to meet the needs of the cocaine industry ... For Washington, Bolivia has become a showcase of what other countries in the region could accomplish if free-market principles are allowed to run their economies ... [but] any downturn in the coca-cocaine economy could have grave consequences for the continued success of Bolivia's highly regarded NEP.[19]

In 1981, the province of the main coca-growing region, Chaparé, had a population of about 84,000 people. By the end of the decade, it was at least half a million. The official unemployment rate jumped from 6 per cent to 22 per cent between 1981 and 1988 (Humberto Campodonico estimates that 'open unemployment' was in fact `35 per cent by the end of 1988); simultaneously the area planted to coca rose from 20,000 to 70,000 hectares. A hectare planted to coca can

earn for its tenant at least US$1200 (£600 pounds sterling) a year –
sometimes much more. Compare this income to the average annual
wage of a miner (US$827); or that of a factory worker ($649); or to
the earnings of a non-coca producing peasant ($150). An EEC briefing
paper notes, 'the New Economic Policy was drawn up by North
American experts and approved by the IMF, but it can only be
carried through by means of the jobs and foreign exchange generated
by the drug traffic.'[20] Bolivian president Jaime Paz Zamora pointed
out that destroying the jobs provided directly and indirectly by the
cocaine economy would be comparable to sacking roughly 50 million
people in the United States.

The coca economy does more than just mop up unemployment.
Bolivia produces few consumer goods and the drug economy also
provides the dollars for vital imports of food, durables and non-
durables sold in markets throughout the country. Coca dollars never
show up in the national accounts, and IMF missions and US officials
keep absolutely quiet about them, but it is an open secret that the
NEP itself took the coca economy fully into account. The influx of
coca dollars is 'the only way we've been able to balance the balance
of payments', explains Professor Rolando Morales, past president of
the Bolivian Association of Economists. He says, 'The government has
promulgated several different measures designed to recycle coca
dollars in the economy.' It has deregulated the foreign exchange
market, lifted all import restrictions, prohibited official inquiries
into the sources of wealth brought into Bolivia and granted tax
amnesties for repatriated capital.[21]

The president of the opposition political party Movimiento
Boliviano Libre, Antonio Aranibar Quiroga, also points out that his
country's economic policy, supported by the IMF since 1985,

> is intimately connected to the existence of the coca and cocaine
> economy. Without the revenues [they] bring in, the New Economic
> Policy would not have had the slightest possibility of success ...
> this great 'success' of economic austerity was sustained directly by
> the narco-dollars that greased the machinery of the Bolivian
> economy.

Aranibar also notes that the huge fortunes made by drug trafficking
have been 'sanctified', since it is now illegal to investigate the origins
of any wealth existing in Bolivia. Laws encouraging drug trafficking
to flourish are on the statute books. 'This legalization of narco-
dollars counts on the complete support and approval of those who

finance the economic policy in Bolivia', which is to say the IMF, and those who follow its lead.[22]

Judged by the criteria of the Fund, the Bolivian experience of austerity has been a huge success. The IMF is pleased indeed with Bolivia as a model pupil. A December 1989 Fund press release announced:

> Since the start of the economic reform program in late 1985, Bolivia has made substantial progress in correcting financial imbalances and economic distortions. Economic activity has expanded for three consecutive years at an annual rate of 2–3 per cent, and inflation was brought down to less than 14 per cent in the year ended September 1989. The current account deficit of the balance of payments has narrowed over the period, and Bolivia has sharply reduced its external debt to commercial banks and certain bilateral creditors.[23]

This citation of merit preceded the announcement of Bolivia's reward: another ESAF, for 'Enhanced Structural Adjustment Facility' loan. Remarkably, the IMF has managed never to utter the dread 'C' word, as Ronald Reagan might say; 'coca' never makes an appearance in its analyses. Yet despite the IMF's fullsome praise, the Bolivian economy is still extremely fragile; Bolivians are still desperately poor and hungry and coca is still the most important and dynamic sector of the nation's 'expanding economic activity'.

The US wants to curb the production of Bolivian cocaine, but can't have it both ways. The Bolivian Ambassador to the US admits 'there are some people in the United States government who would like to eradicate all our coca. But for us, that's impossible to do.' The former director of Bolivia's Central Bank explains why: 'Cocaine is like a cushion that is preventing a social explosion.'[24]

Only the US government and the IMF seem unable, or unwilling, to track the flight path of this debt–drug boomerang.

Peru

Nor do the Fund and the United States seem to comprehend the depth of the drug economy in Peru. Peru is the world's leading supplier of coca, providing over half the raw material for all the cocaine produced in Latin America. The land surface planted to this crop has expanded so fast that no one quite knows if it is 100,000 hectares, or 180,000 (250,000 to 450,000 acres) or something in between.[25]

As in Bolivia, the value of coca production is probably equal to the combined value of all the rest of Peru's agricultural production. The country produces roughly twice as much coca paste as Bolivia, drawing between US$750 million and $1.5 billion to the Peruvian economy. Peru's legal exports are worth only $3 billion in a good year; the drug windfall is a financial blessing.[26]

Coca is Peru's only real growth industry; the single point of light among a thousand points of darkness. In 1979, when the Peruvian economy was already in serious straits but had not yet crash-landed, only 19,000 hectares (47,500 acres) were planted to coca. Cultivation shot up tenfold in ten years. To quote a Peruvian Catholic priest who has studied the drug economy extensively, the 'Peruvian jungle is stained white' by coca production.

He explains why this is no accident. Peru suffers chronic unemployment and coca growing now directly absorbs about 250,000 people, not counting their families. Coca is a labour-intensive crop. In the Alto Huallaga valley where most production takes place, a farm labourer harvesting coca can make US$13 a day, compared to the $3.30 (in 1989) earned by labourers working on other crops in the same valley. The grower employing those labourers can afford to pay them better, since he will earn far more for a kilo of coca than for an equivalent amount of any of the alternative local crops – maize, rice, coffee, or cacao. At 1990 prices, for example, a farmer would need 9.5 hectares of coffee to duplicate the income from 1 hectare of coca. Furthermore, coca production costs are fairly low, earnings are almost pure profit and there are no burdensome bank loans or taxes to worry about.[27] Small wonder that an estimated 70,000 new growers moved into the valley between 1987 and 1990 alone.

Although Peru's economy is larger and more diversified than Bolivia's, the stories of their growing dependence on coca are depressingly similar. Peru holds the further distinction of having fallen into serious debt trouble several years before any other country in Latin America.[28]

Here, too, generals were the chief culprits: they accumulated mountains of debt throughout the late 1960s and 1970s and, as generals are inclined to do, spent 40 per cent of government revenues on the military. Even so, foreign credit sources liked the look of Peru because of its abundant copper and oil deposits. They lent enough to the government to triple its debt between 1968 and 1974. By 1973, debt service already absorbed more than 20 per cent of export earnings; by 1978 the mass of debt had doubled from its already unsustainable 1973 levels to over $6 billion.

The Peruvian balance of payments worsened throughout the 1970s, the expected export boom never happened, and by 1978 Peru's banking system was in the hole by minus $1.2 billion. With foreign accounts awash in red ink, there was no choice but to sign an 'austerity' agreement with the IMF that same year. This move, like the prescriptions of the Fund, did the country little good. Export revenues continued their nosedive, dropping by 25 per cent between 1980 and 1983. But debt service payments continued, absorbing almost half of Peru's meagre hard currency income. The IMF's brief is to organise an economy in such a way that creditors get paid, and this is what it did in Peru. Meanwhile, the debt itself continued to climb, as the government attempted to drag itself out of the recession and bankers kept the faith because they appreciated the 'orthodox' IMF policies Peru was implementing.

Alan García won the presidency in 1985 at the age of 38. When García's predecessor, Belaúnde Terry, had assumed office in 1980, the foreign debt was a shade over $7 billion. Belaúnde more than doubled it, leaving García to deal with a burden of $16 billion. Furthermore, Belaúnde had practically stopped making service payments during his last year in office, so García also found himself lumbered with a billion dollars in arrears. If the new president had tried to pay everything he theoretically owed Peru's creditors, he would have had to hand over to them in 1985 a politically impossible 95 per cent of the country's export earnings. In 1986, assuming he paid all charges due, his debt service ratio would have been an even more impossible 133 per cent.

García, elected as a social democrat from the APRA party, adopted a strategy to deal with the debt mountain which, in retrospect, can only be described as brave but incredibly dumb. Displaying more bravado than sense, he managed to bring upon himself the worst of all worlds. His first move was to announce *urbi et orbi* that he would limit Peru's debt service to 10 per cent of export earnings. In warfare, it is not considered smart tactics to tell the adversary what you intend to do. García's announcement put his creditors on red alert and set them gunning for him. The IMF soon shot off an ultimatum to pay up on the arrears. García refused. On 15 August 1986, barely a year after he had assumed the presidency, the IMF declared Peru 'ineligible' for future loans – the kiss of death in the international financial community.

When a country goes on the 'ineligible' – a.k.a. pariah – list, not only do public credit sources like the World Bank or the Inter-American Development Bank automatically fall into line, but so do the private banks. Dollar-deprived Peru was forced to live day to day, hand to mouth, squeezing a living from exports while slashing imports. Yet despite García's rhetoric and brave declarations, during succeeding years Peru's real debt service payments were hugely in excess of the proclaimed limit. A glance at Table 2.3 causes one to wonder if the Central Bank and the Finance Ministry had in fact ever heard of their president's '10 per cent' declaration.[29]

Table 2.3: Peru's Export Revenues and Debt Service Payments (US$billion)

	1985	1986	1987	1988
Exports	3.0	2.5	2.6	2.7
Debt Service	1.653	1.287	0.775	0.635
Debt Service Ratio (%)	55	51	30	23.5

Service ratios declined, yes, but never reached the 10 per cent García had proclaimed. Thanks to his grave miscalculations, Peru was now not only cut off from the world's credit sources but was also paying extremely burdensome debt service – two to five times more than the fiery young president had threatened. García kept the country going for a while by draining reserves for vital imports, but his reserves too ran out and were exhausted by 1987. The desperate need for cash explains why García made his clumsy and ill-starred attempt to nationalise the banks and insurance companies, thereby destroying whatever credibility he retained. Having infuriated the right by trying to touch the untouchable banks; the left by paying the imperialist creditors far too much and breaking his electoral promises to the people, and the foreigners by open defiance of the international financial community, García was left to preside over the rapid disintegration of the Peruvian economy.

In 1988 miners went on strike and manufacturing and construction slowed markedly as a result of sharp reduction of credit to the private sector (minus 60 per cent). Imported inputs and spare parts were increasingly hard to come by. In December, the fortunate few who still had employment found that their minimum wage was worth half as much in real terms as a year earlier. By 1989, inflation reached 2772 per cent and real wages again fell by half, reaching levels lower than those of 1970. Peru even set a Latin American record for the biggest drop in economic growth ever to occur in a single year: down 20 per cent from 1988 to 1989.[30]

At the outset of the 1990s, all signs pointed to a desperate population. Those who could leave, did – usually Peruvians with capital assets. Legal departures were 120,000 in 1988, four times the figure of two years earlier. Fully two-thirds of the population was either unemployed or under-employed. 'Fujishock' did the rest, leaving Peruvians shell-shocked.

Peruvian presidents can serve only one term so at least García was spared the humiliation of a spectacular loss. In the 1990 presidential race, his compatriots showed that they were sick and tired of politicians in general by electing a total unknown called Alberto Fujimori. He won on a platform promising 'no shock'. Immediately after his election, he instituted, with no outside prompting, a drastic IMF-type shock-therapy programme and embarked on a quest for fresh credit. 'Fujishock', as Peruvians labelled it, included a thirty-fold increase (3000 per cent) in the price of petrol/gasoline, with charges for water, telephones and electricity multiplied by a factor of eight to twelve. Prices of some basic food staples, including potatoes, increased tenfold. The finance minister himself estimated that half the Peruvian population – about 11 million people – were suffering 'critical poverty'. Since this population had already lost most of the purchasing power of a minimum wage under Alan García, this is not surprising. Mr Fujimori's measures reduced what little they had left by a further 70 per cent.

One perhaps unforeseen consequence of these measures has been the collapse of the public health system. This breakdown has been most spectacularly reflected in a devastating cholera epidemic which has spread to the rest of Latin America. Foreseen or not, this epidemic is a logical outcome of austerity measures. Millions of Peruvians, particularly those living in the desert shanty towns around Lima where it never rains, rely on water brought in by tank trucks. With prices sky-high, people use the same water (for dishwashing, for example) over and over again. They cannot afford to wash themselves very often, much less fruits or vegetables. A professor of economics at Lima's Catholic University told the author in March 1991 how escalating prices of water and transport have combined to make life even more unbearable for the poor. In addition to cholera, diseases unknown or believed eradicated have surfaced, including a kind of leprosy which particularly strikes young people who leave their villages to work in the mines or the coca producing areas.[31]

At whatever cost to Peruvians, Fujishock was intended to stop galloping inflation, to spur an export-led economic recovery and to restore external confidence in the Peruvian economy. At the annual World Bank-IMF meeting in September 1990, the Peruvian finance minister gave a credible performance of the return of the prodigal son. Mr Michel Camdessus, Managing Director of the Fund, played the benevolent father. All – or nearly all – was forgiven: Camdessus announced to the Peruvians that they had made 'a clear demonstration of what should, and should not, be done ... from now on, we can support you, and we will.' But not until Peru has reimbursed an outstanding balance of $800 million to the Fund and $1 billion to the Bank.[32] These payments are going to require hustling a lot of cocaine.

Just as in Bolivia, the coca cushion in Peru has provided employment for hundreds of thousands of destitute people and brought critically needed foreign exchange to the empty vaults of the Central Bank. In January 1988, under García, the government completely reversed its previous policy and sought to give drug dollars every encouragement to permeate the 'legal' economy. No boundaries now exist between 'legal' and 'illegal' origins of funds. Anyone can open a bank account in dollars; repatriate capital with no-questions-asked and with tax amnesty, or import, duty free, all foreign goods purchased with dollars.[33]

A huge parallel foreign currency exchange market operates in full view of the authorities on Ocoña street in downtown Lima. The traders of Ocoña are not just petty traffickers in foreign exchange, although small *cambistas* (money-changers) do routinely travel to the Alto Huallaga valley to buy coca dollars and return to the capital to sell them at a slight profit. According to Humberto Campodonico,

> A series of public institutions openly buy their dollars in Ocoña. The President of the Republic, the chief of the National Planning Institute, the Minister of Economics ... all debate whether it's US$300 million, or $500 million or more than a billion a year that drug trafficking provides to the national economy

but there is no debate at all about whether these dollars *should* provide such financial lubrication. In reality, it is now Ocoña that sets Peru's exchange rate, not the Central Bank.

Knowledgeable people estimate that at least $3 million is exchanged on the parallel market every day, virtually all of it stemming from the drug trade. A Peruvian economist who specialises in the workings of the underground economy, Jorge Fernández Baca, said 'If the *cambistas* suddenly disappeared, there would be a huge adverse impact on the country.' Like the Central Bank itself, Peru's major private banks frequent Ocoña, but they buy most of their dollars directly through their thriving branch offices in the Alto Huallaga. Most towns in the valley lack paved roads or decent plumbing, but they circulate more dollars than many of Peru's large cities. Once absorbed into the financial system, these dollars are 'clean', and can be used to buy imports or to service the foreign debt.

In both Bolivia and Peru, the success of IMF 'adjustment' depends upon the success of the coca industry which alone can provide the vital 'cushion' of employment and hard currency income. In both countries, the syndrome is the same: the importance of the drug economy has grown in direct proportion to the decline of the legal economy. Pressure from the international financial 'community' over debt payments has only made matters worse. Yet when asked how the IMF was dealing with the links between poverty and drugs, a spokesperson for the Fund responded, 'We haven't looked at poverty in Latin America in this context.'[34]

Colombia

Columbia is strategically located on the northwest coast of South America at the end of the Panamanian land bridge. To the south lie producers Bolivia and Peru, to the north are the Central American or Caribbean jumping-off points for final transport to US and European markets. Every day, small planes taking off from one of dozens of clandestine air strips transport an average 3500kg of coca paste northwards to Colombia for processing.[35]

Any unskilled *pisadore* ('stomper') equipped with two feet can make coca paste mixing the leaves with chemicals in a plastic-lined pit, but transforming the paste into cocaine requires fairly sophisticated labs with trained technicians. Most of them are in Colombia, though some have been found in remote jungles in Peru and Bolivia, and one lab exploded in a high-class Lima neighbourhood when a major drug baron's 'kitchen' caught fire. Colombia is living proof that the third world should get out of the raw materials business and into value-adding manufacturing activities: Colombia's drug income is probably double that of Peru's, amounting to as much as $2.5 billion a year. The country produces only a small coca crop – perhaps 24,000 tonnes – and prefers to concentrate on processing.[36]

Colombians can do everything but supply their own processing chemicals – from purchasing the leaves to transportation to lab work to marketing. The value added is impressive. According to *The Economist*, 'In 1987, a Colombian refiner could purchase 2.5 kilos of paste for as little as $500, and then convert it into one kilo of cocaine with an export price of up to $6000' – of course the Miami or New York street value is astronomical compared to that sum. Everyone has heard of the Colombian drug cartels but not everyone knows how much they are worth financially speaking. In 1988, *The Economist* noted that the Medellín cocaine syndicate, were it a legal corporation, would be near the top of the list of the *Fortune 500*, right up there with major oil companies. While Medellín's fortunes have lately declined, and those of other cartels risen, its net sales in 1988 were of the order of $20 billion.[37]

Cocaine is now Colombia's largest foreign exchange earner although roughly half the profits do not return to Colombia but are laundered and invested in real estate and businesses in the US and elsewhere. Cocaine's place in the Colombian economy has become especially critical since 1989 when the price of coffee – previously Colombia's major export – plunged by half. Colombia immediately lost $300 to $400 million in one blow and the price of coffee has not recovered since. The Colombian president bitterly blamed the United States for allowing the International Coffee Agreement to collapse. But the Bush administration's answer to everything is military: rather than let Colombia earn an honest living and do its own policing, it offered $65 million in military aid – a fifth or less of the amount the country is guaranteed to lose because of the coffee crash.

About 300,000 Colombians are directly or indirectly employed by the cocaine trade, whether as security guards or accountants, pilots or chemists. A report to the US Congress explains:

> Employment in the cocaine industry has served as an avenue of upward mobility in a country where advancement through opportunities in the legal economy is limited. Wages in the cocaine trade are considerably higher than for comparable work in the legal economy.[38]

Colombia is often cited as a Latin American model of sound economic management and close cooperation with foreign creditors. It is that South American *rara avis* – a country that has never needed to reschedule its debt and has thus so far escaped the grasp of the IMF. *The Economist* suspects a positive debt-drugs link: 'In Colombia, the cocaine boom is probably a big reason why the government has been able to avoid rescheduling foreign debt.' Colombia integrates drug dollars into the national economy in a straightforward way. Many of them go through the so-called 'left window' – the Central Bank's *ventanilla siniestra* which happily accepts dollars with no questions asked. This *ventanilla* is not exactly a teller's window where you queue up, but it is a policy. The government long ago decided that dubious dollars might as well be put to the good of the nation and spur economic activity – legal or not. R.T. Naylor reports, 'Allegedly (thanks to the huge cash flow from drugs) thousands of businesses came into existence – everything from contraband imports and illegal emerald mining and exports to simple textile production – that were not captured in the official data.' Thus the left window also serves as a bridge between the above-ground economy and the under-ground one.[39]

The Colombian economic boom began to wane in the mid-1980s and once again coca came to the rescue. In 1988, the last year for which figures are presently available, Colombia paid its creditors $1.3 billion in interest and $1.6 in amortisation. Despite this perfect record, bankers are once burnt twice shy when it comes to the Southern hemisphere. They are leery of lending to anyone in Latin America and are not rewarding Colombia for good behaviour. Faced with rising costs, no fresh loans and prices for legal exports in the doldrums, successive Colombian governments have officially condemned the cocaine cartel while quietly encouraging the repatriation of cocaine dollars. These dollars are then hidden under anodyne headings in the national accounts. Colombia seems to be, for example, an astonishingly popular destination for 'tourism'.

Whenever the government makes one of its periodic crackdowns on the drug cartels, significantly fewer dollars are shoved through the *ventanilla siniestra*. When the presidential candidate Luis Carlos Galán was murdered in August 1989 and the government decided to get tough with the drug barons, dollar deposits dropped by nearly two-thirds. When the repression lessened in early 1990, deposits recovered.

Eduardo Sarmiento, the Colombian economist who tracked these levels of deposits according to political events, also concludes that it will be extremely difficult to curb the drug trade so long as there is an open window for drug dollar deposits and no financial system regulations against them. His study notes that the influx of drug dollars has allowed Colombia to 'avoid the huge devaluations of other Latin American countries and reductions in real wages'. Cocaine revenues give the government financial flexibility. 'No government is about to compromise its economic leverage ... they have implemented all the mechanisms to facilitate' drug dollar deposits. Why should a strapped government with a heavy debt burden and balance of payments problems do anything else?[40]

Feedbacks

There are often instances where one debt boomerang accelerates another. A major feedback is the far-reaching and multiple impact of drugs on the environment. The drug plague is causing deforestation, soil erosion, genetic wipe-out and devastating pollution from dumped toxic processing chemicals which are poisoning the Amazon and other waters. According to Marc Dourojeanni, formerly a professor at the National Agrarian University of Lima, now with the Inter-American Development Bank and a specialist on the ecological impact of cocaine, coca growers have already invaded and destroyed huge areas of national parks, national forests and designated 'conservation areas' in Peru.

Dourojeanni's observations on this little-noticed phenomenon are striking:

> The deforested areas include: (1) actual coca plantations [over 200,000 hectares/450,000 acres]; (2) plantation of susbsistence crops by the coca growers; (3) exhausted lands abandoned by the growers; (4) areas used by peasants who have fled regior dominated by narcotics traffickers and terrorists; (5) land used by coca growers fleeing police repression; and (6) areas deforested for landing strips [which number over 100], camps and laboratories. Based on detailed reports ... One can safely deduce that since the coca boom began ... coca production has directly or indirectly caused the deforestation of 700,000 hectares [1,750,000 acres] of jungle in the Amazon region.[41]

Coca has thus been directly responsible for about 10 per cent of deforestation in Peru and all the pressures listed by Dourojeanni remain. Deforestation, in turn, causes drastic changes in water regimes and flooding; it leads to the extinction of genetic resources, soil erosion, air pollution from burning, and it contributes to the greenhouse effect (see Chapter 1). Coca is harvested between three and six times a year – each time the soil is hoed and stripped of all protection. The crop is also a natural soil-exhauster. One Latin American agronomist calls it 'the Attila of tropical agriculture'.

Intensive cocaine production also calls on large quantities of pesticides and herbicides which run off and contribute to poisoning waterways. Yet 'dangerous as these agrochemicals are, the environmental impact of the manufacture of coca paste is much worse', says Dourojeanni. The cocktail of chemicals used in processing includes sulfuric acid, ether, kerosene, acetone, toluene, acetic acid, ammonia and others – bound together with thousands of metric tons of – would you guess? toilet paper. All of this is dumped after use.

In Bolivia alone, says the nation's League for the Defence of the Environment, drugs create 38,000 tons of toxic wastes every year. Processing requires a lot of water, so the labs are set up beside streams where the expended chemicals are dumped. Kerosene is a major offender because it does not break down and spreads over the surface of the water, inducing asphyxiation of aquatic life. Three million gallons of it are dumped in Bolivia each year, 15 million in Peru.[42]

Dourojeanni concludes that the 'result will be fewer fish, fish which are dangerous to eat, and polluted water for irrigation and consumption'. Waterways of the upper Amazon Basin have already become sterile. And because the coca-growing regions are havens for lawlessness and terrorists and are so hard to penetrate, deforestation and dumping are completely uncontrolled.

Cocaine can't be processed without these chemicals and most of them are not manufactured in the drug-producing countries. Any 'war on drugs' should logically target the suppliers of the indispensable solvents, but this did not occur to the US authorities. Throughout the 1980s, 70 to 80 per cent of the processing chemicals were exported from the US to South America. As one critic testified before a Congressional committee, 'In short, we've been providing the ingredients of our own poison.'[43]

One raid on a Colombian jungle lab unearthed a cache of thousands of gallons of solvents, some still in containers bearing the names of Shell, Mobil and other US manufacturers.[44] A videotape of this raid, and these containers, appears to have helped concentrate the minds of legislators. At long last, in November 1989, the US introduced mandatory export controls on the major drug ingredients. But the 'Chemical Diversion and Trafficking Act' may not do much good. Already, in 1990, German chemical exports to the cocaine countries rose by an extremely suspicious 438 per cent. Hoechst, Dow and BASF are building a major chemical production complex in Cartagena, Colombia, scheduled to begin full operations in 1993. Although there is no proof they intend to manufacture and sell chemicals used to process cocaine, there is no proof either that they don't.[45]

Operation Blast Furnace, Operation Snowcap, and Other Military Imagery: The Failure of the US Drug War in the Andes

Hundreds of thousands of Latin Americans count on jobs and incomes provided solely by drug production and trade. The governments of the three countries we've looked at desperately need the cocaine cushion – only Colombia, with a larger, more diversified economy and higher foreign reserves, could survive without it. The International Monetary Fund through its 'adjustment' programmes creates deep recession and imposes drastic belt-tightening on people who can sacrifice no more. Thus does it entrench the drug economy as the single effective survival mechanism, the only game in town.

As long as the consumer countries continue to demand drugs, the supply will find its way to them one way or another because so many livelihoods, so many lives, depend upon it. These are the stark economic realities reflecting, if you will, people's normal, self-interested market behaviour and governments' normal pursuit of state objectives. To survive, people have to take risks. Sometimes, with the ultimate entrepreneurial spirit born of desperation, they risk, and lose, their lives. The private-enterprisers, the free-marketeers presiding over official Washington, the structural adjusters of the major inter-national financial institutions with their monetarist doctrines – if they are ideologically consistent – should actually admire such behaviour. At the very least these policymakers who have helped to make the drug economy indispensable should understand, if anyone can, that you can't argue with the marketplace.

But the United States government, the World Bank and the IMF want it both ways; they seem to assume they can encourage economic 'privatisation' and the entrepreneurial spirit of the 'informal sector' in all spheres – except for the drug economy. First, their programmes close off all legal avenues of escape. Then, when people have been driven into the *cul-de-sac* of illegal activities, their crops are destroyed and the forces of repression are set on them.

Since the early 1980s, US administrations have consistently ignored the debt–drug link and proclaimed it possible to attack the scourge of drugs directly, in the Andes. When President Bush relies on US and Andean armies and police forces to cut off the cocaine flow at the source, he has about as much chance as King Canute ordering the tide to roll back. One fears that the lightning success of Operation Desert Storm may strengthen Bush's resolve to impose a military and repressive 'solution' in the drug 'war'.

Is there any hope that the US people and their representatives can be convinced they should not follow the president in the Andes as they did in the Gulf? In September 1990, Bush claimed a partial victory in the war on drugs, pointing to 'clear signs of progress'. He must have meant signs of progress in overall drug use, since the signs of any reduction in supply are far less clear. Inside the US, drugs may be correctly regarded as a security problem, but it will do no good to regard them as one outside. Fortunately, at least some members of the US House Committee on Foreign Affairs appear sceptical of the law-enforcement approach, aimed at 'disrupting' and 'interdicting'. At this Committee's hearings in May 1990, the Administrator of the

Drug Enforcement Agency (DEA) was asked by Rep. Gilman about the results so far:

> *Mr Gilman*: What have we reached at this point, what reductions [in supply] since you started?
> *Mr Westrate*: Well, the production has not reduced at all really yet. But I think that what we are seeing ...
> *Mr Gilman*: Has there been any reduction in supply?
> *Mr Westrate*: What we are seeing is disruption. And I think that there are a lot of signs out there.
> *Mr Gilman*: I know that you are disrupting, and I know that you are interdicting, and I know that you are raiding, but I am asking you, Mr Westrate, has there been any reduction in supply?
> *Mr Westrate*: I cannot say at this point.[46]

Another Congressional committee, the US House Committee on Government Operations, in its capacity as the authorising body for the Office of National Drug Control Policy (the formal title of Bush's latest programme, headed by the so-called 'Drug Czar') carried out an extensive review of the US anti-drug and law-enforcement strategy in the Andean region. Committee members and their aides visited the three cocaine countries and spoke extensively with government officials, the military and the police, and some ordinary citizens; as well as with local US diplomats and DEA personnel. The Committee's conclusions are not encouraging.[47]

The total US anti-drug budget for 1990 was $9.6 billion. In an era of budget cutting, this figure proves that the problem is taken seriously. Although 'demand-side' measures do figure in the overall plan, 70 per cent of the money is set aside for supply reduction and for law enforcement efforts. A small percentage of the available funds are earmarked for 'source country' programmes, including the Andean Initiative.

> The Committee's investigation ... raises serious questions regarding the feasibility of a strategy designed to cut the supply of drugs in the source countries ... If, as the Committee's evidence suggests, there is reason to believe that this strategy is unworkable, then the policy must be reassessed or a convincing case made to Congress and the American public for a continued investment in the current strategy.

The evidence gathered further leads the Committee to the following conclusions:

Specifically, the Committee's preliminary investigation suggests that (1) the policy has been ineffective to date in meeting counter-narcotics objectives; (2) there are serious reasons to doubt that the strategy can work within the political and economic constraints of the host countries; and (3) the consequences of continuing and escalating the policy may be counter-productive not only to anti-narcotics efforts, but to long-term US security interests in the region.

The Congressional team recognises the same economic and social handicaps we have outlined here. They fault the US approach because they believe it

lack[s] a serious long-term strategy for economic development as an alternative to the coca and cocaine economy. In addition, the increase of US military assistance to the region under the Andean plan will strengthen the hand of military institutions with long records of corruption and abuse, and little proven commitment or ability to conduct effective narcotics control programs.

Simultaneously, the Committee expects the plan to further undermine civilian, democratic governments. 'Neither the counter-narcotics objectives nor the long-term security interests of the US would be served by weakened Andean economies or by the collapse of civilian governments to military control.'

Connoisseurs of the language of Congressional Reports and of the dependably dull documents habitually emerging from the US Government Printing Office may appreciate that all this constitutes an extremely sharp indictment. But considering what is actually happening in the region, on the ground, it is not too sharp.

For example, 'the Committee delegation heard details of countless examples of corruption in the counter-narcotics operations of the police and armed forces.'

An army colonel from Lima told a US Border Patrol agent at a drug checkpoint in Peru,

I have the opportunity while I'm here to make $70,000 by looking the other way at certain times. You have a family, they are protected in the United States, you have a proper pension plan. My family is not protected and I don't have a proper pension plan and I will never have the opportunity to make $70,000 as long as I live. I am going to make it.

The man has a point, in fact several points. He too is seizing a free-market opportunity. As do law 'enforcement' personnel in Bolivia, where police officers accept assignments in the inhospitable coca-producing jungle region of Chaparé because of the manifold opportunities for pay-offs.

The US drug war in Peru also continues to escalate. A major clash in April 1990 at the 'Santa Lucía Base', constructed in Peruvian coca country at a cost of over a million dollars, had US pilots flying Huey helicopter gunships with Peruvian soldiers aboard firing M60 machine guns against Shining Path (*Sendero Luminoso*) guerrillas. After the fight, US officials were 'pleased with their successes in the firefight and in their overall effort'. 'We gave 10 for every one we took.'[48]

Perhaps so, as far as the firefight was concerned. But Shining Path was the real winner. The *Sendero* can show that it is defending the peasants and every time the *gringos* intervene against the peasant coca growers, *Sendero*'s recruiting figures go up. A Peruvian historian and expert on Shining Path, Gustavo Goriti, says military-style intervention can only bolster *Sendero*'s 'anti-imperialist' claims. 'It is throwing gasoline on the fire', he says. 'The [US anti-drug] bases are visible symbols for recruiting propaganda.' As peasant coca growers and their crops are defended, so they then defend the guerrillas, who already control many functions of the state, not to mention much of the economic activity in this part of Peru.

Shining Path has gained political and military ground thanks to the explosion of drug production in the Andes. It levies cocaine taxes which allow it to replenish and add to its stocks of arms. Rarely does a plane full of coca paste take off for Colombia without having acquitted a tax of up to $4000. Drug traffickers obviously resent these taxes, nor are they happy when *Sendero* forces them to pay peasant growers higher prices for coca. In this way, Shining Path acts as a kind of obligatory 'armed union' for coca growers who have little choice but to turn to the guerrillas.

These growers are caught between the US-supported anti-drug war waged by the Peruvian military – one of the most repressive in the world – and the *Sendero* guerrillas, who play Robin Hood only so long as they get absolute obedience from their 'protégés'. According to the Peruvian National Coordination for Human Rights, *Sendero* has assassinated over 15,000 people in the past decade, the overwhelming majority of them peasants and ordinary townspeople. Shining Path also targets civil servants and other authorities. State officials – judges, sub-prefects, mayors and the like – constantly resign and leave their posts in the coca areas. This is the best way not to be killed.[49]

The US has graphically given its Andean interventions names like Operation Snowcap or Operation Blast Furnace. In Colombia, it doesn't give its operations names because they are mostly undercover. Here, the warfare is infinitely more complex. We cannot pretend to give a full account of the Colombian case here, but it is important to point out that not one but several wars are going on there. One is aimed at protecting the cocaine cartels' prerogatives. This is the war that assassinates anyone who might try to interfere with those privileges – especially judges, officers and other high-ranking officials. One was the front-running presidential candidate Luis Carlos Galán, gunned down in front of the television cameras in 1989.

Another war is being waged by an alliance of convenience composed of the rich traditional landowners, the military and the drug cartels against the organised left in general. It has claimed over 8000 lives since 1986: peasants, workers, opposition politicians and social activists. These civilian targets are more or less aligned with – but also sometimes directly opposed to – various guerrilla groups of various Marxist persuasions.

Galán's assassination was interpreted by the Colombian political class, and the wealthy in general, as a 'signal ... that the drug traffickers were not only fighting those elements of the state who directly threatened their commercial interests or their welfare. They were now actively employing violence to influence the course of politics on the national level.'[50] Before Galán was even buried, President Bush rushed an emergency $65 million package of 'anti-narcotics assistance' to Colombia. Colombia is now the largest recipient of US military aid in the hemisphere where the line drawn between 'anti-narcotics' and 'counterinsurgency' can be exceptionally thin.

Conclusion: Breaking the Debt-Drug Chain

So far, US attempts to stanch the supply of drugs in the Andes have been wholly, and deservedly, unsuccessful. These efforts have, however, helped to empower corrupt and brutal military forces at the expense of civilian rule.* Just as Northern economic policies have served to entrench the drug economy, so the 'law-enforcement' approach to drug supply and trafficking has exacerbated human rights abuses – committed either by the military and the police or by the guerrilla insurgents who also profit from the drug trade. Ordinary people, the rule of law and democracy are the chief casualties of this

* For other relationships between debt and violence see Chapter 6 on conflict.

war in which – except for the forces of official or unofficial repression – there are no winners. IMF and United States strategies are clearly part of the problem, not of the solution.

The debt crisis has not, perhaps, directly caused the drug crisis but we believe we have shown that recourse to drug production and trade has definitely been fuelled by debt. We do not intend to propose here detailed alternative policies to alleviate the disastrous situations we have described, both in the producer and the consumer countries. We do, however, want to stress that any alternative drug control strategy abroad must, necessarily, include major debt relief. At present, Andean governments have neither the will nor the capacity to halt drug cultivation and trafficking. Military 'quick-fix' 'solutions' are doomed to worse than failure.

A former Peruvian foreign minister, Guillermo Larco-Cox, proposed in front of the UN General Assembly in 1989 that coca farmers be provided with alternative ways of earning a living and that Peru's foreign debt be transformed into resources to break up the drug cartels. We believe that debt cancellations could indeed be used for legal, environment-enhancing, employment-creating development. Nothing is to be gained by criminalising and attempting to prosecute hundreds of thousands of peasants and petty traders whose range of economic alternatives is presently close to zero.

We further believe that debt reduction should be directly tied to better targeted development aid, transmitted primarily through reputable non-governmental organisations. They, in turn, would be held responsible for making sure the aid reached organisations of peasants, women, workers and environmentalists.

Such policies could not, of course, 'solve' the drug crisis by themselves, because the real roots of this crisis are to be found on the demand side, in the consumer countries' social failures that encourage the use and abuse of drugs. A realistic attack on the supply of cocaine has to be based on an understanding of the situation in producer countries, and in economic cooperation with them. Nothing can be accomplished until the deadly debt–drugs link is severed.

The Third Boomerang:
How Northern Taxpayers are Bailing Out the Banks

Research and Documentation by John Denham, assisted by Helen Long

In this world, nothing is certain but death and tax breaks.
Benjamin Franklin, revised

A billion here and a billion there and soon you're talking real money.
The late Senator Everett Dirksen

Northern taxpayers have carried commercial banks through the third world debt crisis from the start and virtually all of them are blissfully unaware of the fact. This chapter explains some of the ways in which citizens of the creditor countries have unwittingly or unwillingly provided financial support to private banks throughout the 1980s. And, as if this involuntary financing were not bad enough, government support to the banks supplied by taxpayers has not even been used efficiently or effectively. It has not, in particular, lightened the burden of the debtors.

However the debt crisis is eventually resolved – assuming that it is – it will entail some financial costs to the North. This much is clear and a premise dictated by realism. Massive debt forgiveness or reduction – the polite way of saying 'cancellation', or 'wipe-out' – will inevitably fall on Northern creditor countries. Their taxpayers will, one way or another, ultimately foot the bill of official debt reduction. The banks which made the mistaken, misguided loans are unlikely under present circumstances to pay the full consequences of their bad decisions; but even if by some quirk they did, taxpayers would still indirectly lose the benefits of tax revenues assessed on the banks if bank profits dropped as loans were no longer repaid.*

* Naturally, we are speaking here only about immediate *financial* costs to Northern citizens. This whole book is devoted to showing how many benefits they would derive from a different debt strategy, including deep debt reductions – from a healthier planet to increased employment whose taxed revenues could then compensate for tax losses on bank profits.

Many argue, we think correctly, that most third world debts have already been abundantly repaid, for long enough, and that Northern citizens can easily withstand these losses. Perhaps so. But at present, the said Northern citizens are channelling funds to the banks and getting nothing in return for their money. Tax compensation to the banks serves only the banks – not the debtors themselves. We shall try to show how this system works in several countries. We highlight how taxpayers support commercial banks while receiving nothing in exchange, because *no direct mechanism exists to bring commensurate benefits to the debtor countries*. Four cases in which taxpayers' money is used to benefit the creditor banks are:

- Tax mechanisms enabling banks to claim tax credits against third world debt, with no commensurate reduction being required.
- Tax regimes encouraging bank participation in capital flight, thus undermining debt crisis solutions.
- Costs and increased risks born by taxpayers arising from official (public) lending to third world governments being used to finance debt service payments to private banks.
- Inefficient use of public financial resources in debt reduction strategies like the 'Brady Plan'.

We also make the case that taxpayer support for the banks is prolonging the agony of the debt crisis and unnecessarily increasing future costs which the public is likely to bear.

Cautionary Note

In the course of our research, we have discovered that no other exercise of this kind has yet been published – least of all by the large and powerful public and private institutions which possess the relevant information but have no incentive to disseminate it. Frequently, too, the information one really needs cannot be obtained since legal disclosure requirements are not all they might be. One unfortunate consequence is that the figures estimated here have to be treated with some caution, particularly when one is speculating about the possible costs of future events. Further intensifying the methodological thicket are the different requirements and tax regimes in different creditor countries.

The wall of silence surrounding the issues and the difficulties inherent in breaking it down have so far stifled debate. We want to encourage that debate, and though parts of this chapter may seem rather technical, we will do our best to use layperson's language. The banks have got away with a great deal partly because the issues are so complex and their implications have been so successfully hidden from public scrutiny. We hope to throw light on these issues and their implications. There is nothing banks hate more than having the public see that it is 'bailing them out' – because there is nothing the public/taxpayer hates more!

That, however, is precisely what is happening.

Tax Relief for the Commercial Banks

In most creditor countries, the tax and regulatory authorities have set up mechanisms enabling banks to treat third world debts as 'losses' for tax purposes, *without any requirement to reduce the debt of the debtor countries* on their books and, in some cases, with no actual cash loss suffered by the bank.

The chief mechanism allowing this sleight of hand is called the 'provision' or the 'loan-loss reserve'. In nearly all creditor countries, banks are allowed, usually encouraged, sometimes forced, to make reserves or provisions against possible future losses on their third world loans.

A prudent banker, faced with a loan that seems to be going bad, will set aside at least part of the value of the loan before he finally has to admit to himself and to his Board that it will never be repaid. At that point, the loan gets wiped off the books as a dead loss. The banker draws these 'provisions' from the bank's income. They allow the bank to spread the cost of bad loans over a longer period of time than the one covered by the annual balance sheet.

If, as the banker feared, the loan is not repaid, then the provision is used to cover the loss and thus protect the bank's capital. If, in the more cheerful scenario, the loan is repaid, then the provision is not required and can be taken back into the income of the bank.

Whether the provisions relate to an overall general estimate of the bank's vulnerability to bad third world loans (in several shaky debtor countries, for example) or to specific individual loans (such as 'the Brazentina Hydro-Electric Power Company') tax authorities now accept 'sovereign' (foreign government) risk provisions as tax deductible. Rules vary from country to country.

In some creditor countries, it is up to the banks to decide when and if they should make provisions; in others, banks receive informal advice from bank regulators; in still others, the regulators establish mandatory provision levels. In practice, at the top levels, bankers and their regulators talk to each other all the time – particularly since the onset of the third world debt crisis – so most regulatory regimes actually represent some combination of the three and a consensus between the banks and the authorities on the best way to proceed.[1]

In the first case, when banks themselves have the most responsibility for deciding on levels of provisioning, they are influenced by several factors. A banker will ask himself:

* What is the tax treatment of provisions?
* Will provisions be regarded as part of the capital and reserves of the bank, or not?
* Will the shareholders prefer a bank that tries to cover its bad debts prudently, or will they punish it for reducing profits and therefore diminishing dividends?

There are two basic answers to the banker's first question on tax treatment of provisions. Under some tax regimes, a bank can treat the act of making a provision against some future – and unconfirmed – loss as if the bank had actually already made a loss on the loan. If the bank decides to set aside, say, $500 million against the $1 billion it has loaned to Brazentina, the bank will decrease its declared taxable income by $500 million. If corporate tax is 40 per cent, the bank will thus decrease its tax liability by $200 million in that year.

This is where the sleight of hand comes in: Note that the bank has neither lost the $500 million, nor has it reduced Brazentina's debt by $500 million, nor has Brazentina even necessarily ceased to pay back at least part of its interest. There is a risk, of course, that the bank may take a loss in the future, and this risk is probably greater than the risk of a banker being run over crossing Threadneedle or Wall Street. But the bank gets its tax relief (i.e., tells the tax authorities that its loans to Brazentina are worth less than 100 cents on the dollar, and shows them that way on its books) while still retaining a 100 per cent claim on Brazentina.

In most European countries, such tax relief can be obtained through the simple act of provisioning. In the United States and the United Kingdom, and in quite different ways, things are a bit more complicated as we shall describe in due course. Nonetheless, wherever tax break rules apply, and whatever their nature, the process of provisioning with subsequent tax relief is often defended on two grounds. We think both arguments are specious.

First, say its beneficiaries, tax relief is an incentive to make higher levels of provisions and thus protects the banking system. The obvious response to this argument is that the banking system would be best protected if bankers did not make silly loans to begin with, as they consistently did during the go-go years of the late 1970s and the early 1980s. The bankers then found themselves in one of two possible cases: either they knew that the money they were loaning was being largely squandered on military hardware, current consumption and capital flight, and were thus guilty of negligence with regard to their directors, their shareholders and their employees; or they did not know these things and were simply foolish. But under the present regulatory system – the term is to some degree an abuse of language – nothing succeeds like failure. Since banks did and do make silly loans, sometimes with startling regularity and dogged persistence, the question is then how best to deal with their improvidence. We think the best way is simply to create higher levels of provisions directly, without fiscal incentives, by having state regulators legally require them.

The second argument generally advanced in favour of tax relief has to do with the nature of 'sovereign' lending (loans to governments as opposed to loans to companies or individuals). Bankers want sovereign loans treated like any other loans for tax loss purposes, and this desire has often been satisfied by regulators, but in fact they are not the same. A company in trouble usually recovers or goes bankrupt quickly. If it goes bankrupt, the provisions made against its bad debts will have to be called up quickly too. The loan is then *ipso facto* written off. With sovereign loans, however, banks can maintain provisions for years and years without writing off the loans. This difference was actually underscored by that banker's banker, the former president of Citicorp, Walter Wriston. He is reported to have observed, as a justification for huge bank exposure in the third world, 'Countries do not fail to exist.' In other words, companies can go bust but countries cannot. Sovereign loans are different and should not give rise to the same tax breaks. In a few countries this is recognised; in most it isn't.

Secondary Markets

Another way a bank can obtain tax relief on poorly performing loans is through the 'secondary market'. Many people unfamiliar with the *arcana* of debt may find it bizarre that even third world loans can be bought, sold or traded like gold, coffee or pork bellies. The so-called 'secondary market' in debt works like any other market, except that it deals in second-hand loans. If Banker A thinks, for example, that Peru is going to hell in a handcart and that he will be lucky to sell the loans he holds for 5 cents on the dollar; whereas Banker (or Speculator) B thinks that the IMF and Fujishock will do great things for the Peruvian economy and improve Peru's ability to pay back, then

B may buy A's Peruvian paper in the hopes of Peru's later paying back more than 5 cents on the dollar.

When Banker A sells his Peruvian loan at a discount on the secondary market, he is making a loss with regard to the face value of the loan. But, just as with provisions, Peru itself gets no debt relief – the new owner of the loan still holds the country responsible for 100 per cent reimbursement and may try to exert whatever leverage he can to make sure Peru does not backslide any further. If Banker A has already received a tax credit for making provisions on a loan he later sells, he can usually get a further tax credit on the same loan when he sells it if his loss exceeds the level of his provisions. If he has not already made a provision, then he will receive a tax-break corresponding to the entire amount of the loss.

Between 1985 and 1990, an estimated $195 billion of debt was traded on the secondary market (this of course includes trading at a profit as well as at a loss). Where banks incur genuine losses, the usual tax deduction rules apply as they would to any other business: this is normal. Our question is whether state regulators should allow tax relief without corresponding relief to debtors.

Prices for much third world debt have deteriorated badly, yes, but if you had hung in there, you could have done well if you bought Chilean, Costa Rican or Jamaican paper in 1987 (or sold Argentina, Côte d'Ivoire or Ecuador short, which you can also do, just as on stock markets). The recovery in some prices between early 1990 and mid-1991 was quite surprising and shows that markets may regain confidence in those countries where the IMF really plays the tough cop. Table 3.1 shows how secondary market debt prices for some Highly Indebted Countries (HICs) evolved between the end of 1987, the beginning of 1990 and mid-1991.

To sum up, OECD creditor country banks receive tax breaks when they make provisions against possible bad third world debts or when they sell them at less than face value. Taxpayers pay their share of these costs. First, the money 'handed back' to the banks obviously comes from the governments their taxes support. Second, the public services that could have been supplied through the bank's taxes, had it paid them, must be forgone. Yet the taxpayer does not even have the moral satisfaction of knowing at least that the Brazentinians or the Peruvians are better off. Would you support a charity guaranteed not to channel the money you gave it to the children or the elderly you were trying to help? The banks will reply that they are not charitable institutions. Quite so, and they have manoeuvred intelligently to avoid benefiting anyone but themselves.

Table 3.1: Secondary Market Prices in per cent of Face Value of Loans

Country	1987 4th Q*	1990 1st Q	1991 2nd Q	Per cent change 1987–90 Q1	Per cent change 1987–91 Q2
Argentina	34	11	24	-68	-29
Bolivia	11	11	11	0	0
Brazil	47	24	34	-49	-27
Chile	61	66	89	+8	+46
Colombia	65	60	85	-8	+30
Costa Rica	15	21	47	+40	+213
Côte d'Ivoire	40	6	6	-85	-85
Ecuador	37	15	25	-59	-32
Jamaica	33	39	72	+18	+118
Mexico	50	40	55	-20	+10
Morocco	52	39	48	-25	-8
Nigeria	29	26	42	-10	+45
Peru	7	5	7	-28	0
Philippines	50	49	50	-2	0
Uruguay	59	45	62	-24	+5
Venezuela	57	40	61	-30	+7
Group of HICs	46	33	NA	-28	NA

* Q = quarter
Source: Salomon Brothers, 4 May 1990; Merrill Lynch Capital Markets, June 1991.

Even worse, the very existence of these tax breaks gives banks an incentive not to participate in any debt reduction deals. Let's take another example. If the bank has set aside $500 million on the $1 billion it holds of Brazentina's debt, and has received its $200 million tax break already, it will receive no further tax credits if it sells off the loan at a 50 per cent discount. If 50 per cent is the going rate in a debt reduction scheme, it is tempting for the banker to think, 'Why not let the other banks sell their debts, and hope that the value of the remaining debt I hold picks up?'

No Freedom of Banking Information

Now we will try to estimate the costs of the mechanisms described above to taxpayers of individual creditor countries. Our figures, again, are estimates only – partly because we did not have three years and a hundred thousand dollars for research on this chapter, but mostly because the necessary information simply is not publicly available.

Banks are not democratically run institutions. They are rarely required to disclose the level of their loan exposure in the third world, except, sometimes, for their total lending to the largest debtor countries. Usually it is not possible to identify levels of provisions or sales of debt against particular country loans. Press coverage of this subject, even in the specialised financial media, is spotty at best.

Even national financial institutions of creditor governments, like Central Banks, theoretically open to citizen scrutiny if the said citizens are willing to dig hard enough, provide extremely limited information. Bank exposure in smaller debtor countries is almost never identified. Central bank statistics on exposure are usually given in the aggregate and are often months, even years, out of date. It is usually impossible to relate known information about *average* provisioning levels to *actual* provisioning for specific countries or for specific banks. Government lists of 'problem' debtors officially triggering certain levels of provisioning vary from government to government, and in any case these countries are not often identified. So it can become mind-numbing to figure out which countries any particular set of banks has provisioned against. And, of course, not all banks have lent to all debt-distressed countries either.

Finally, the legal right to claim tax relief does not necessarily mean that tax relief has been granted. Some creditor governments have set limits on the rate at which banks can claim tax relief. And some banks may be in such poor financial shape that they are not making enough profits to set tax credits against. This is an important point. Tax relief is not a payment from the government to the bank, but rather an agreement that the bank need not make a payment to the government. Some banks have been so unprofitable that they haven't even had the opportunity to consider making these payments to the government. Thus they may hold substantial unutilised tax credits which have not yet given rise to genuine relief.

In the absence of an exhaustive – and exhausting – bank-by-bank study, which we think would yield only marginally improved numbers anyway; and in the light of the difficulties just described, we will move towards an estimate of the tax credits arising from provisioning by the major banks in the major OECD countries. These estimates are based on World Bank data. In the other chapters of this book, we generally use OECD data and we exclude Eastern European and Middle Eastern sovereign debt. Here, the debtors included are somewhat different in order to make them consistent with existing data on provisioning.

Table 3.2: Selected OECD Countries' Commercial Bank Exposure to all Developing Countries (US$ current billions, rounded)

Banks of	1984	1990	% change
USA	141	70	-50
Japan	74[1]	84[2]	+13
UK	63	47	-25
Germany	46	113	+146
France	72	86	+19
Switzerland	13	22	+69
Italy	15[3]	20[4]	+33
Canada (in US$, converted at $1.15)	22	13[5]	-41
Total	446	455	+2

1. First quarter 1987.
2. 1988.
3. 1986.
4. 1989.
5. 1989.

Table 3.3: Selected OECD Country Commercial Bank Exposure to SIMICs; and to SILICs, MILICs and MIMICs (US$ current billions, rounded)

Banks of	1984			1990			% change 1984–90
	SIMICs	Others	Total	SIMICs	Others	Total	
US	92	21	113	47	10	57	-50
Japan	39	13	52	41	14	55	+6
UK	34	12	46	21	10	32	-30
Germany	20	11	31	36	26	62	+100
France	29	11	40	28	21	49	+22
Switzerland	7	3	10	7	5	12	+20
Italy	5	0.7	5.7	6.4	0.7	7.1	+17
Total	226	71.7	298	186	86.7	274	-8

Tables 3.2 and 3.3 provide some basic information on commercial bank exposure in the third world. Table 3.2 gives the total levels of banks' exposure to all developing countries in 1984 (or earliest available date thereafter); then its exposure in 1990 (with the relevant quarter indicated); and finally the per cent change from 1984–90. Table 3.2 refines this information by indicating bank claims on

- the Severely Indebted Middle-Income Countries (SIMICs) and
- on the *combined* categories of the Severely Indebted Low-Income Countries (SILICs); Moderately Indebted Middle-Income Countries (MIMICs) and Moderately Indebted Low-Income Countries (MILICs).

These figures are also given for 1984 and for 1990, followed, again, by the per cent change. The SIMICs are generally the most dangerous countries for banks and thus the highest provisions are most likely to be made against their debts.*

There is one other point to make when asking the reader to explore these tables. Aggregate World Bank figures for 1990 show total commercial bank claims on developing countries of $615 billion. However, their total claims on SIMICs, SILICs, MIMICs and MILICs – those countries the Bank thinks might normally cause the banks some trouble – is only $355 billion. In other words, in the considered view of the World Bank, 58 per cent of total debt held by the banks is conceivably problem debt, 42 per cent is not. In only two and a half years, from 1988 to mid-1990, the banks managed to reduce their outstanding debt held on the dangerous SIMICs substantially. With the curious exception of the German banks, they seem determined to continue on this route.

How is *YOUR* Country Treating the Banks?

(Please keep Tables 3.2 and 3.3 handy – they will make this section easier to follow.)

The United States

As the tables show, US banks have been more successful than those of any other country in reducing their third world exposure over the years, even if they still hold a lot of dubious debt. By 1990, they had got rid of half of all developing country debt on their books in 1984, and had also reduced by 50 per cent their exposure to the four most dangerous groups of debtors. Recall, however, that most of this debt has not been written off as far as the debtor is concerned.

---

* Although we follow the World Bank's categories, it has to be said that we find them sometimes unfathomable. The Bank's list of SIMICs includes Argentina, Bolivia, Brazil, Chile, Congo, Costa Rica, Côte D'Ivoire, Ecuador, Egypt, Honduras, Hungary, Mexico, Morocco, Nicaragua, Peru, Philippines, Poland, Senegal, Uruguay, Venezuela. So far, so good. But its list of 'Other' countries – those which are not Severely nor Moderately Indebted Low- or Middle-Income Countries (i.e., they are neither SIMICs or SILICs, MIMICs or MILICs) is constituted by China, Colombia, India, Jamaica, Korea, Malaysia, Nigeria, Thailand, Turkey and Yugoslavia. Collectively, these countries owed banks $111 billion in 1984 and $124 billion in 1990. Among them, certainly Jamaica, Nigeria and Yugoslavia are having serious repayment problems; while India has lately admitted to being severely strapped for cash and has, for the first time, addressed a plea to the IMF. Had we included these four debtors in our tables, we would have added a further $29 billion to the shaky loans column for 1990.

Unlike European banks, US banks do not generally obtain tax credits simply by making loan loss provisions. In the United States, government regulators must unlock the door to tax relief. The regulatory body holding the key is called the InterAgency Exposure Review Committee, or ICERC (pronounced 'I-Kirk') which was created in 1979 by federal bank regulators. A former World Bank consultant, now a partner in a major financial services firm, explains ICERC's purpose:

> The aim of the group was to highlight concentrations of credit to economically weak countries so that boards of directors of banks could make their business decisions with more complete information about their banks' relative exposure to those countries. The intent was, and is, not to restrict or allocate credit, but to make judgements about the appropriate value at which to carry existing loans.[2]

The US Agencies that give ICERC its InterAgency nature are the Federal Reserve, the Office of the Comptroller of the Currency and the Federal Deposit Insurance Corporation. Regulators from these bodies do their homework, talk to bankers, then meet three times yearly to discuss the state of several third world debtors. On the basis of ICERC's investigations, these countries are classed as 'strong', 'moderately strong' and 'weak'. Further classifications are then made of the outstanding loans themselves which can be 'substandard', 'value-impaired' or 'loss' – i.e., forget about collecting.

The 'substandards' and 'value-impaireds' are classed that way because they show varying degrees of tardiness in interest payments and non-compliance with IMF programmes. If a country hasn't remitted full interest for six months and is paying no attention to the IMF, ICERC tells banks either to 'charge off' a certain percentage of their claims or to establish specific provisions against these loans. The required initial levels of provisions are generally 10 to 15 per cent. Each time the country is reviewed and found still delinquent and still disobeying the IMF, ICERC ups the charge-off or provisioning levels by a further 10 or 15 per cent.

As of mid-1990, 14 countries were reportedly on the ICERC list, but their identity and details about the provisioning levels their debt triggers are not public. Bankers, however, know which ones they are and no banker in his right mind would loan them any further funds in the absence of an unlikely, spectacular and sustained financial recovery. Judging from information provided by various press accounts, internal documents and unpublished studies, it appears that by mid-1990, ICERC had reached these decisions concerning federally mandated provisions:

- Five countries require 100 per cent reserve levels: Liberia, Peru, Zaire, Sudan and Nicaragua.
- Côte d'Ivoire weighs in at 75 per cent; Ecuador and Argentinian debt must be provisioned at 60 per cent and Brazil's at 20 per cent.

According to the British private banking analysts IBCA, between 1987 and 1989 US banks charged off $14,231,000,000 against their third world loans. In the first half of 1990 alone, ICERC appears to have stimulated charge-offs of $5.6 billion for the 12 major US banks, the giant ones that together hold 88 per cent of outstanding third world debt. In July 1990, to these charge-offs in the neighbourhood of $20 billion were added more mandatory charge-offs against Brazil and Argentina, for $2.8 billion.[3]

Taking all the known factors into account, it appears that during the three and a half year period from 1987 to mid-July 1990, *over $20 billion of US bank debt on the third world was charged off and provisioned under federal mandate. Since the corporate tax rate on US banks is 34 per cent, this sum would give rise to total tax credits of at least $6.8 billion.*

One neat trick employed in gaining federal tax credits – but a manoeuvre that could only be definitively documented if one were in on the deals – is the reported propensity of US banks to trade debt with each other. For example, if two banks sell each other debt held on the same country at, say, 50 per cent of its face value, each of the banks can record a 50 per cent loss, thus generating a tax credit. On the books of both banks, the loan shows up at 50 per cent of its previous face value, but of course the banks retain the same 100 per cent claim on the debtor. *The US Treasury may have lost over $2 billion in tax credits on such inter-bank debt transactions.*[4]

Naturally, the largesse of the United States Treasury is not the only factor stimulating the banks' active interest in reducing their stock of third world debt. Banks must have adequate reserves if they are to be perceived as 'sound' – and they compete with each other on just such grounds. When a bank makes provisions, in accounting terms the provisions go into its reserves and the bank cannot in principle lend out the money it holds in reserves. Although it theoretically still has the cash, the mere fact of making a provision means that the bank has reduced its own estimate of the funds it has available for lending. So a bank that wants to increase the volume of its business has other incentives besides federal regulation and tax relief to use creative financing with regard to reducing its stock of third world debt.

Citicorp started the reserves ball rolling in 1987 by announcing large voluntary loan loss provisions. It was quickly followed by the other so-called 'Money Center Banks', the heavies with the most third world debt. Meanwhile, middle-sized and smaller banks began extricating themselves from the third world with dispatch – for example, the Wells Fargo bank reduced its 'less developed country' exposure from $1.7 billion in 1987 to zero in 1989. Even the giant banks often decided to take a painful hit in earnings one year in order to improve the looks of their portfolios.

Now the major US banks are all provisioned at levels corresponding to at least a third of their total medium- and long-term exposure, with the aristocratic house of J.P. Morgan in the lead at fully 115 per cent. Citicorp, which initiated the movement, is now at the bottom of the heap, with only 30 per cent, and bank analysts are after it to catch up. One of them says, 'We are more interested in the cushions everyone has to deal with the problem rather than the fact that they're selling [debt] or the price they're selling it at.'[5]

Aside from getting rid of whatever they can on secondary markets, many US banks like the 'debt-for-equity' swap. Small wonder – the swap can be a vehicle for picking up valuable assets at fire-sale prices. The principle is simple: debt is cashed in at an agreed (discounted) price with the Central Bank of third world country X and the proceeds are used to buy companies – public or private – up for sale in that country. Debt, and the desire of both debtors and creditors to get rid of it is often the driving force behind massive privatisation programmes. The sale of the nationalised Argentine phone company ENTel is absorbing large chunks of Argentine debt all by itself. In late 1990, Citicorp made the biggest single debt–equity deal in history, buying 60 per cent of ENTel's southern division in partnership with Telefónica de España for $114 million in cash and $2.7 billion in debt. Manufacturers Hanover got the northern half of the same phone company in partnership with Atlantic Bell Telephone and on roughly the same terms: $100 million cash, $2.7 billion in debt.[6]

Other multi-million dollar debt-for-equity asset purchases by US Money Center Banks include shares in a Venezuelan aluminium plant, a pulp and paper company in Argentina, national airlines and a brewery in Mexico, fertiliser and paper companies in Chile, automobiles and airlines in Brazil, and many, many more. These swaps may be extremely profitable for banks, but with few exceptions (the case of Chile comes to mind) they don't make much of a dent in the debt itself. Even the huge ENTel deals in Argentina wiped out less than 10 per cent of the country's total debt.

Debt–equity swaps may not even change the debtor's financial condition at all if one considers the longer term. Profits on all these ventures can presumably be repatriated by the foreign purchasers later on. To a nation as a whole, it doesn't matter much whether the cash outflow takes place in the form of interest payments or repatriated profits. For example, Bankers Trust, an early swapper, in 1986 made a $60 million debt–equity investment in Chile's largest pension fund. In 1990 Bankers Trust collected nearly $50 million in profits on this investment. This bank also 'points to a special interest in *maquiladora* financing along Mexico's northern border' (see Chapter 1 on the environment for the social and environmental impact of such investments in the *maquiladora* zone).[7]

Japan

Believe it or not, the US regulatory regime, which has probably granted some $8.8 billion in tax credits to US banks between 1987 and mid-1990, is one of the two *least* favourable regimes with respect to this corporate capacity to gain such credits. Japan is the other one.

Japan, in fact, seems to be the only genuinely capitalist country in the OECD group. Basically it is saying to its banks, 'If you make smart loans, you take your profits. If you make stupid ones, you take your lumps.' Japanese banks can only claim tax relief on provisions up to a measly 1 per cent of the face value of their loans.

Japanese commercial bank exposure to the Severely Indebted Middle-Income Countries and to the SILICs, MINICs and MIMICs was $55 billion in 1988, up 6 per cent from a year earlier. Its exposure to the SIMICs alone was $41 billion, or three quarters of the potentially troublesome debt it holds. Assuming a round figure of $45 billion dollars' worth of possible needs for provisions, assuming further that Japanese banks provisioned themselves at the almost utopian level of 100 per cent; and given the corporate tax rate applied to Japanese banks of 38 per cent, the maximum allowable tax relief under the present regime would be $171 million – hardly worth doing the paper work!

Japanese banks have been offered a small but apparently little-used sweetener. The government has allowed them to set up a tax shelter company in the Cayman Islands. With the previous approval of the tax authorities, banks can sell up to 4 per cent of their total loans to this company at a market-related (i.e., discounted) price. The loss made on the sale is tax-deductible. The bank is also authorised to receive dividends paid by the Cayman company, based on any interest payments it may receive on the loans. It seems the banks haven't much availed themselves of this facility, and to our knowledge, no estimates of its tax advantages have been reported.

On the other hand, and unlike most other regulators, Japanese government authorities do encourage debt reduction transactions. There have been at least two cases of 'buybacks', in which the governments of the debtor countries – here Chile and Bolivia – have repurchased their loans at a discount. Japanese banks that sell back the loan to the debtor in this manner obtain tax relief on the full difference between the face value of the loan and the actual cash price of sale.[8]

This regime is fairer to the debtors than those of other OECD countries because a direct connection is established between genuine relief for the debtor – who has effectively cancelled his own loan by repurchasing it at a sharp discount – and tax relief for the bank.

The United Kingdom

A rather dense thicket. Until 1987, the UK Inland Revenue severely restricted tax relief allowable on provisions against shaky third world debt. As a result, British banks tended to have perilously low provisions – less than 10 per cent of their exposure. However, when Citicorp sounded the alarm in May 1987, the echo was heard across the Atlantic and UK banks followed suit, beginning seriously to build up their loan loss provisions. The government then acted to allow higher levels of tax relief and, at the same time, the Bank of England issued what it called a 'Matrix' – a sort of country rating system of risk factors.

The Matrix has slots for risk-determining elements like the third world country's economic problems, its interest-rate payment record and its compliance with IMF structural adjustment programmes. These general categories are then broken down into 16 differently weighted variables. The variables determine a score which in turn determines the appropriate range of provisions. The more 'points' a country has, the more dangerous it is deemed for the banks.

The Matrix was revised in January 1990 and its 'scores' now start at 10–24 points which trigger a minimum 5 to 13 per cent reserve. The highest possible scores, 120–145 points, are awarded to not merely distressed but virtually brain-dead countries for which provisions should scale dizzying heights of 97 to 199 per cent. Just to make things simpler, the Bank of England's provisioning requirements will henceforward be based on a moving average Matrix score over 15 months, not just the score at a given moment. Tennis, anyone?

Or perhaps the Matrix should be compared to a quite sophisticated parlour game, one which is supposed to provide 'a uniform framework for assessing provisions against LDC claims'. But it doesn't do that really, because final responsibility for the decision to set funds aside must still be assumed by the individual bank. As the executive director of the Bank of England told an audience of bankers in November 1989,

> First, the responsibility for determining the level of provisions for loss rests with the management and directors of each institution. Secondly, and most important, provisions are essentially and ultimately a matter of judgement and no amount of analysis will avoid the need to make that judgement.[9]

In fact, the Bank of England is consistent in telling the bankers to make up their own minds, for both its 1987 and 1990 Matrices were simply devices to catch up, in regulatory terms, with what the banks had already decided to do anyway. The chief concern of the Old Lady of Threadneedle Street seems to be to provide *post facto* justification for reserve levels already achieved.

The thicket becomes even more impenetrable with the degree of subjectivity introduced by the Inland Revenue's rules as to what constitutes 'bad' or 'doubtful' debt. The Matrix is supposed to be the starting point for determining what bad debt is, but individual tax inspectors have a lot of leeway in deciding if it really is bad and how bad it really is. They can then decide how much relief is due on it. The tax people have frequently taken the position that 'sovereign' debt cannot be 'bad' because countries do not go bankrupt. Furthermore, the Finance Act of 1990 allows the Inland Revenue to develop its *own* Matrix for tax purposes. According to IBCA Banking Analysis Ltd,

> The release of the [1990] Matrix was delayed by several weeks, supposedly on account of wrangling on this subject between the Bank of England (the banks' champion) and the Inland Revenue. When the major UK banks raised reserve levels during 1989, they almost certainly counted on gaining a substantial increase in tax relief. If, for reasons political or otherwise, the Inland Revenue declines to increase tax relief, the the UK banks will be facing a much larger tax bill than expected.[10]

Aren't you glad you're not a tax adviser to a major British bank? You can leave them, however, to worry about the details: the other rules established by the 1990 Finance Act with regard to third world debt are even more complex and we do not intend to explain them, although we know of someone who can.[11]

Although the bottom line may still be a bit hazy, after confronting and comparing with other sources, we think IBCA gets it right when it shows that UK banks, to be in line with the Matrix, would have to make total provisions of $20 billion on outstanding loans to 34 countries (this list includes all of Eastern Europe, Turkey and South Africa). IBCA concludes, *'Using a 35 per cent tax rate, the Inland Revenue will bear about US$7 billion of the US$20 billion of provisions.'* By 1991, the big UK banks would have received tax credits for about half their sovereign debt exposure. Those that have provisioned more than 50 per cent will ultimately receive full tax credits, but they will get them only gradually. John Denham, our researcher for this chapter, estimates that their total relief will then rise to $8.5 billion.

Germany
Germany's case is intriguing. It is the only OECD country lender whose exposure to the debt-distressed has vastly increased since the debt crisis first surfaced. This exposure is up by nearly 150 per cent with regard to all developing countries and has doubled with regard to the four danger-prone groups of SIMICs, SILICs, MIMICs and MILICs. Part of the increase in German banks' outstanding loans can of course be attributed to Eastern Europe, where they have shot up from a little over $9 billion in 1984 to nearly $34 billion in late 1990 – a rise of 268 per cent. But during the same period, German claims on other areas also showed remarkable increases, in total contrast with the numbers for other OECD creditors; for example Africa +104 per cent, Asia +122 per cent, Latin America +82 per cent. Either German bankers know something the others don't or there is a good reason for passing out all those deutschmarks.

There are various plausible ways to account for this phenomenon. Perhaps German banks aren't really passing out that many deutschmarks and the jump in their 'claims' simply reflects the rise in value of their currency vis-a-vis the US dollar (World Bank figures used here are all expressed in dollars). Or perhaps German bankers have been inactive on secondary markets and the arrears of interest payments by their third world debtors have piled up and pushed the levels of their total exposure higher. Or maybe the German government has continued to guarantee third world export credits granted by banks at a higher rate than in other countries? One or more of these explanations may be enough to account for the quite staggering rise in German third world loans since 1984. Possibly.

But the answer to the riddle could also lie in the tax regime. In Germany, *all provisions against country risk are tax deductible*; the banks make up their own minds on what they want to set aside and then merely inform the authorities of what they have done. The regulatory and tax authorities set no guidelines of their own. In mid-1990, provisions were estimated to range between 50 and 85 per cent on possible problem debt from all sources. If we take *only* the Severely Indebted Middle-Income Country problem debt ($36 billion); assume a conservative provisioning rate of 60 per cent and a corporate tax of 45 per cent, *German bank tax credits on the third world part of their portfolios would be close to $10 billion*. If we include SILICs, MIMICs and MILICs as well, then German bank exposure of $62 billion could give rise to tax credits of $16.7 billion. Note that these figures do not include most of the doubtful loans outstanding in Eastern Europe.

It seems fair to estimate that German banks have probably been granted at least twice as much tax relief as their American or British counterparts. Perhaps German bankers find it profitable to continue to loan, knowing that heads they win, and tails they win too. State foreign policy objectives may well be served by these financial rules – keep the money flowing towards certain areas and certain nations, but do it quietly, behind the shield of 'commerce'. This is speculation – we hope German colleagues will try to elucidate the matter!

France

French banks have the highest proportion of total outstanding loans to Africa of any OECD country in their third world debt portfolios – $21 billion, or 40 per cent of total African commercial debt. By comparison, German bank exposure in Africa is $11 billion, British $5.5 and American only $2.5. In 1990, French banks remained just as heavily exposed to the Severely Indebted Middle-Income Countries as they had been in 1984 ($28 billion) and their claims on the three other dangerous groups were also higher than those of any other creditor country except Germany ($21 billion). So it's not surprising that the French Treasury's list of worrisome countries is much longer than that of any other national regulatory body, and includes 77 debtors.

The Banque de France stipulates that individual French banks must have a reserve level at least equal to the average provisioning level of the French banking community, which, in 1990, was about 55 per cent. Provisions against loans to any of this particular 'Group of 77' are currently tax deductible up to 60 per cent. The three largest French banks are all known to hold reserves at this tax-relief limiting level, whereas IBCA says that 'banks in France can easily obtain tax deductibility on provisions to LDC reserves which cover up to 60 per cent of exposure.' Using a base of $49 billion in dubious debt, a conservative provisioning level of 55 per cent and an effective tax rate of 37 per cent, the tax credits gained by French banks would be about $10.9 billion.[12]

Switzerland
Swiss banks, like German ones, write their own ticket. They decide levels of provisioning and then tell the authorities what they've done. All provisions are tax deductible. This may be why, as in Germany, the Swiss have increased their exposure to debt-distressed areas, albeit by a far more modest 20 per cent. Their exposure to dangerous debt was $12 billion in 1989 and Swiss banks are believed to have made provisions of 60 per cent. With a corporate tax of 35 per cent, their tax credit gains would amount to $2.5 billion.

Italy
Foreigners tend to think of Italy as tax-heaven, but in the case of third world loans owed to banks, the Italian regulatory authorities are much more restrictive than those of other European countries. Tax relief can only be claimed up to a maximum of 20 per cent of provisions. Italian banks are thought, however, to have exceeded that level. Exposure to the debt-distressed in 1989 was $7 billion. With provisions at 20 per cent and the corporate tax rate 36 per cent, tax credits generated would have been about $515 million.

Canada
The Canadian government's policies on tax relief for loan loss provisions are straightforward. In 1989, the regulatory authority known as the Office of the Superintendent of Financial Institutions (OSFI) determined a 'basket' of 42 developing countries (up from 32 in 1986) on whose loans the banks must set aside mandatory provisions of 35 per cent minimum. As of March 1990, the upper limit for obtaining tax relief was 45 per cent; banks can, of course, make provisions beyond this level if they so choose.

And on the whole, they have so chosen. Canadian third world bank exposure was reduced by a quite drastic 39 per cent between 1986 and 1989, when it came down to less than Cdn$16 billion. Simultaneously, as they got rid of their outstanding loans, Canadian banks rapidly set aside provisions against the ones they kept. These provisions reached an average 70 per cent in 1989. Of the six largest Canadian banks, the least provisioned one is at a level of 60, the highest at 87 per cent. Compare this with Citicorp's 30 per cent. Although Canadian banks did not get tax credits over and above the 45 per cent limit of their provisions, they have still received more than Cdn\$3 billion. If, at some future time, the ceiling on tax relief is raised to cover real levels of provisions, Canadian taxpayers would forfeit another Cdn\$2 billion.

As in other tax regimes, like that of the US, Canadian banks' provisions and tax credits do not result in any corresponding relief for the debtor countries involved – there is no connection between the two processes.[13]

Other OECD Countries

Several other smaller countries with much lower exposures also allow tax relief on provisions. Austrian banks can claim credits on 60 per cent provisions on the face value of their third world debt. The Belgian Commission Bancaire et Financière requires 60 per cent coverage against exposure to a list of 45 countries. The three largest Belgian banks have made provisions approaching 100 per cent of their claims on these countries. Dutch banks can claim relief on all provisions, which are set in accordance with Central Bank guidelines. Spain grants tax credits on provisions up to 35 per cent.

The findings for the major creditor countries are summed up in Table 3.4:

Table 3.4: Total Probable Tax Credits Against Loan Loss Provisions Obtained by Banks in Major OECD Creditor Countries, 1987–90 (\$US billions)

Country	Probable Tax Credit
United States	\$8.8*
Japan	0.17
United Kingdom	8.5*
Germany	10–16.7
France	10.9
Switzerland	2.5
Italy	0.5
Canada (in \$US)	2.7
Total:	44.1–50.8

* The figure for the US includes \$2 billion probable tax credits obtained through interbank purchases of loans on secondary markets; the one for the UK includes credits that will be received in future on provisions already made.

The bottom line here is quite literally that, in the three and a half years from 1987 until mid-1990, taxpayers of North America and Europe provided their banks with up to $50 billion in tax relief. But to err on the conservative side if at all, we will give the banks the benefit of every doubt by using the lowest conceivable figure. We will use the lower end of the possible scale for Germany and subtract credits US banks probably received by selling debt to each other on secondary markets as well as credits in the pipeline to UK banks for which they must wait a while. Thus we can assume a rock-bottom figure of about $40 billion in tax relief.

'How much' is $40 billion? It's much more, for example, than the Gross National Product of nearly any third world country you care to name except for the really large ones like India, China, Indonesia, Brazil, Argentina, Mexico and some of the Newly Industrialising Countries (NICs) like Korea. It's 55 times UNICEF's budget for 1990. It is more than the combined average 1990 after-tax incomes of 5,750,000 Americans among the poorest 20 per cent. It is much more than the $34 billion of Official Development Assistance (ODA) accorded to all developing countries in 1987.[14]

In each of the 42 months from 1987 to mid-1990, tax credits to the banks averaged nearly a billion dollars – thus they received more every month than the total annual budget of UNICEF ($721 million) which serves to counteract some of the harm done by the banks. In each of these 42 months, every North American or European, including infants and children, was theoretically assessed $1.60 to cover tax relief to the banks on their third world debt.

We have all unwittingly remitted to the banks an average $67 for this three and a half year period, or, put another way, forfeited $67 worth of services their taxes could have provided. If the less conservative, though more probable figure of $50 billion in tax relief is used, then the assessment on every OECD citizen was $84.*

There is no question that, strictly speaking, the OECD governments and banks are within their rights, since under most tax regimes, provisions or losses may legally attract tax relief. Tax breaks on third world loans have, however, been granted on an unprecedented scale, because the loans themselves were unprecedentedly massive and the bankers' judgement uniformly – though perhaps not unprecedentedly – foolish. Furthermore, because their so-called 'sovereign' loans are treated like any other category of business, banks can

---

* $40 billion divided by 595 million people (275 million North Americans and 320 million Europeans) = $67 divided by 42 months = $1.60 per month. Using the higher estimate, the monthly charge to us all was $2.00.

greatly reduce to themselves the costs of setting aside provisions while granting no comparable relief to their sovereign 'customers'. They can carry these loans on their books for much longer periods than they could do if they were dealing with comparable levels of corporate or individual debts.

As IBCA Banking Analysis Ltd said in February 1990:

> Given the determination of all banks to get out of LDC lending, it may well be that some further provisioning is necessary; however we have no doubt that most of the pain associated with LDC lending is now history as far as the banks are concerned. In the UK, it seems likely that total losses on LDC lending are going to end up in the region of 10–15 billion pounds, while world-wide these losses will be in excess of US$100 billion. Both in the UK and elsewhere, this data confirms that LDC lending was the largest commercial bank mistake in history.[15]

But Northern taxpayers everywhere have already compensated and will continue to compensate the banks for their 'mistake'. If, as we believe, IBCA's figure of $100 billion in overall losses is reasonable, then each of us in the creditor countries will be assessed about $157 in the end so that the banks' 'pain' can be forgotten and their 'mistake' thrown into the dustbin of history. The pain of the ordinary taxpayer – much less that of the hungry, the homeless, the jobless in the third world – is of no concern. Meanwhile, as we shall shortly show, the banks have already received, and continue to receive, not only huge tax credits – in fact subsidies from the public purse – but consistently enormous sums from the third world.

It is a triumph of modern statecraft and of international economic management that neither borrowers nor lenders need play by the rules of traditional free market, entrepreneurial capitalism. It is a triumph of the media's capacity to miss the really big stories that so few people are aware of it. Third world governments and elites borrowed heedlessly but can now force their poor majorities to reimburse their debts. Banks lent recklessly but instead of facing the music can fall back on the forced generosity of society at large. The difference between the privileged and the penalised in the South and the North is one of degree, not of principle. Few Northern taxpayers realise how costly the 'largest commercial bank mistake in history' has actually been for them, but it is entirely legal that these taxpayers should be made to pay for it.

Do the Banks Really Need the Taxpayer?

The financial pages of the US and the European press focus on the banks' pain or praise them for their prudence in setting aside reserves against the proverbial rainy day. Official and unofficial handwringing over the continuing third world debt crisis concentrates on the dangers faced by banks and by the North in general. The media and officialdom are, however, remarkably silent on two interesting subjects:

- First, since the debt crisis broke in 1982, and however much they may whine and claim the opposite, banks have received extremely generous returns on their outstanding loans in less developed countries. Third world service payments to banks have not only held steady but have lately even tended to increase, despite the fact that most banks have stopped lending the South any new money.
- Second, as the banks have continued to receive these large remittances, the overall burden of third world debt, which has stabilised at around $1.3 trillion, has been gradually shifted from the private to the public sector, that is, from the banks to you and me.

These trends can be seen with figures drawn from OECD data in Table 3.5.

Table 3.5: Bank Loans to and Returns from LDC Debtors ($US billions)

Year	1982	1983	1984	1985	1986	1987	1988	1989
Total LDC debt (public and private)	854	937	961	1.078	1.194	1.329	1.313	1.322
LDC debt owed to comm.banks	493	516	520	554	584	630	625	629
% of total debt held by banks	57.7%	55%	54%	51%	49%	47%	47%	47%
LDC debt service to banks	82.2	69.7	77.9	83.6	69.3	66.5	84.5	82
New bank lending to LDCs	37.9	35	17.2	15.2	7.0	7.0	5.8	8.5
Service to banks as % of debt held by banks same year	16.7%	13.4%	15%	15%	12%	10.5%	13.5%	13%

Source: OECD, *Financing and External Debt of Developing Countries 1989 Survey*[16]

Total service payments received by banks between 1982 and 1989 amounted to $615 billion (both interest and amortisation). This figure does not compare at all unfavourably with the total third world debt banks held in 1982 ($493 billion) nor with the debt they held seven years later ($629 billion). It is, in fact, astonishing that third world countries could pay their commercial creditors an average of nearly $77 billion a year; more than $6.4 billion a month – yet find themselves as a group fully 28 per cent more in debt to these creditors than they were in 1982, in spite of a dearth of new lending.

In stark contrast to this $615 billion outlay from the poor countries to the banks, the bank's new third world loans for the same period of 1982–9 came to only $133 billion – with 55 per cent of that sum loaned in 1982 and 1983 before the banks had fully caught on to what was happening. Subsequently, their new loans were scarcer than unicorns and had to be painfully extracted by governments touting various rescue plans.

During all the years of 'crisis', as Table 3.5 shows, banks received healthy rates of return on their loans (both interest and amortisation) averaging 13.6 per cent from 1982 to 1989. This is certainly a comfortable margin compared to what the banks would themselves have to pay in interest to borrow fresh funds on capital markets. In other words, the banks *as a group* were never in genuine danger on their aggregate third world portfolios, although many individual banks – US and British ones in particular – were in deep trouble vis-a-vis individual debtors, especially in the early 1980s. One can still legitimately, some might say angrily, ask if the banks really needed the generous relief provided by taxpayers as well.

How the Boomerang Lands in the Public Court

The second little noticed trend, also shown in Table 3.5, is the shift of the debt burden from the private to the public sector. At the beginning of the 1980s, banks held roughly 58 per cent of all third world loans. By the end of the decade, their share was down to 47 per cent. This downward trend has continued. Hobart Rowen, writing in the *Washington Post*, explained:

For the first time, more than half of the total Third World debt is now held by the World Bank, the International Monetary Fund and the other official lenders and less than half by the commercial banks. It is the reverse of the situation that used to prevail. This 'officialisation' of Third World debt is likely to grow – with strong political fallout. In effect, the risk of lending money to poor countries is being transferred from commercial bank stockholders to the backs of taxpayers.*[17]

This reduction of the banks' share has been achieved even though the third world's total debt burden went up by 55 per cent (from $854 to $1322 billion) from 1982–9 and the amount owed to banks went up by 28 per cent (from $493 to an estimated $629 billion). Virtually none of this increase was due to new loans but represented rather a pile-up of arrears. For example, in the five years from 1985 to 1989, banks received $386 billion in payments from the third world while supplying it with only $43.5 billion in new funds.

There is strong evidence that these exceptionally high remittances from poor countries to banks since 1982 could never have been made without the help of public money – taxpayers' money – from national or international public agencies. Loans from official creditors seem to have transitted via the books of third world countries but were in fact used to pay back the banks, not to fund 'development' or provide for human welfare.

For example, more World Bank money than ever before, and practically all IMF funds, are lent under the vague heading of 'structural adjustment'. The recipient government need not necessarily apply these funds to any particular internal purpose. John Denham argues, with long tables too complex to reproduce here but available on request, that Latin America and the Caribbean, from 1983 to 1989, provided 'an effective transfer of $32.7 billion from new official lending to commercial banks. This represents 17 per cent of the total debt service received by commercial banks from this region over the period.' His calculations show that this further subsidy of nearly $33 billion from public purses to private coffers was drawn from official bilateral (government) sources for one-third and from multilateral institutions like the Bank and the Fund for two-thirds.

It would be simpler, and much more help to the debtors, if these public lending bodies simply bought back third world debt from the banks instead of going through this rigmarole. At least that way the weight of the debt burden would be reduced. As things stand, the debtors will remain in bondage forever. Or could this, perhaps, be the whole point?

Jeffrey Sachs, the Harvard economist with hands-on experience advising major debtors, laid out the mechanisms of public-to-private

---

* According to the OECD figures for 1990, one proportion of debt held by commercial banks was further reduced that year, to 42 per cent.

transfers to members of Congress with such clarity that we cannot do better than paraphrase or cite rather large chunks of his testimony.

When money is owed to 'official' sources, explains Sachs, it is ultimately and indirectly owed to 'taxpayers'. So if the total amount of debt is too large for a debtor to pay, theoretically the commercial banks and the taxpayers will share the loss. The more this loss is absorbed by the banks, the less by taxpayers and vice-versa. If the claims of the banks are fully protected, then the taxpayers absorb the whole loss.

'Under the debt management strategy of this Administration, *the commercial banks are not expected to absorb any losses'*, declares Sachs. So guess who does? These losses, however, have never been presented to the public for what they are, but have rather been

> very well hidden in the form of new loans, reschedulings and so forth. Basically, the Administration, together with other creditor governments and the official institutions, has supported various mechanisms to make sure that the official creditors do not receive much repayment on their claims, so that the debtor countries can devote the great bulk of their debt servicing to the commercial banks.

Some of the 'various mechanisms' are new loans from the IMF or the World Bank – which then demands, and gets, from the same taxpayers a General Capital Increase of $75 billion in order to sustain these loans. 'Paris Club' countries – the official government creditors – also

> forgo much or all of the interest that is due on government-to-government loans. Thus, while the commercial banks receive their interest payments from the debtor countries, the official creditors allow the debtor countries to postpone the interest payments that are due.

Some governments (Japan, for example) have also made new loans which directly or indirectly help debtors to keep on servicing old commercial debts. Official cancellation of part of the African debt at the Toronto Summit in 1988 was another ploy. 'Importantly, and interestingly', says Sachs, 'the creditor governments apparently did not even suggest that the commercial banks should share in a *pro rata* cancellation of the debt owed to the banks.'[18]

He thinks taxpayers should be protected by making the banks share the burden. In that case, the urgent need for huge new appropriations like the Capital Increases for the Bank or the Fund, and public money put into Paris Club reschedulings, could be substantially reduced.

Jeffrey Sachs doesn't put any specific numbers on these gifts from taxpayers to the banks, but clearly they are for all intents and purposes roughly equal to any official relief accorded to the debtors. Denham's figures show that these disguised subsidies were of the order of $11 billion extracted from OECD countries directly and another $22 billion from multilateral agencies. Since multilaterals get their funds not only from member country (taxpayer) capital subscriptions but also, in the case of the World Bank, from bondholders, Hobart Rowan wonders if its bonds will not find their 'vaunted Triple A rating threatened' as the Bank involves itself more intimately with bad third world debt.

Aside from losses which might be incurred by the Bank's bond-holders (many of which are pension funds and other institutional investors), one can state unequivocally that every dollar of public money – bilateral or multilateral – devoted to reimbursing the commercial banks is a dollar not put to use to satisfy human needs. Other chapters in this book show how much Northerners stand to lose from chronic poverty in the South. Surely the payment of indirect subsidies to banks is an inefficient, indeed fraudulent use of their money.

At the World Bank-IMF meeting in Seoul in 1985, Mr James Baker, then US Secretary of the Treasury, launched the plan that bears his name. The backbone of the Baker Plan was the banks, who were supposed to lend quite a lot of fresh money, particularly to 15 major debtors. They did nothing of the kind, but rather cut their lending to the drastically low levels where it remains to this day. Why not, especially when the Administration was not threatening them with anything but rather making every effort, as detailed above, to guarantee their revenues. Banks are not philanthropic institutions, as Mr Baker, a fourth generation banker himself, is doubtless aware.

In 1989 the new US Secretary of the Treasury, Nicholas Brady, attached his name to another Plan. It is not important to describe here the financial ins-and-outs of the Brady Plan – negotiations for its implementation have been known to take months of complex wrangling. This plan essentially sought to persuade the banks that they should exchange a theoretically 'high value' but insecure loan for a lower value but safer loan; or that they should lend enough money to debtors so that they could buy back their own debt at a discount. By the time the plan has made the rounds of all its prospec-tive clients, at least $20 billion of World Bank and IMF money will have been mobilised to support Brady-type deals.

This is not just a time-consuming and inefficient use of 'development' money at a time when calls on public financing are coming from all quarters and growing more pressing every day; it is also far too little and far too late. The Brady Plan is intended to apply to just a handful of countries (Mexico and the Philippines are the largest). Nor has it, so far, got the banks to cooperate any more than the Baker Plan did. For instance, after protracted negotiations with its creditors, the Philippines signed a Brady agreement widely estimated to have saved the country ... $70 million a year in debt service.

Capital Flight: Those Who Talk Don't Know; Those Who Know Don't Talk

One of the major stated goals of the Brady Plan is to encourage flight capital to return home. A country cannot even be considered for Brady relief – such as it is – until it has signed on for the whole series of IMF-type measures: deregulation of markets, fiscal austerity, currency depreciation, lower wages and higher interest rates. Since the advent of Brady, the IMF has added a further item to this list of requirements: its support for future debt relief will be made conditional on success in reversing capital flight.

But Manuel Pastor, in his study on 'Capital Flight and the Latin American Debt Crisis' finds such a reversal highly unlikely. Pastor says that in fact, 'the debtor countries are being placed in a "Catch 22" dilemma in which they are going to be judged on their success in achieving a goal, while being required to employ a set of policies that have proven to be ineffective in achieving that goal.'[19]

He estimates the exit of capital from Latin America at a rather suspiciously precise '$151 billion in the years 1973–87'. Other sources would cite a higher figure; for example, the former president of the Inter-American Development Bank says that capital flight from Mexico alone, from 1979–83 only was $90 billion. Until 1989, the OECD subtracted flight capital from its tables on resource flows to developing countries: it gave a total of $185 billion for the period from 1980–8.[20] Whatever its amount and its provenance, capital flight is frequently and correctly identified as the shadowy partner of the third world debt crisis.

When official creditors like the IMF are criticised for their draconian debt management policies, they like to remind their critics that debtors could easily pay off their debts if they encouraged assets outside the country to return home. (See Chapter 2 on the policies of the cocaine growing countries which do just that.) But if the creditors really wanted flight capital to go back where it came from, then they would stop providing the positive encouragement they have always given to flight capital.

Such capital is a boon to bankers, but another loss to taxpayers. Northern governments do not tax the earnings on assets belonging to foreign nationals. As two experts from the Washington DC Institute for International Economics note,

> Most developed countries, including the United States, have now abandoned taxation of most non-resident investment income. For example, the United States has long exempted from taxation interest on bank deposits owned by non-residents; it does not even impose a refundable withholding tax. In 1984, it exempted interest on Treasury securities held by non-residents from withholding as well – a move swiftly followed by France, Germany and Japan.[21]

Capital that flees its own country may derive from illegal or corrupt activities but it may also simply be the rational response of the legally wealthy to crisis-wracked economies. The promise of no taxes in the safe haven is an added attraction. Given the make-up of most debtor country governments, it is unlikely that they will themselves show much enthusiasm for mutual tax treaties with creditor countries which would help to stem capital flight.

We can give only a ballpark figure on the amounts of tax revenues theoretically lost on this capital. However, using a conservative estimate of $250 billion held in OECD countries by debtor country nationals; and assuming that earnings are 10 per cent and the tax rates 35 to 40 per cent, tax losses to Northern governments and citizens would be in the neighbourhood of $8–10 billion a year.

As Manuel Pastor explains, to be persuasive, debt relief must come before capital flight goes into reverse gear, not after. 'Capital will not return if investors fear that a debt-burdened government might be forced to seize dollar assets.' And each IMF-required devaluation is an invitation to keep one's money in non-devalued dollars, marks or francs – the best way to become automatically richer at home.

Conclusions

Since 1982, Northern taxpayers have contributed to banks, or simply lost:

- Between $44 and $50 billion in tax relief on bank provisions and losses. Further tax relief to banks is likely, according to IBCA.

- At least $33 billion – far more when World Bank and IMF Capital Increases are counted – in disguised subsidies from public entities to private banks.
- A minimum of $8–10 billion a year in taxes forgone on capital flight, or some $80 billion for the decade. (Banks have, however, presumably made money on these deposits and such earnings have, theoretically, been taxed.)

Meanwhile, between 1982 and 1989, banks received service payments of $615 billion from the debtors.

The debtors, on the other hand, by 1991 were 61 per cent more in debt to all creditors than they were in 1982; and 35 per cent more in debt to the banks themselves.

This whole process of transfers to the banks from the ordinary citizen in both North and South has occurred entirely within the law. The banks, the creditor governments and the international lending agencies have committed no crimes. The question of justice is another matter entirely.

The Fourth Boomerang:
Lost Jobs and Markets

Research and Documentation by Cameron Duncan and Indra Wahab

When the produce of any particular branch of industry exceeds what the demand of the country requires, the surplus must be sent abroad and exchanged for something for which there is demand at home. Without such exportation, a part of the productive labour of the country must cease, and the value of its annual produce diminish.
Adam Smith, *The Wealth of Nations*, Book Two, Chapter 5

Just as a debtor country, in order to make a foreign debt payment, must sell to foreigners more goods and services than it buys from foreigners, so a creditor nation, in order to receive a completed debt payment, must be prepared to buy from foreigners more goods and services than it sells to them ... The degree to which such a creditor country accepts an import surplus measures its willingness to receive debt payments ... One thing is certain – a country which is unwilling to receive payments cannot be paid.
Harold G. Moulton and Leo Pasvolsky, *War Debts and World Prosperity*, the Brookings Institution, Washington DC, 1932

A change afoot in the late twentieth century may prove as momentous as the historic shift that took place in the eighteenth and nineteenth centuries when agrarian capital gave way to industrial capital. Just as the great landowners of England lost their pre-eminent economic place to the rising urban bourgeoisie, so it seems today that industrial capital is staggering under an assault of finance capital, led by the banks. In the previous chapter, we saw how the banks have transformed their 'historic mistake' into a near-bonanza and how they have managed to make the public pay for their ill-conceived third world adventures.

Industry and agriculture – and their workers – have managed nothing of the kind. Although they took no part in creating the debt crisis, they, like so many others in both North and South, have become its inadvertent victims. Because of debt, farming and manufacturing have lost significant markets, just as those employed in these sectors have lost their jobs by the hundreds of thousands.

Third world earnings remitted to banks are lost to commerce and fewer goods sold mean fewer jobs. This much is obvious. But the effects of the debt crisis are more perverse and far-reaching than that. To earn the dollars for those remittances, debtor countries must invest in export production and their goods then often enter into competition with goods produced in the North. Debtors have no choice but to run structural trade surpluses or they will necessarily default on their payments.

Surpluses for some, however, imply deficits for others because trade is a zero sum game. Creditors cannot have it both ways – they cannot both sell more to the debtors and receive higher interest payments from them. If they want the interest, then they must accept the debtors' goods. If the creditors do not export, then, as Adam Smith pointed out, 'a part of the productive labour of the country must cease'; and as the other two authors cited at the head of this chapter, writing during the debt crisis of the 1930s, said, 'A country which is unwilling to receive payments cannot be paid.' Such is the choice. A country that *is* willing to be paid – or rather wants its banks to be paid – must sacrifice export sales. And the United States, at least, has clearly opted against exports – and thus against its own 'productive labour' – and for the banks.

For the debtors of our era, just as in the 1930s, it is catch 22. Countries struggling to export their way out of the debt crisis ought at least to earn a fair price for their wares, and be able to sell them without undue encumbrance. Neither condition holds true today. Raw materials' prices have fallen into the Slough of Despond, never, it would seem, to emerge. The IMF's own data prove this.

The Fund's index of 34 non-fuel commodities shows that throughout 1989 and 1990, after a short-lived boomlet, their prices suffered consistent decline. In the IMF index, a value of 100 is assigned to 1980 commodity prices. At the end of 1990 the curve had plunged below 80 and the downward slide seemed destined to continue towards the historic depths of 1985–6, themselves the lowest levels attained since the Great Depression. Prices for the 34 commodities expressed in Special Drawing Rights, the Fund's composite currency that avoids the distortions of an oscillating dollar, dropped 13 per cent in 1990 alone.[1]

This decline is especially worrying because at the very time commodity prices were in free fall, the volume of world trade was expanding – by 7 per cent in 1989 and by a further 6 per cent in 1990 – according to GATT. However, 'the expansion of world trade (throughout the 1980s) was largely concentrated in North America, Western Europe and Asia, while the share of the Middle East, Africa and Latin America in world trade declined.' Even the so-called Asian tigers – the countries GATT calls the 'dynamic exporters' – in 1990 'registered a sharp slowdown: their export volume expanded by less than the global average'.

Naturally it is the largest debtors who have had to make the most heroic efforts to generate trade surpluses, but they too seem to be running out of steam. GATT reported in 1990 that 'The growth of merchandise exports from the 15 highly indebted developing countries decelerated sharply.' Nonetheless, for these big 15, *'foreign exchange earnings ... were almost $20 billion above the predebt crisis peak in 1981, while imports were more than $20 billion below their 1981 peak.'*[2]

This statement from GATT succinctly conveys the dilemma the third world debt crisis poses for the North. On the one hand, much of the extra $20 billion (compared to 1981 levels) earned by the 15 Highly Indebted Countries went straight to the banks (with a portion to official Northern creditors as well); while the symmetrical $20 billion slash in their imports was almost entirely subtracted from the potential sales of Northern farms and factories. In the drive to export and to earn hard currency, something has got to give, and what has clearly given in the 1980s and 1990s are the jobs and markets of the creditor countries.

People who criticise present debt management policies on ethical, economic or ecological grounds have generally tended to be identified with the political left. Where vanishing markets and glaring trade deficits are concerned, however, Establishment voices have also taken the floor. The causal connections between the debt crisis and these losses were recognised almost from day one and their impact measured early on. Third world debt is well known to be a culprit contributing to deficits and unemployment.

Everyone – from Secretaries of Commerce to the trade unions to the United States Senate – has lamented the depressing effect of other peoples' debts on the US economy, but no one, apparently, has had the political clout to do anything about it. One easily drawn conclusion is that a genuine, if muted, conflict now exists between the banks on one side and the productive sectors of the economy on the other. So far, the banks have won hands down.

Benefits to Banks or Business but not Both: The Decline of Western Hemisphere Trade

As early as 1983, barely a year into the debt crisis, an expert writing in the *Quarterly Review* of the Federal Reserve Bank of New York diagnosed a sharp drop in US exports to Latin America. He expected them to fall that year by 40 per cent from their 1981 levels, with the consequent loss of a quarter of a million jobs. According to this economist, Sanjay Dhar, the loss of employment in 1983 would be additional to the 225,000 jobs already wiped out in 1982 because of 'financing constraints' in Latin America. Worse still, these jobs would be 'concentrated in some of our most depressed industries', like machinery and transport equipment where rates of unemployment were already running between 11 and 15.3 per cent.[3] Sophisticated high-tech industries suffered too. Previously fast-growing exports of 'scientific and business machinery' to Latin America dropped precipitously, by nearly 40 per cent. So did farm exports.

Meanwhile, the banks were happily raking in extra receipts.

The state of play as it stood in the early part of the decade, at the outset of the debt crisis, is shown in Table 4.1.[4]

Table 4.1: Changes in US Export Revenues to, and US Bank Receipts from Latin America (US$ billions)

	1980	1981	1982	1983 (first half)
US exports to 20 Lat. Am. countries	36	39	30	11
(of which farm sales incl. food & animals)	(4.5	4.7	2.8	1.7)
Private receipts (almost entirely banks)	12.3	20.5	25.6	10.7

Between 1981 and 1982, at the same time export earnings from sales to Latin America plummeted by $9 billion, bank receipts increased by $5 billion. One can, of course, argue that previous purchases of Northern goods by Latin America were partially fuelled with borrowed money, and so they were. For much of the 1970s, banks were, in a roundabout way, effectively providing credits to industries in their own countries. They took their own back with a vengeance in the following decade.

Since the mid-1980s, Stuart Tucker, a fellow of the Washington DC Overseas Development Council, has constantly chronicled the negative impact of the debt crisis on US jobs and markets. His testimony to a US Congressional committee in 1985 showed that job losses were in fact much worse than those predicted by Sanjay Dhar in 1983, and that the situation had continued to deteriorate. Tucker told the Committee:

In 1984, the United States had 560,000 fewer jobs due to the decline of exports to the Third World since 1980. Additionally, another 800,000 jobs have been lost which would have been created if the growth trend of the 1970s had continued after 1980. Thus *nearly 1.4 million US jobs have been lost due to the recent recession in the Third World. Adding up the losses each year since 1980, the poor performance of US exports to the developing countries has cost a total of 3.2 million person years of employment – an average of 8.4 per cent of official unemployment during the period.*[5] (his emphasis)

In a report released a few months later, Tucker expanded on this testimony and provided detailed information on the US manufacturing sectors hardest hit by the debt crisis. Aircraft, trucks and tyres, earth-moving and construction machinery and parts, iron and steel, and tractors had taken the brunt of the shock. But Tucker turned up other vital evidence the significance of which was to become even clearer in the following years.[6]

In 1985, the balance sheets of the vastly overexposed US 'Money-Center' banks were still shaky and US authorities were on the lookout for policies able to buy them time and provide them with an escape route. The initial attempt, known as the Baker Plan, had yet to be unveiled. (It was launched at the World Bank/IMF meeting in Seoul in September 1985.) Tucker noted that the future of the banks 'appears risky' but also that the 'US banks have compensated for the rising uncertainty and risk. Unlike other US activity abroad, income from the banking sector has ... profited greatly from the [developing world's recession].'

That is putting it mildly! Commerce Department figures in Table 4.2 show how much more profitable it was to be a US banker than a US manufacturer investing in the third world, even in a time of 'crisis'.

These double-digit rates of return on invested capital in banking are not misprints. Banks really did routinely make more than 40 per cent per annum on their investments in developing countries. Even when the 'crisis' hit, banking brought stunning rewards – easily three to four times as large as those received by companies engaged in actual production. Tucker also calculates that even as manufacturing profits plunged into the red, in constant 1980 dollars, 'income of the US banking sector's direct investment in developing countries grew by 26 per cent from 1980 to 1984.'[7]

Most people will be astonished to learn that anyone's return on any investment, aside from the most speculative gambles on the most

volatile stocks, can scale such dizzying heights. The banks, still
making a usurious 18 to 22 per cent on their foreign direct investments *worldwide* in 1983 and 1984, not to mention a hefty 28 to 35
per cent in developing countries in the depths of crisis, are the
selfsame banks that came whining to the government – and through
the government to the taxpayers – for 'relief'. And relief is what they
got, at the expense of hundreds of thousands of suddenly jobless
people.*

Table 4.2: Rate of Return on US Direct Investment Abroad (%)

	1979	1980	1981	1982	1983	1984
Manufacturing						
World	16.6	12.6	8.9	5.7	6.4	7.8
All Developing Countries	13.5	15.3	12.2	4.5	2.5	9.5
Latin America	12.1	14.9	11.1	1.9	(1.4)	7.2
Africa	16.0	16.0	13.5	9.6	1.8	5.3
Asia/Pacific	21.6	18.1	18.3	16.3	20.4	19.1
Banking						
World	27.7	27.4	26.3	28.2	22.5	18.4
All Developing Countries	40.5	42.4	42.8	38.6	33.9	28.3
Latin America	40.8	41.2	43.5	36.9	34.9	29.3
Africa	32.6	33.1	23.1	29.5	26.1	18.3
Asia/Pacific	38.8	45.9	41.6	40.4	29.9	24.1

Source: US Department of Commerce, *Survey of Current Business and Selected Data on US Direct Investment Abroad*, Washington DC in Tucker, *Update: Costs to the United States of the Recession in Developing Countries*, Working Paper no. 10, Overseas Development Council, Washington DC, January 1986. The rate of return is defined as 'income for the year divided by the year-end direct investment position'.

* By the end of the decade, however, returns on banking were down to more realistic though still remunerative levels, while manufacturing returns were, like banking returns a decade earlier, creeping towards indecency. According to the 1990 *Survey of Current Business*, the percentage rates of return for all developing countries were:

	1987	1988	1989
Manufacturing	16.3	20.5	19.0
Banking	5.6	14.6	9.3

Manufacturers made money on the small amount of capital they had invested in Africa, whereas bankers took three straight losses on that continent. For both US manufacturers and bankers, Asia was the bright spot, with returns as high as 33 per cent for banks and 27 per cent for industry.

Meanwhile, Down on the Farm ...

During this same period, at the outset of the 1980s, the farms of North America were also sorely tested by the drying up of their export markets, particularly in Latin America. In retrospect, it is easy to argue that the record levels of US food exports in 1980 and 1981 could not have lasted; that they had been artificially created by subsidies and by the easy money then coursing around the world. True, farm exports had taken off in a suspiciously short time. Between 1978 and the peak in 1981, they grew by 47 per cent, from $29 to $43 billion dollars' worth of sales worldwide. In Latin America they doubled. This boom was, however, the basis upon which US farmers were themselves encouraged to borrow, to expand production and to take advantage of the opportunity. No one in a position of public or private authority was responsible enough to warn them off heavy indebtedness. When the debt crisis hit, farmers were left in the lurch, with huge carryover stocks, depressed prices and global sales down by 15 per cent – with a decline of minus 30 per cent in sales to Latin America.

Since 1982, these farm sales have never completely recovered. By 1990, after a disappointing decade, they had inched their way back up to $40 billion worldwide; while sales to the less developed countries of $16 billion finally equalled those of 1981 – the best year ever. One should remember, though, that these sales figures are expressed in 'current', not 'constant' dollars, and that real gains have been much eroded since 1981.[8]

When US agricultural export sales hit new records in 1980–1, Latin America by itself absorbed almost half of the huge growth. The continent was the United States' third largest client, ranking just behind Western Europe and Japan. The debt crisis unfortunately coincided with another disaster for US farmers – a sharp drop in sales to the Soviet Union. But as a Congressional staff study explains, Latin American sales fell off much more than those to the USSR, to the point that 'the Latin American debt crisis was nearly five times as damaging to US farmers as reduced sales to the Soviet Union.'[9]

To compound the plight of the US farmer, all-out export drives by major debtors like Brazil and Argentina resulted in more agricultural commodities flooding the market and lower prices for everyone. Many US farmers were so deeply indebted that when agricultural prices fell, they could no longer service their debts and faced bankruptcy. Meanwhile, the debtor countries, desperate for hard currency, ate into their market shares. The same 1986 Congressional staff study also looked at these trends. It found that in the 1981–2 crop year, the

United States supplied 48 per cent of world wheat needs and Argentina only 4 per cent. By 1984–5, however, the US share was down to 35 per cent and Argentina had doubled its exports. The story for soybeans was the same. During the same period, US exports fell 36 per cent while Brazil quadrupled and Argentina doubled its exports. Together, these two debtor countries came to control 27 per cent of the world soya market compared to only 9 per cent three years previously.[10]

For US farmers, the unkindest cut of all was perhaps the announcement made early in 1985 by the giant agribusiness and grain trading firm Cargill. Cargill stated it intention to import 25,000 tons of Argentine wheat into the US at prices US$30 dollars less per tonne than US prices. The trader could do such a deal and still make a profit in spite of shipping costs and high tariff barriers. Although later withdrawn, Cargill's threat was plausible, since wheat production costs at the time were only US$50 per tonne for an Argentine farmer compared with $110 for the heavily indebted US farmer. The overwhelming market shares US farmers used to enjoy for major commodities now seem to have vanished for good and third world debt goes a long way towards explaining why.[11]

As more farms fail, North American farm communities wither and die with them, precipitating further job losses and the destruction of a traditional way of life in the US heartland. The accelerated demise of the family farm is reflected in mounting suicide, divorce and mental illness rates. Farm bank failures, for example, rose by 900 per cent between 1982 and 1985. Farm banks suffered more than half of all bank failures during this period, even though only a quarter of US banks are classed as 'farm banks'.[12]

Perhaps sustained exports to the debtor countries, and less competition from their produce, would not have entirely prevented these dire consequences for North American farmers, but they could have substantially alleviated them.

Meanwhile, as the debtors ship more and more food abroad, hunger takes over on the homefront. Malnutrition has grown alarmingly in Brazil and even made serious inroads in Argentina where nutritional problems were virtually non-existent prior to the debt crisis. And, predictably, commodity prices for everyone have plunged and remain at depressed levels.

Dim Policymakers or Deliberate Policy?

Twice more, in 1988 and in 1990, Stuart Tucker appeared as a witness before US Congressional committees. His testimony on both occasions was depressingly similar. On the first one, he told a subcommittee of the House Foreign Affairs Committee that by 1987,

> about 860,000 US jobs had been lost because of the decline of US exports to Latin America ... About half these jobs once existed in 1980. The other half could have been created had US exports continued to grow at the trendline pace of the 1970s.

When he returned to Capitol Hill in 1990, this time for a subcommittee of the Senate Finance Committee, it was to tell the legislators that

> US exports to developing countries are now about $60 billion less than they could have been in the absence of debt and recession in developing countries in the 1980s ... due to these lost exports, we lost 1.8 million jobs – well over one-fifth of our current level of unemployment.[13]

Tucker thinks the reason US policymakers have been 'slow to react to the implications of the current Third World debt crisis' is 'due to a dim understanding of the relevance of the debt crisis to US prosperity'.[14] One might beg to differ. The debt-induced drag on US prosperity is not due to a lack of comprehension or to some deficit of rationality. US policymakers have, on the contrary, displayed a keen understanding of the significance and the workings of the debt crisis and they have consciously decided to play their hand entirely on behalf of the banks – both US and foreign.

Next to the banks, hundreds of thousands of sacked workers pounding pavements in search of hypothetical jobs weigh little in the balance. As one economist expressed it, 'The unemployment and industrial disruption in the US rust belt are not due solely to industrial inefficiencies ... US workers may lose jobs so that Brazilian debts to Swiss bankers that manage accounts for Arab interests can be repaid.'[15]

It is true that the Swiss, and other Europeans, and Japanese have all profited from the US policy of putting banks first. Somehow, somewhere, someone has to shoulder a trade deficit so that debtors can build up trade surpluses with which to make their payments to all and sundry. Europe and Japan are running trade surpluses. The only other likely-looking candidate for bearing the burden of deficit is the USA, and this it has done with the greatest enthusiasm throughout the Reagan and Bush years. When Reagan first sat down at his desk in the Oval Office in 1980, the United States was the world's largest creditor nation. Its trade account surplus was $166 billion.

When Reagan left the White House, the trade deficit was a resounding, round $500 billion. These vanishing $666 billions were obviously not all due to the third world debt crisis, but it certainly didn't help.[16]

The Democratic staff of the US Congress Joint Economic Committee came up with a more cogent explanation for falling US exports. The drops were neither inevitable nor unavoidable, and they were not the result of ignorance or stupidity. As bluntly stated by the Committee staff, the drying up of markets and jobs is 'the direct outgrowth of administration policies which are tantamount to telling debtor nations that they must promise to continue paying interest and stop purchasing US products.' Administration officials proceed exactly as if they begin by calculating how much interest each debtor owes and then pressure them to make whatever trade adjustments are necessary in order to have that amount of foreign exchange on hand to make their interest payments.

> In effect, by sacrificing their sales and jobs so that debtor nations can fully meet all interest payments, US exporters and workers have been subsidizing the bad lending policies of US and other money center banks. To add insult to injury, US workers and exporters are also bailing out European and Japanese banks.[17]

But that news was already stale in 1986 when this study appeared, and since then nothing much has changed. Every billion dollars' worth of exports lost still means between 20,000 and 30,000 jobs forgone, depending on the industry concerned.[18]

What Might Have Been

Europe and Japan have traditionally had weaker trade links with Latin America where the debt crisis hit first and hardest. Consequently, their loss of jobs and markets has been less noticed than that of the United States. Noticed or not, the debt crisis has clearly diminished opportunities which, had they continued to expand as in the 1970s, would have provided much more flourishing commerce for the EC and Japan with the South. Africa, which ought normally to be a natural trading partner for Europe, has virtually dropped off the map as a factor in world commerce during the 1980s, whereas Asia has, to a certain extent, taken up the slack. Thus an examination of figures for Europe's or Japan's trade with 'the South' as a whole is not as revealing as a more detailed look, continent by continent or even country by country.

When trade figures are translated into constant dollars and simulations of 'what-might-have-been' are performed, as they have been here for us by Dr Indra Wahab of Amsterdam University (see Table 4.3), one can more accurately judge the full impact of third world debt on Northern exports as a whole. We use throughout the cut-off point of 1982 – the first year of the crisis – and look at trade trends from 1969 to 1981, then from 1981 to 1988. The first and most striking fact is the sharp fall-off in everyone's trade with the Southern hemisphere during the second, deeply recessionary period of the 1980s.[19]

Table 4.3: Growth of Exports to Developed and Less Developed Countries (Per Cent Per Year)

To:	1969–1981		1981–1988	
	DCs	LDCs	DCs	LDCs
From:				
EEC	5.5%	8.8%	5.7%	-2.3%
North America	4.6	8.7	4.8	0.6
Japan	8.3	10.4	8.3	-0.9
World	5.0	7.9	4.0	-0.2

Instead of increasing by an average of 8 per cent a year as they did in the period from 1969–81, growth rates in the world's exports to the less developed countries ground to a complete halt in the 1980s and even went into sharp reverse where Europe is concerned. The reason the North could absorb such a severe blow is because intra-North trade – exports from developed countries to other developed countries – went on growing much as before.

Meanwhile, the third world lost out across the board, with its place in world trade dwindling. Table 4.4 shows the importance of third world trade for the North during three significant periods.

Table 4.4: Relative Share of Exports to LDCs in Total Export Revenues of the Developed Countries (%) (includes exports to OPEC)

Averages for	1969–71	1979–81	1986–8
EC	14	18	13
North America	23	30	25
Japan	41	45	32

As Table 4.4 shows, just prior to the debt crisis, in 1979–81, the US was earning almost one third of its export revenues from the South;

Japan received a sturdy 45 per cent of its export receipts from LDCs (mostly in Asia), while Europe was approaching one fifth. By the end of the 1980s, these proportions for all but North America had dropped below their 1970 levels.

What would have happened to export growth had the debt crisis not occurred? Indra Wahab's simulations indicate that if exports to the third world had continued to increase at the same average rate as they did between 1969 and 1981, then the average (simulated) growth of *total* exports between 1982 would have been as shown in Table 4.5

Table 4.5

	Simulated annual growth of exports to LDCs (%)		Real annual growth of exports to LDCs (%)
Europe	6.4	instead of	4.6
North America	5.0	instead of	2.5
Japan	9.1	instead of	4.8

North America and Japan could have doubled their export growth and Europe's could have increased by almost 40 per cent. Japan-bashers should also take note that whereas Japan previously sent 45 per cent of all its exports to the third world, when the debt crisis hit, this proportion had to be brutally scaled back to only 32 per cent. For a nation as export dependent as Japan, the goods suddenly in excess had to be absorbed somewhere. Unsurprisingly, Japan sought further to penetrate US and European markets.

Two factors were at work in cutting back imports in the South: the drop in oil prices which caused OPEC countries to restrict their imports in the 1980s and, of course, the debt crisis. If OPEC countries are totally excluded from the simulations, there is still a drop but it is less pronounced. Such a distinction is, however, in many ways artificial and arbitrary since countries like Nigeria, Indonesia, Venezuela or Algeria – and even some wealthier Arab oil producers – are also major debtors. Clearly the debt crisis was a poor deal for industry and agriculture throughout the rich countries.

These rich countries, however, lost less revenue than they might have done because the share of Non-OPEC (NOPEC) countries in their total export revenues was traditionally fairly small, especially for Europe. The situation for the same three significant periods as those given in Table 4.4 is seen in Table 4.6

Table 4.6: Relative Share (%) of Exports to LDCs in Total Export Revenues (excludes OPEC)

Averages for	1969–71	1979–81	1986–88
EC	11	10	9.5
North America	19	23	21
Japan	35	31	27

At first glance, Table 4.6 would seem to show that the impact of the debt crisis in the NOPEC countries on Europe's exports, and therefore on Europe's jobs, could not have been especially harmful – what, after all, is 10 per cent or less of exports for an entity like the EC? But when we look not at percentages but at the actual amounts of cash that could have been generated from exports if Europe had continued to expand them in accordance with the trend established between 1969 and 1981, we get a quite different picture.

In that case, in constant 1985 dollars for the period 1982–8,

- Europe's total exports to Latin America would have been worth $52 billion more than they were;
- Europe's total exports to Africa would have been worth $112 billion more than they were (this figure includes North Africa but excludes South Africa);
- Europe's total exports to Asia – where growth largely continued – would still have been $7 billion more than they were.

This comes to a *total of $171 billion in unrealised European exports for the period 1982 to 1988*.

Finally, we can take the average for those seven years – about $24.5 billion in lost sales – and apply to it the same rule of thumb as for the United States, that is, 20,000 to 30,000 jobs generated for every billion dollars' worth of exports. The bottom line is that Europe lost between 490,000 and 735,000 jobs per year as a *direct* result of debt-induced recession in the third world. We have not attempted to quantify the extra economic activity – and jobs – which this additional employment would in turn have generated.

Has it really been worth it?

Privatisation: Panacea or Trap?

As the IMF and World Bank have gained leverage over dozens of third world economies they have called for across-the-board privatisation, a doctrine practised with a vengeance by Margaret Thatcher and heartily espoused by Ronald Reagan before being spread throughout the poorer countries. Privatisation has been a favourite neo-conservative rallying cry, amplified by the collapse of the 'command' economies of Eastern Europe. According to British researcher Brendan Martin, by 1988 no fewer than 83 governments had taken steps to privatise at least one public industry or service.[20]

Although many people would give Margaret Thatcher the credit for putting privatisation on the world map, Martin points out that the pioneers were the famous 'Chicago Boys', the economists who used the opportunity of the 1973 CIA-backed *coup d'état* in Chile to impose a brutal restructuring of the Chilean economy according to the free-market principles of their University of Chicago mentor Milton Friedman. The privatisation prize for the 1980s does, however, go to Britain, followed by the US, where official political and economic theory has been reduced to the Me-Tarzan-You-Jane level of 'Private Good, Public Bad'.

During the 1980s, the only thing that was socialised rather than privatised was debt itself. As we saw in the previous chapter, the banks have offloaded most of their bad risks onto the public in general and onto public lending institutions in particular. Not content to discharge the banks of their burdens, these same institutions – the Bank and the Fund – have used their clout to dismantle the public sector wherever and whenever possible, thus offering attractive investment opportunities to the same banks and causing many employees of the privatised sectors to lose their jobs. Does the Bank find poetic justice in the fact that the debt–equity swaps it also encourages allow transnational corporations and banks to buy up formerly public companies in the debtor countries (for example the Argentine telephone network)?

Such is the vogue for privatisation that a whole new industry has grown up around it – at least some jobs have been created in this way! Squadrons of experts, accountants, auditors, bankers, management consultants and indeed official aid agency personnel have been quick to seize this particular market opportunity. In 1986, USAID held a landmark international conference on privatisation attended by representatives of 60 third world nations. In succeeding years, as soon as Eastern Europe showed signs of crumbling, the same squads rushed in. By late 1989, for example, Price Waterhouse already had a bureau with dozens of employees in Budapest and became an official adviser to the Hungarian government. As Martin notes,

The resulting privatisations programme currently includes 20 companies ... and is planned to expand rapidly in a fiver-year plan aimed at reducing state ownership by more than half. Among the beneficiaries will be historic owners of the industries concerned, who will be compensated for the expropriation from the privatisation proceeds.

Don't throw away your great-grandmother's 1919 Hungarian stock certificates! Alas, the high hopes of the Hungarians, and others, are often based on grossly distorted information about the impact of privatisation in the pioneering countries. Mrs Thatcher's privatisation guru, John Redwood, told his Budapest audience for example that the results of privatising British bus services were 'stunning: lower fares, more travellers, better quality services'. He omitted to inform them that these effects occurred only on a few well-travelled routes, whereas most of them – including socially necessary routes in more deprived neighbourhoods – have suffered effects that are exactly the opposite.[21]

Jeff Faux, president of the Economic Policy Institute in Washington, confirms similar failings in the United States. Less has been recently privatised in the US than in Britain simply because so little was ever under public ownership, but that little was still too much for the ideologues. Reagan administration 'studies' – the quotes are Faux's – purported to show that privatised urban transport would save the public money. Instead, it became both financially and socially more costly because it was no longer concerned with safety, convenience or environmental protection.

> Privatization confused efficiency of transportation *systems* with lowering costs of individual *routes*. Privatization policy assumed that urban transportation networks are merely a collection of separable routes rather than complete systems. But, in fact, the measure of the success or failure of urban transportation lies in its ability to move travelers between *any* two points in the metropolitan area, not just between two points on a given single route.[22]

Faux also stresses that contracting out of public services to private firms often creates private monopolies with prices to match, that 'private contracting is by far the single most important source of political corruption' and that 'private contractors are less flexible than public employees because they need not perform any work not specified in the contract. Costs thus rise in unforeseen emergencies'.

Private contractors or new owners of previously public companies often find in privatisation remarkable opportunities for windfall profits. They invariably increase working hours and cut both staff and wages – not to mention fringe benefits. Contractors can employ inexperienced, unqualified, unsupervised – and of course non-unionised, sometimes illegal – personnel unlikely to complain about low incomes and unsafe working conditions. And when a public service has gone private, it has usually done so for good. As one Chief Executive of a British District Council put it,

> A major factor in going private is the risk involved. Once you have handed all your equipment over and closed your depots you have burnt your boats. Suppose it does not work out, suppose the private company decides at the end of the contract to double its price?[23]

Although neo-conservative doctrine claims that high public expenditures will cripple the economy, a survey by the OECD covering the role of the public sector in the overall economies of its member countries from 1960 to 1982, found otherwise: 'There is no relationship between public sector size and economic performance as reflected in GDP growth rates, or between public sector growth and inflation rates.'[24]

Despite the lack of evidence that privatisation improves overall economic performance; in the teeth of much evidence that it doesn't; and with emphatic proof that it does further polarise societies and marginalise the elderly, the young, the female and the poor, jobs throughout the world are under heavy assault because of it. Had the debt crisis not provided the opportunity, one doubts that the World Bank and the IMF – however faithfully they might try to carry out the mandate of their richest and most powerful shareholders – could have so successfully pressed this doctrine in the South. Their leverage over countries that have no real choice in the matter helps to create the mistaken impression that privatisation is the only possible path – and the proof is that 'everybody's doing it'.

Privatisation is merely one aspect of the drive to reduce all working people's incomes and conditions to the lowest common denominator. In the North, *we should worry* when in the South people are sacked and wages are cut, because this is how, sooner or later, everyone's wages are forced down as the world marketeers seek the cheapest and the weakest workforces. The feedbacks between the demolition of the public sector and the other 'boomerangs' are apparent. Sacked public sector workers 'invade' forests, as in Brazil and Peru; or move into illegal drug production as in Bolivia. They also try to emigrate. Privatisation provides new and profitable opportunities for the banks.

How has privatisation, like so many other dogmatic 'new right' measures, gained such tremendous momentum? Why does it seem to be part of the natural order of things? This has not happened by accident. The right has understood something which, alas, the progressive community, including the unions, has not. There has been a concerted effort, an extremely well-funded ideological effort, to make privatisation and all that goes with it seem beneficent and necessary.

You fund people to create an ideological climate which becomes the life-support system for the doctrine. It becomes the water for the fish – the fish doesn't even know he's swimming, he can't imagine breathing air. You put enough people with the 'correct' ideas into universities. You create the institutes and the foundations. All these people come together in the colloquia and symposia, open to the press, that you sponsor. And they all write in the journals that you also fund, and from there they get on the editorial pages and on the air. Pretty soon, you have those three-man (they almost always are men) pseudo-debates on television between the raving radical right, the extreme right and the right of centre. Anyone who thinks differently soon begins to seem a pariah, or someone who at the very least must make apologies for his or her beliefs. Those who hope to keep their jobs, and those who represent them, should be building the counter-institutions that will help them to do so.

On the other hand, those who are convinced of the overwhelming virtue of the marketplace, those who trust the capacity of the private sector to provide all the public goods we may require, should heed the words of an economic founding father, frequently invoked by many of them who have not read him carefully:

> The interest of the dealers, however, in any particular branch of trade or manufactures, is always in some respects different from, and even opposite to, that of the public ... The proposal of any new law or regulation of commerce which comes from this order ought always to be listened to with great precaution, and ought never to be adopted till after having been long and carefully examined, not only with the most scrupulous, but with the most suspicious attention. It comes from an order of men whose interest is never exactly the same with that of the public, who have generally an interest to deceive and even to oppress the public, and who accordingly have upon many occasions, both deceived and oppressed it.
>
> Adam Smith, *The Wealth of Nations*,
> Book One, Chapter 11, Conclusion

The Fifth Boomerang:
Immigration

Research and documentation by Claudio Jedlicki, David Pedersen
and Susan George

Once we had a country and we thought it fair,
Look in the atlas and you'll find it there:
We cannot go there now, my dear, we cannot go there now ...

Came to a public meeting; the speaker got up and said;
'If we let them in, they will steal our daily bread';
He was talking of you and me, my dear, he was talking of you and me.
W.H. Auden, 'Refugee Blues'

Auden wrote this poem in March 1939. His refugees were German
Jews condemned to wander with no documents

> The consul banged on the table and said,
> 'If you've got no passport you're officially dead':
> But we are still alive, my dear, but we are still alive.

and little hope of shelter

> Dreamed I saw a building with a thousand floors,
> A thousand windows and a thousand doors:
> Not one of them was ours, my dear, not one of them was ours.

Fifty years later, although the colour of the wanderers is darker than
that of Hitler's refugees, their plight has scarcely changed at all.
Unprecedented, however, are the sheer numbers of people now on
the move. Are these numbers causally linked to the third world debt
crisis?

From the earliest planning stages of TNI's 'Debt Boomerang'
project, we were convinced that the hot and sensitive topic of third
world immigration to Europe and North America would necessarily
show up as a major – perhaps *the* major – boomerang. We

hypothesised that debt must have forced ever-greater streams of people to escape the growing misery of their homelands.

There are some places where this is clearly the case. We mentioned one, for example, in the chapter on drugs – Peruvians who can afford to leave are leaving their country in droves. But on the whole, with more documentation and a closer knowledge of the question, we have to declare that of the six boomerangs examined here, migration is perhaps the one hardest to link to debt *per se*. The cut-off date – 1982 – that we have used elsewhere works well for phenomena like drugs or deforestation and yields natural and oper-ational pre-and post- debt-crisis categories. The areas we have looked at so far do indeed show significant quantitative and/or qualitative changes before and after the onset of the crisis.

Not so immigration. The factors determining mass movements of people do not seem to undergo a decisive push from 1982 onwards. People simply continue to move; debt and the consequences of structural adjustment policies are only one element accelerating the flight from poverty, steadily swelling a tide so full and inexorable as to appear unstoppable. This vast human displacement is more like a majestic river broadening as it flows to the sea than like a flash flood precisely traceable to a particular landmark event like the onset of the debt crisis. Migrations are, certainly, linked to the general failure of the dominant development model – one which has displaced huge numbers of people from the countryside, in particular. Their rural-to-urban migration often appears as a prelude to the longer and more perilous journey they will eventually undertake Northwards.

Coping with the Human Tide

If past experience is any guide, the Northern leadership will not readily recognise or comprehend the mass movement underway. The rich country governments are thus unlikely to take proper, timely and humane remedial measures to slow the flow, let alone turn it around by helping to provide people with genuine opportunities at home. The reaction of these governments is more likely to be based on police methods and perhaps ultimately on military force to protect 'fortress Europe' and 'fortress America'. The 'moat and drawbridge' mentality is already becoming so pervasive and insidious that if present policies continue, one can predict a drive towards worldwide apartheid in the twenty-first century.

People do not usually lightly take the decision to leave their homes. Massively, they are doing so today because they have no real choice. Only the most inhospitable natural environments – deserts, mountains, ice – oblige a person to keep moving or die. Today, ever-widening areas of the third world are becoming the economic, political and social equivalents of the Sahara, the Himalayas, or Antarctica. Millions faced with dehumanising poverty, shooting wars, or ecological collapse find all their previous means of livelihood vanishing. What option have they – besides death – but to move? The UN Environment Programme (UNEP) fears, at the start of the next millennium, as many as a billion environmental refugees. The International Labour Organisation (ILO) estimates that there are already about 100 million legal or illegal immigrants and refugees today. Very few of them have, as yet, arrived in the North.[1]

The North is, however, where many more of them would go if they could; and where many more of them will come one way or another. Faced with this situation, reflex responses of both right and left are wholly inadequate. The right-wing, knee-jerk 'we shall fight them on the beaches' riposte is as inappropriate as the 'liberal' or 'progressive' notion that the rich countries can somehow maintain open borders. The former socialist prime minister of France Michel Rocard took a lot of flak from his own party and the rest of the French left when he said, 'Nous ne pouvons pas accueillir toute la misère du monde' ('We can't take in the whole of the world's misery') but he was speaking the literal truth. If only to ensure a decent living – and at least relative freedom from racism – for those immigrants who are already in the North, we must try to deal with immigration by making it less necessary. This is the only strategy that can possibly work, and the sooner it is put into practice the better. One obvious starting point in allowing people to work and live – decently and with dignity – in their own countries is to resolve the debt crisis.

Otherwise, clashes in the North are likely to become not only more frequent but far uglier. The stakes are rising rapidly, as are violent or overtly fascist counter-attacks. A story in the *New York Times* tells how well-off California residents suddenly find themselves living much further 'south' than they thought. 'Homeowners ... complain that the migrants, who line the roadsides seeking jobs and who camp out at night within shouting distance of their homes, bring crime, unsanitary conditions and a breath of the Third World to their carefully tended communities.'

The migrants, on the other hand, have their own serious complaints. They say they are 'routinely abused by people who shout and throw garbage at them, destroy their campsites, cheat them at work and sometimes attack them physically.' A social worker – Hispanic himself – with the American Friends Service Committee says, 'What I've observed is that as the [housing] developments have encroached into migrant areas, we are seeing more tension and more incidents', including random murders and other serious crimes against Hispanics. A local police lieutenant calls the migrants 'perfect victims': they don't speak the language well and usually fear authorities who could help them; they sleep out in the open and carry all the money they have on them.[2]

The situation is also rapidly deteriorating in Europe. Several racially motivated murders of young Arabs, some involving the police, have occurred in the tougher French *banlieues*. In 1990, a French government-sponsored survey showed that 76 per cent of 1000 people questioned thought there were too many Arabs in France; 46 per cent complained of too many blacks, and 40 per cent said there were too many Asians. The same survey showed that 51 per cent of the sample thought politicians campaigning for election should be allowed to state that 'North African Arabs and blacks are racially inferior to Europeans'. (Anyone now making such statements in public can be legally prosecuted.) Since 1984, the ultra-right French National Front has routinely won 10 to 15 per cent of the vote – in isolated cases up to 30 per cent – in local and national elections. Although many people would not buy the Front's whole programme, a third of the French electorate does share its hardline views on immigration, according to the conservative Paris paper *Le Figaro*.[3]

In Italy, the newspaper *La Repubblica* carried out two surveys on immigration – the first in January 1989, the second in March 1990. In both cases, the questions were the same. People were shown a picture of an African and asked, 'If you could choose and decide, what would you do for this person?' Four possible types of laws were suggested, with multiple answers possible. In the scant 14 months elapsing between the two polls, the number of people responding that they would 'make a law preventing any more immigrants from coming here' rose from 20 to 42 per cent; those who would 'make a law to send them back to their country of origin' shot up from 8 to 37 per cent. Laws to 'protect them better' or to 'improve regulation of their activity' lost support.[4]

If a law to send *émigré* Italians back where they came from were promulgated and applied, the United States, Canada, Brazil and Argentina, among other places, would lose a sizeable part of their populations! Europeans now seem to have forgotten how, for more than two centuries, they solved many pressing social problems of the industrial age through out-migration. Some, like the French, conquered vast empires and dispatched large numbers of settlers. Australia was initially a dumping ground for British convicts. After the catastrophic crop failures and famines of the 1840s, two million destitute Irish who had escaped set sail for Britain or for the New World.

'Send these, the homeless, tempest-tossed to me ...'

The fast-expanding United States was the biggest receptacle of all. By 1930 the US had taken in 7 million Germans, 5 million English or Scots, 5 million Irish, as many Italians and even 4 million Canadians. Lesser numbers, though still well above the 1 million mark, came from Russia, Austria, Hungary, Sweden, Norway and France. Between 1890 and 1915 alone, 12 million new Americans – 'the tired, the poor, the huddled masses yearning to breathe free' extolled in Emma Lazarus' verses on the base of the Statue of Liberty – arrived in the United States via Ellis Island.[5]

During every new wave of immigration, the outcry is the same. Germans will be unable to live next door to Brits and Scots and will soon have us speaking their barbaric tongue. The Irish will spoil the neighbourhood with their drinking and brawling; the Italians will do the same with their noise and crime. The culture of East Europeans and Jews is too different from that of already settled Americans and will pose a grave threat to the social fabric. Etcetera. The same routine discourse is now applied to Hispanics and Asians. Newcomers without exception are abused. Each new cohort of immigrants has been well and truly beaten up by the previous one – historically speaking, such behaviour is as American as apple pie. Some immigrants have fared even worse. Recall the fictional heroes of *West Side Story*, or the real Sacco and Vanzetti who fell victim to hysteria about 'bolsheviks' and 'anarchists'. And yet, in spite of it all, the melting pot has somehow continued to bubble.

The recurring US debate about immigrants does not even take place along cleanly predictable political fault lines. At the beginning of the 1980s, an article on 'Coping with Illegal Immigrants' in the Establishment journal *Foreign Affairs* summed up the dilemma of politicians who try to please anyone on the issue of immigrants:[6]

> Some conservatives say keep them out, we don't need any more people to create social problems and soak up scarce welfare dollars. Other conservatives say let them in, to discipline the domestic labor force and provide workers for the stoop labor that Americans simply won't do. Some liberals say let them in, we have a duty to share our riches with poorer people ... Others say keep them out, our first duty is to maintain social welfare for poor people already here.

Ten years later, in 1991, *The Economist* reported that *plus ça changeait, plus* it was decidedly *la même chose*. In the new decade as in the previous one, the pro-immigration lobby in the US

> covers an extraordinarily wide political spectrum, stretching from right-wing scholars at influential political think-tanks ... through various ethnic and religious associations to some more left-wing Americans who want to open their country's doors to more of the world's poor.

And, as usual, the 'antis' are just as diverse: common or garden racists are allied with some blacks, some environmentalists and some trade unionists, but the 'antis', *The Economist* reports, are 'less organised and far less coherent' than the 'pros'.[7]

Whichever conservative/progressive position one cares to adopt, the fact remains that before the debt crisis broke in 1982, the United States was already experiencing an uncontrolled, perhaps uncontrollable, influx of immigrants, half of them Mexicans and a lot of them illegal, in spite of the liberalised immigration law voted in 1965. At the outset of the 1980s, the net illegal inflow was probably at least half a million a year, a tenfold increase from 15 years previously. The accumulation of 'undocumented aliens' amounted to a total pool of 4–6 million people, living physically and socially unprotected lives on the margins of American society.

During this same pre-debt crisis period, the rate of inflow of both legal and illegal immigrants was 'near the highest level ever experienced in American history, reminiscent of the years before the First World War'. If then-current rates of influx were to be sustained, Los Angeles could well become '75 per cent Hispanic in the year 2000 with unemployment rates quite possibly as high as 12 to 15 per cent. Such hardships would then make Hispanics the most easily targeted scapegoats for the economic grievances of "indigenous workers".'[8]

Forcing People Out – with Bayonets or La Miseria

By the early 1990s the foreign-born population of the United States had never been higher, standing at about 18 million. Although the economic 'development' model championed by the United States has certainly played its part in marginalising people in the third world and uprooting them from their homes, a good part of this foreign influx could be directly traced to American military adventures abroad. Of the more than 2.5 million Asian immigrants who arrived in the US after 1975, several hundreds of thousands were Indochinese whose lives had been tragically altered by the Vietnam War.

When the Washington DC Mount Pleasant neighbourhood, heavily populated by Salvadoran immigrants, erupted in riots in May 1991, writer Christopher Hitchens, who lives there, reported in his regular column for *The Nation* that

> The population of one Salvadoran town, named Intipuca, moved here some years ago, having given up life back home as a bad job ... Conversation with these immigrants discloses, without much prompting, the most appalling tales of forced conscription, near-slave labor, the disappearance of family members and the general *miseria*. Nor are the victims often in much doubt as to the source of the hardship and the fear from which they fled. They blame the Salvadoran oligarchy and its patrons in Washington, who donate $450 million annually to the predatory armed forces and have no cash left to spare for Mount Pleasant.[9]

Aside from military adventurism, out-migration also tends to stem from a rapid and largely forced rural–urban exodus. This process gains special momentum when poverty and indebtedness have made countries an easy target for 'export-led growth' and structural adjustment policies imposed from outside. No region fits this description better than the Caribbean which, if all the islands are taken together, sends more migrants to the United States every year than any other place in the world, including Mexico.

It is no accident that most of these islands are living in debt bondage, owing staggering amounts compared to their small populations and slender means. No matter how much or how long they pay,

Table 5.1: Debt and Debt Service, Selected Caribbean Countries 1982–8 (US$ millions)

	Debt 1982	Debt 1988	Per cent change	Total service paid 1982–8	Debt per capita (US$)
Barbados	220	664	+202	425	
Dominican Republic	3218	3865	+20	2866	552
Haiti	667	888	+33	347	139
Jamaica	2936	4550	+55	4235	1895
Trinidad & Tobago	1440	2025	+40	1983	1557
Other West Indies	741	1787	+141	1296	
Total	9222	13,779	+49	11,152	

Source: OECD

they slide deeper and ьeeper into debt – as does the rest of the third world. Table 5.1 shows how much these island nations owed in 1982 and in 1988, how much they paid their creditors in total debt service in the seven calendar years between 1982 and 1988; and (where available) their debt per capita in 1988.[10]

As these figures show, the Caribbean paid out substantially more – 21 per cent – in debt service in the 1982–8 period than the total debt it owed in 1982. The region's reward for sending its creditors over US$11 billion in seven years was to find itself half again as much in debt at the end of the decade as at the beginning. In spite of drastic structural adjustment measures rigorously applied, one cannot point to a single example of a diminishing debt burden. As the table shows, these burdens have, instead, increased by anywhere from 20 to 200 per cent.

Nor can one argue that the debt mountain has grown because the Caribbean countries are somehow welshing on their debts. Without giving detailed figures here, we have calculated that for the group of countries in Table 5.1, service payments on debt outstanding in any given year ranged from 11.5 to 14.4 per cent, averaging 12.9 per cent for the seven year period. By any standards, this is a generous, bordering on the usurious, rate of return for the creditors – but still not enough to keep debt from escalating.

Naturally, these simple financial observations cannot render the enormous and prolonged human suffering that has made such payments possible. They do, however, show that World Bank-IMF claims are shoddy and pretentious. In spite of repeated failures and crushing factual evidence, these institutions and the major share-holders who make their policy still pretend that countries like those in the Caribbean can somehow 'work their way out of debt' by supplying cheap labour and raw materials; by relying on 'the market' and the private sector. Uniquely blessed by nature and geography (though too close for comfort to the United States), the Caribbean is also expected to rely on import-export trade in people – namely tourism and migration.

Because the island economies are especially diminutive, defence-less and debt-ridden, the structural adjusters are having a field day. Their activities are orchestrated by a regional body known as the Caribbean Group for Cooperation in Economic Development (CGCED), led by the Bank and the IMF, which coordinates adjustment programmes for 22 Caribbean states. The devastation that has followed in their wake can only be compared to that wrought by the tropical storms that periodically rip through the region.[11]

The Aid Establishment, nominally concerned with development, in fact *wants* people in the Caribbean to leave it and go somewhere else. In practice, 'somewhere else' can only mean the United States, though this fact is not generally referred to in polite structural adjuster society and the final destination of migrants is coyly kept quiet. As the senior World Bank economist for Jamaica stated, 'There is no doubt that emigration is an essential part of any development strategy for the region.'

The locals may, however, tend not to want to leave, or not in large enough numbers to make a difference. To hasten their departure, one must first destroy their means of subsistence, making it hard for them to produce their own food and impossible not to participate in the export economy. With the dismantling of local agricultural production for home consumption, the food import bill has been steadily rising ($2 billion for the English-speaking Caribbean alone in 1988) and the trade deficit is expanding. Theoretically, one of the jobs of the Bank and the Fund is to help countries establish a positive balance of payments. Yet, according to another World Bank economist, 'Barriers to protect local food don't make sense for anybody.' In other words, let them plant bananas or flowers on their former food producing land and pastures; let them further eat frozen imported chicken if and when they can afford it, which is not often.

Making rural people redundant and throwing them off their land creates plenty of cheap labour for export processing zones. As the World Bank 'Country document' said about Haiti – the third-ranking country for sending immigrants to the USA: 'Haiti's long term future will be urban. This [rural–urban internal] migration will sustain the development of assembly industries, cottage industries and other urban labor-intensive activities consistent with export-led growth.'[12]

This Bank document omits to mention that the initial transformation of rural people into under-employed wage labourers in their home country is also the first step in transforming them into immigrant labourers for the United States. They are 'encouraged' to leave because they can't earn a decent wage for their labour at home. This, too, is not aberrant, but policy: the former World Bank programme director for the Caribbean says that governments in the region must accept 'the need to keep wages low and exchange rates realistic (by devaluing their currencies). Otherwise, they'll destroy investor confidence.'

Although the search for employment abroad has been a constant in the Caribbean 'sending' countries that supply so many US immigrants, a series of other 'push and pull' factors specific to the 1980s are also evident, including debt. These factors have been especially pervasive in Jamaica, Haiti and the Dominican Republic, all of which have witnessed dramatic rises in out-migration since the beginning of the 1980s. As Kathy McAfee sums it up,

> High unemployment, the decline of food production for local needs, and rising land prices – all exacerbated by structural adjustment policies – have accelerated the loss of talents and skills. Increased dependency on imported food and consumer goods raises the need for cash, while US [media] promote US [products and lifestyle]. All these factors [encourage] young adults, potentialy the most productive members of society, to move from rural to urban areas and from their countries of birth to the United States.

As the younger, more dynamic, more skilful members of society migrate, the stay-at-homes become dependent on remittances. As an agronomist working on the island of St Vincent notes, 'You see many people sitting by the roadside, waiting for the mail van that they hope will bring that cheque from their relatives working abroad, because that is all they have to sustain them.' And anyway, why fight it? One official from USAID, speaking of the Caribbean, simply dismisses the whole region: 'None of these islands is viable. The best way to solve their problems is to subsidize their exports and allow the people to emigrate. Other than that, their best shot is tourism.'

Well, maybe. But one has to wonder how these islands survived for several hundred years in their 'unviable' state before the World Bank, the IMF and USAID interfered; before migration was seen first as an acceptable, then the preferable and finally the only solution to their economic problems, not as a last resort to be avoided as much as possible. Export-oriented policies, based on foreign investment, free-trade zones and the like do help service debts. They also destroy people's livelihoods and displace local investment as well as local workers. In such small economies, the human consequences are more drastic than in larger, more resilient ones. Today, more migrants leave the Caribbean as a percentage of the population than any other part of the world. And nearly all of them end up in the USA.

Now, Voyager ...

Until 1965, half of all immigration to the US came from Europe. At the end of the 1980s, a mere 10 per cent of the annual 600,000 to 640,000 immigrants were Europeans. Except for a few Canadians or Australians, the balance came from the third world.

Here is the ranking of countries sending immigrants to the US in 1988: nearly all these countries also sent 10,000 or more people to the

US during each of the six years 1983–8. The lowest and highest immigration numbers for that six year period are given in column three.[13]

Table 5.2: Rank of Countries Sending Immigrants to USA 1988; Range of Number Sent 1983–8 ('000s, rounded)

	1988	Range 1983–8
(Total Caribbean	112	73–112)
1. Mexico	95	57–95
2. Philippines	51	41–52
3. Haiti	35	8–35
4. Korea	35	33–35
5. China	29	23–29
6. Dominican Republic	27	22–27
7. India	26	22–28
8. Vietnam*	26	24–38
9. Jamaica	21	19–23
10. Cuba	18	9–33
11. Iran	15	11–16
12. United Kingdom	13	13–15
13. El Salvador	12	9–12
14. Canada	12	11–12
15. Laos**	11	7–24
16. Colombia	10	10–12
17. Taiwan	10	10–17

* 88,500 Vietnamese were admitted in 1978; 72,500 in 1982
** 90,000 Laotians were admitted 1980–3; a considerable drain on a country of only 4 million people.
Source: US Immigration and Naturalization Service.

This ranking for 1988 shows relatively few changes compared to the ranks for the decade 1970–9. In the 1970s, Italy, Portugal and Greece still figured among the top 15 sending countries; by 1988 they had disappeared and were replaced by Haiti, Iran and El Salvador. The biggest numerical jumps were accomplished by Mexico and Haiti – often because of adjustments in the status of people who had in fact been living in the US for several years.*

Where do the immigrants go once they get to the United States? Overwhelmingly, they head for cities and only a few cities at that. The preferred destinations, in descending order, are the urban areas of New York, Los Angeles, Miami, Chicago, Washington and San Francisco. Nationalities tend to stick together as well – Dominicans go massively

* The full ranking for the decade of the 1970s is Mexico, Philippines, Cuba, Korea, China (including mainland China and Taiwan), India, Vietnam, Dominican Republic, Italy, Jamaica, UK, Canada, Portugal, Greece, Colombia.

to New York and Asians to California, except for Indians who like New York and Chicago. Koreans divide themselves between the Eastern seaboard and Los Angeles. Mexicans, predictably, go to California and the Southwestern states. The real surprise, however, in immigrant destinations is how few end up in 'nonmetropolitan destinations'. Only 1 per cent of Cubans, 3 per cent of Chinese or Dominicans or 4 per cent of Vietnamese have anything to do with the countryside. Even among Mexicans immigrants, whose image is that of the sweated fruit-picker, only 12 per cent are to be found in rural areas.[14]

Before they can go anywhere, however, migrants have to get in, and getting in has become a growth industry from which handsome profits are now made. The World Bank, the IMF and USAID, all vigorously engaged in promoting free enterprise in the third world, should rejoice at the number and scope of entrepreneurs trafficking in human beings. In mid-1989, the *New York Times* reported that these 'multinational rings fronting as travel agencies and using safe houses, fake or illegal documents ... are growing in size, confidence and expertise.' Smuggling people used to be an artisanal trade; now, 'as economic and political conditions throughout the third world worsen and legal entry to the United States becomes more difficult', this trade is, in the words of one US Immigration and Naturalization Service official, 'a big business, a series of highly organized and sophisticated networks'.[15]

The basic unit in these networks is the Mexican 'coyote' who actually takes you across the border, but plenty of other people of varying nationalities are involved along the way. Prices for a long voyage with a lot of stops – from, say, China – can attain $30,000. In 1988, more than a million people were arrested trying to enter the US illegally across the Mexican border. US immigration officials estimate that for every one who gets caught, at least two illegal immigrants make it. Most of the clandestine entrants are, not surprisingly, Mexicans, but in 1988, those apprehended came from 60 different countries. Mexico is a wide-open staging area for the coyotes, since the country requires no entry visas for most foreign nationals. Until they try to get into the US, the smugglers' clients are nothing but legitimate travellers.

According to the *New York Times*, the economic woes of major Latin American debtors weigh heavily on illegal immigration: 'Argentina, Brazil and Peru, all of which are fighting inflation of over 1000 per cent and soaring unemployment, are becoming significant sending areas.' Not content to sit back and wait for clients, the smuggling networks are now also directly recruiting potential immigrants. Candidates who cannot pay a lump sum can purchase their border-crossing on the instalment plan. Some who naively accept this offer find themselves stuck in Mexico for long periods in virtual servitude – hired out by the networks as contract labour – and 'the brothels here (on the Mexico–Guatemala border) are full of nothing but Central American women' forced to sell themselves to pay off the coyotes.

The stereotype of the Mexican 'illegal' as an illiterate peasant is widespread, and wrong. Although by US standards their attainments may be modest, Mexicans who attempt to slip into the United States are consistently at or above average levels for Mexico. The very poorest people can't afford to migrate. One example of a couple who made it to the United States shows that even decently paid professional people may decide to take the plunge. This couple was directly influenced to emigrate by conditions brought on by the debt crisis.

Alicia now teaches Spanish part-time in Washington DC. She and her boyfriend arrived in 1986:

> I have been in Washington for four years ... I just wanted to leave. I didn't want to stay in Mexico. It wasn't that I was poor. I had a good job with a newspaper and my own house. My family was well off. We (my friend and I) were journalists and because of that we saw a lot, the poverty, the people without jobs, all the problems. I remember the crisis in 1982. My friend and I saw that things were getting worse. I just didn't want to face that for the rest of my life. By 1986, things were *much* worse so we decided to leave. I had one friend who was living in Washington DC so we came here. I wanted to go to Spain. That's my dream, but my friend said come to Washington and earn some money. And we're still here! Trying to get money![16]

The bottom line is that most people emigrate – legally or illegally – because they need work. Work at a decent wage and indeed any work at all has been in short supply since the structural adjusters took over. Former Mexican president Lopez-Portillo was fond of responding to Americans who complained about undocumented Mexicans in the United States, 'It is not a crime to look for work and I refuse to consider it as such.'

The European Scene

The United States prides itself on being a 'nation of immigrants' and during the 1980s accepted more of them than in any other decade of its history. In 1990, 18 million Americans were foreign-born, but this still amounts to only 6 or 7 per cent of the total US population.

In Britain, over eight per cent of the population is foreign born, and in France the figure is 11 per cent (including both naturalised citizens and non-citizens).

Europe's historical experience with immigration has been recent, brief and geographically limited. Suddenly – in the past decade – having to cope with unprecedented numbers of foreigners, Europe is not handling the task with particular aplomb. True, there were some pre-war, intra-European migrations like that of Poles coming to work in the French mines in the 1920s and 1930s, but no massive influxes of migrants really occurred until post-war economic growth caused drastic labour shortages in Northern Europe. Many of those who went North were Southern Europeans.

From the late 1950s until the brutal door-slamming on euphemistically named 'guest-workers' in 1974, over 30 million people were given 'temporary' status in the European labour force. The major 'sending' countries were Ireland, Italy, Portugal, Spain, Finland, Greece, Turkey, Yugoslavia and the North African countries (especially Algeria and Morocco). The 'receiving' countries were Germany, France, Britain and the Benelux countries, plus Sweden and Switzerland. The governments of these countries assumed that migrants could be shunted back and forth as demand for their muscles and for their capacity to shoulder the dirtiest and worst paid jobs rose or fell. They were wrong. As the Swiss author and playwright Max Frisch said at the time, 'We asked for workers, but human beings came.'[17]

By the early 1970s the Swiss were astonished – some of them alarmed – to learn that over one-third of their workforce was foreign. Total numbers of 'guest-workers' ranged from over 2.6 million in Germany to 200,000 in Sweden. In 1973, the final year before the clampdown, worker remittances to their home countries amounted to over US$6 billion. The energy crisis and the sudden economic crunch that ensued put a stop to all that.

Or so the Northern Europeans thought. A 1990 Council of Europe study sums up what actually happened after 1974.[18] Immigration *for work* was stopped almost completely, yes, but this did not mean that immigration itself stopped. Obliged to deal with mounting unemployment, some European countries provided incentives to encourage foreigners to go 'home' – in so far as they might still have one in their country of origin. Other countries tried to intimidate them, keeping a watchful eye on their papers – with the slightest violation providing a one-way ticket. Neither bribes nor threats worked very well. One way or another, most of the workers managed to stay. Just as Frisch said, they turned out not to be walking robots with wind-up keys in their backs but human beings with spouses, children and the usual needs for work and shelter.

Measures allowing 'family regrouping' were subsequently instituted in several countries, allowing wives to join their husbands, parents their children and vice-versa. Whereas migration began as a phenomenon concerning working-age males, after 1974 it became 'feminised', and younger. Former 'sending' countries turned into 'receiving' ones – by 1989, about 3 million migrants were living in Italy, Spain, Greece and Portugal, nearly half of them illegally. Clandestine immigration remains a big headache in Europe and it is on the upswing. Refugees and candidates for political asylum – once negligible in number – have also become a significant component of new migration flows and the fastest growing one. Finally, some countries – France, Holland and Spain in particular, have legalised the situation of significant numbers of formerly illegal residents. Such is the big picture.

> *What would one say of a shepherd who did not know the number of his sheep? It is as easy for a king to know the number of his people, if he so wills it.*
>
> Fenelon (1651–1715), tutor to the Duke of Burgundy

Enormous confusion reigns in Europe about the number of immigrants. The confusion seems destined to get worse, not least because xenophobic movements and right-wing political parties want it to be. The obvious increase in the number of people of non-European origin living in Europe leads public opinion to call for precise information – or to believe whatever the local racist party tells it. And every time 'public opinion' opens a newspaper, it gets a different answer. Accurate statistics are remarkably hard to come by.

This is partly because nobody seems to be talking about the same thing. Let us attempt here at least minimum precision of language. An 'immigrant' is someone who has the administrative and legal status of an immigrant. He and she are persons living legally in a country other than the one where they were born and intending to stay there for some time, usually to work. Once people are naturalised, however, whatever their country of origin, they are no longer counted in the 'immigrant' population because they are full-fledged citizens. In several European countries, children born to non-citizen parents of any statute can (or at least could until recently) become citizens automatically through *'jus soli'*.

Although these first, second (now even third) generations may still be referred to by the longer-standing, European-origin population as 'immigrants', they are not legally foreigners, though some may still be a far cry from being integrated. 'Integration' is the hot topic and the key political word in Europe today – France even set up a new Ministry of Integration when Edith Cresson was named Prime Minister in 1991.

There is a further, huge, foreign population with no rights to becoming 'integrated' – that is, to receive training, health benefits, unemployment compensation and the like – because it has no official existence. These illegal, clandestine workers should not, strictly speaking, be called 'immigrants' at all since by definition they have no legal or administrative status. The term is, however, so entrenched that it is hard to discuss the subject without using it.

Every country in Europe – albeit in different ways and to different degrees – is confronted with the same dilemma: if you don't integrate the foreign – or naturalised but culturally different – population, social tension and eventual explosion are guaranteed. If you do try to integrate them, and do so fairly successfully, your very success will cause a lot of other, poor foreigners to want to move to your country. Your social services risk being swamped and the efforts you are making to integrate the foreigners already there can be jeopardised.

European countries furthermore have quite different policies vis-a-vis immigration which have not been harmonised with an eye to Europe 1992. One country's actions can cause unforeseen problems for another. For example, in May 1985, Great Britain decided for the first time to demand an entry visa from Sri Lankans even though they came from a Commonwealth country. Within a month, Sri Lankan entries to Britain dropped by 90 per cent. Simultaneously, the then Federal Republic of Germany, which did not prevent entry of people coming from the then German Democratic Republic, allowed thousands of Sri Lankans to use its territory for transit. No longer able to go to Great Britain, they chose France because its political asylum laws were known to be the most lenient. Well-organised and profitable networks ferried them, always by the same route: Colombo-Moscow-East Berlin-West Berlin-West Germany, and thence to France and the OFPRA: the French Office for the Protection of Refugees and Stateless Persons – all as a result of a unilateral British decision, taken without consultation.[19]

Political asylum is a tricky subject. There is no doubt that this concept – a noble one if ever there was one – is being abused and therefore discredited in the eyes of many Europeans. Hundreds of thousands of third world people want to move and don't much care how they manage it. Fair enough. Most of them don't come from countries with democratic traditions or respect for human rights that gave rise to the concept of political asylum in the first place.

With legal immigration almost entirely curtailed, it has become widely known among those who want to enter Europe by any and all means that one promising avenue is to claim political asylum. Thus it is not surprising that the number of people claiming they are 'fleeing political persecution' has grown tremendously. The annual number of people asking for asylum has risen thirty fold in France in the past 15 years. In 1987 there were 27,000 requests; only two years later the number of asylum-seekers reached 61,000 and in 1990 the average monthly requests continued to top 5000. Similar increases have occurred in other European countries; for example, between 1989 and 1990, requests in Switzerland were up by 50 per cent and in Belgium by 60 per cent.

Many of these asylum seekers are indeed in danger if they remain in their own countries. French Constitutions have constantly stipulated the right first promulgated in 1946: 'Anyone persecuted because of his action in favour of liberty has a right to asylum on the territory of the Republic.' However, a thorough enquiry by the French Senate into the phenomenon of immigration concluded that the situation was getting completely out of hand:

> Throughout its work, its hearings and its visits, the mission noted the omnipresence of a recurring theme: widespread abuse of the right of asylum. Normally this means of entering and remaining on the territory of the Republic should be limited to some individuals who are under threat because of their actions in favour of liberty; in fact the right of asylum has been transformed in just a few years into a major means of clandestine immigration.[20]

Reiterating their attachment to this right, and expressing the fear that the onslaught of abusive demands can harm the cause of those who are genuinely being persecuted, the report of the French Senate mission explains in detail how an overwhelming proportion of those claiming asylum are in fact purely 'economic refugees'. In France at least, the mere fact of asking for asylum gives the candidate the right of residence while the dossier is being processed, the right to work, payment of 2000Fr cash and numerous other financial and social benefits. Even if the person's request is rejected, as it lately has been in 90 per cent of the cases, there are various appeal procedures that have been known to be strung out for up to seven, sometimes ten years! And even if the final appeal is denied, the candidate still isn't necessarily made to leave – often he (it usually is a man) can't even

be found. In other words, a large number of those who have managed
to get in by this method have also managed to stay in.

> ... a delegation of the Mission spoke with members of a very
> large group of petitioners, most of them Malians, in two enormous
> waiting rooms placed at their disposal by the Seine-Saint-Denis
> Prefecture. Asked about their motives for claiming asylum, several
> quite naively admitted that they just wanted to work, or that the
> economic situation in their country had become too difficult for
> them to be able to take care of their families ... These foreigners,
> obviously economic refugees, were quite oblivious of the seri-
> ousness of the abuse of human rights law they were about to
> commit and seemed rather to think they were merely carrying out
> a banal bureaucratic procedure which would automatically give
> them a right of residence and of work, with the corresponding
> monetary benefits.[21]

France is not the only European country coping with unprecedented influxes of asylum seekers. Elsewhere, particularly since
1987–8, these movements have swelled. Germany has had the most
requests in absolute numbers – they doubled between 1987 and
1989 to more than 120,000. Much of this increase was due to of
Eastern Europeans fleeing their countries before the Berlin wall came
tumbling down. But even leaving Germany entirely out of the calculations, the numbers of requests for political asylum rose by 56 per
cent as a whole in Europe between 1987 and 1989, to nearly 200,000.[22]

These figures do not include refugees, for which most European
countries have a separate quota. The OECD (from whose 'Permanent
Observation System of Migrations' – SOPEMI – this information is
drawn) says that its member countries are worried lest the 'abuse of
the asylum procedure for immigration harms the people who are
genuinely persecuted and who fulfil the criteria required to obtain
refugee status'. The OECD also says that all its member countries are
experiencing the same general problem – trying to sort out what has
actually happened to the high proportion of those to whom asylum
is refused. Many go underground and stay; others may start the
petitioning process all over again in another European country since
there is no EEC-wide central registry. The sheer number of asylum
seekers – whether economic or genuinely political – seems certain to
push Europe to tighten up procedures.*

---

* As we delivered this book to the publisher (1991), France was taking steps to
tighten the 'droit d'asile' laws drastically.

Aside from entries under this pretext (as it turns out to be in a high percentage of the cases) which ends up swelling the clandestine population by thousands; the 'no frills', common or garden illegal immigration is also on the rise, particularly in Southern European countries. The Northern ones have been 'receiving' countries for decades and have acquired considerable experience in spotting illegals, but Spain, Portugal, Greece and Italy were until recently 'sending' countries themselves. They have not yet established efficient means of controlling entries. Italy in particular still has more illegal immigrants than legal ones, in spite of two opportunities, in 1988 and again in 1989, for them to legalise their situation without penalty.[23]

Lucrative enterprises of human traffickers and counterfeit paper suppliers also exist in Europe, though they may not yet have the transnational status of the Mexican-based networks. Some people simply enter as tourists or students and then disappear into the woodwork when their visas run out. Illegal migration grows partly because, in most European countries, sanctions against it punish the immigrant, not his (occasionally her) employer. Virtually all the illegals have jobs, or depend on someone who does; they are, of course, ideal candidates for the sweatshop or the scullery with wages as low as the traffic will bear and no health or employment benefits of any kind. If Europeans want to put an end to the major 'pull factor' – the possibility of work whatever the cost – that keeps immigration pressures at their peak, then they should be targeting their own nationals who employ this modern variant of slave labour.

Other ways the non-European population grows in Europe are through so-called 'family regrouping' policies and through demographics. The major receiving countries have, on humanitarian grounds, instituted the possibility for legal immigrants to bring their immediate family members – especially wives and children – to live with them. For example, about 150,000 people moved to the United Kingdom under these circumstances between 1985 and 1988; 235,000 settled in France under this programme between 1983 and 1989. The immigrants who bring their families are overwhelmingly young and male – of child-rearing age. Immigrants, at least at the beginning, have a lot more children than Europeans. Data about migrants to Belgium is particularly revealing on this score, as seen in Table 5.3.[24]

Note that women from earlier 'sending' countries like Italy and especially Spain, both supposedly devoutly Catholic, have significantly lower birthrates than do Belgians themselves, and this after a single generation of immigration. Non-EEC migrants, on the other hand, are much more recent and their fertility rates still characteristic of their countries of origin. It will be interesting to watch them plunge, as they seem destined to do, after another generation or so. In 1988, births to foreigners represented 15 per cent of all births in Switzerland, about 11 per cent in France and Germany, 7 per cent in Holland.[25]

Table 5.3: Average Number of Children per Woman According to Nationality (All Belgian cities, 1983–8)

Belgians	1.42
EEC	1.18
of which Italians	1.32
of which Spaniards	1.03
Non-EEC	3.72
of which Turks	3.57
of which North Africans (Maghrebins)	4.64

Meanwhile, mortality rates for immigrants to Europe show no significant differences from those of native Europeans – at least not for legal migrants, the only ones who can be counted. In fact, 'life expectancy for foreigners is extremely close to that of nationals, perhaps even superior.' This may be due to a kind of 'natural selection' – those who migrate know they will have tough jobs and tend to be physically hardy specimens. Older men may also return to their countries of origin when their working lives are ended – they are thus not counted in the statistics.[26]

Immigration: Whose Good Fortune and Whose Responsibility?

Such are some of the reasons why the current net increase of foreigners in Europe is happening and will continue. Is this good or bad or both – and for whom? First of all, the phenomenon of immigration and the figures given here should be kept in perspective: foreigners of non-European origin represent no more than 3 or 4 per cent of the total EC population of 320 million. Second, European birthrates are shrinking; the population is already beginning to decline. Europe needs – or will soon need – more labour power. Recent or future immigrants are the only ones who can provide it. Their financial contributions to retirement funds will also take up the slack left by an ageing population and they will sustain many European pensioners in their old age.

Nor should Europe be so smug about the 'great' number of refugees it is supposed to be welcoming. Whether they have fled their homelands for political or for economic reasons, or were simply caught in the crossfire of war, refugees have been welcomed in far greater numbers in the poor third world itself, where several countries have been much more generous than European ones in taking them in. Afghans moved massively to Pakistan; Turkey has taken in hundreds of thousands of Kurdish refugees (Turkish Kurds are persecuted in Turkey, but that's another problem) and 650,000 Mozambicans fled to Malawi during the civil war.

The problems, when there are such – and when these are exploited by racist movements – lie not in numbers of immigrants but in their spatial concentrations, in 'ghettoisations' that can, if allowed to fester, marginalise some non-European populations for generations to come. The phenomenon has now been widely recognised. People arriving in Europe settle where their friends and relatives already live. They haven't much money so they crowd together. They change the local scenery with their shops and places of recreation or worship. They send their children – who at home speak a whole medley of non-European languages – to schools which may literally have to cope with the cultural differences of dozens of nationalities.

Through no fault of their own, children who at five or six do not already speak the local European language fluently, draw heavily on teaching resources and – in a highly competitive educational environment – slow the progress of the children whose mother tongue is the local language. At that point, European families move out if they possibly can and the concentration of foreigners grows even greater. A story in the *New York Times* describes the case of one French high school in the crowded Belleville area of Paris:

> The result [of the concentration of foreigners] is evident in the patio below Mr Desvaux's [the principal's] office ... At different times of the day, teenagers of 28 nationalities and 5 religions and many races take breaks there between classes, but hardly a white French child is to be seen. 'The ghetto phenomenon is a permanent danger to us', Mr Desvaux said.[27]

In an earlier era of intra-European, South-to-North migrations, the Catholic Church played an important role in helping uprooted Italians, Spaniards and Portuguese feel more at home in their new countries of residence. When religion is no longer a unifying factor, schools are still the best way to integrate people into a new culture and bright students have always seized whatever opportunities were

on offer to improve their economic situation. However, in the transitional phase Europe is currently undergoing, lots of young
immigrants did not enter the European educational mill as toddlers.
Some who have come to Europe in 'family regrouping' schemes
received whatever meagre education they may have had in a variety
of overcrowded and underfunded third world schools. Many others,
even if they started school in Europe, lack cultural advantages at home
and experience repeated school failures. By the age of 12 or so, they
can find themselves hopelessly behind their European counterparts,
yet can't possibly be sent back to younger children's classrooms.

If they are extremely lucky, they may leave school for a dead-end
job, but unemployment is also increasing among the foreign born
or those of non-European parentage and is particularly concentrated
among the young. These are the disappointed and disaffected youth
who succumb to violence and despair. For the first time, France is
getting a taste of how life is in the American underclass, as ethnic
minority children as young as ten organise in neighbourhood gangs
specialising in robbery, rape and harrassing the police.[28] In Italy,
10,000 foreigners were in prison in 1988 (Yugoslavs, Tunisians,
Moroccans, Algerians and Senegalese were, in that order, the most
incarcerated nationalities), 70 per cent of them for theft or drug
offences.[29]

So there is no point pretending that all is rosy with immigration
in Europe, but on the other hand, no European country has yet made
the systematic effort or invested the considerable resources needed
to include these New Europeans in the New Europe.

They must be included because they are not going to go home in
any significant numbers. So long as the debt crisis and economic
stagnation persist, governments of the sending countries are unlikely
to put up any barriers to migration and will encourage their citizens
to stay put once they go to Europe, for the simple reason that they
bring in money. Remittances from migrant workers are, for many
indebted countries, major sources of hard currency. When the Gulf
War forced hundreds of thousands of foreign workers to flee Kuwait
and set them wandering in the desert, countries like Egypt, Sri Lanka
and the Philippines suffered major drops in income. Filipino Airways
reportedly lost $800,000 in revenues in a single month on its Gulf
flights. In 1988, Turks in Germany sent home 2.5 billion marks
while Moroccans remitted nearly 4.5 billion French francs to their
families in Morocco.[30]

And yet, tens of thousands of immigrant families have been
reunited in Europe. Available figures would seem to indicate that many
workers had hoped eventually to return home but have now decided

against it. Otherwise, it is hard to explain why, 15 years after the end of officially sanctioned 'guest worker' immigration to Europe, family regroupings should remain at virtually the same levels as at the beginning. Either the immigrant worker in Europe has decided he and his family have no future in the country of origin, or the economic situation of the family at home – in spite of remittances – has deteriorated to the point that he is prepared to assume the extra financial responsibilities of taking care of them in Europe. This is a subject on which more research could usefully be done, since it seems clearly linked to the debt crisis and the ensuing stagnation.

Immigration may bring the deeply indebted home countries desperately needed hard currency but beyond that it constitutes a further drain on the poor countries' resources. Immigrants are overwhelmingly the younger, stronger and cleverer members of a given population. An African explains why he thinks emigration is not an opportunity for his country, even though it may solve some individual problems:

> African migrants who go to Europe are between 17 and 40 years old. They are the most vital people in our countries. Look at the valley of the Senegal river where they're talking about putting 240,000 newly irrigated hectares [600,000 acres] under cultivation. Right now, in that valley, we have 370 groups of producers and 70 per cent of them are women. We can't develop our country without the men – if we only have the women and the old people … I think Europeans should think more about why people migrate to begin with. The reasons are economic … If people were able to get training in Europe that would help them to help their countries when they returned, that would work in favour of development. If the immigrant only gets training that integrates him into French industry, it may be France's good fortune, but I don't think it's ours.[31]

The Future: Crossing Thresholds

President François Mitterrand was ill-advised to take up the cry of the right in France and to speak in public about 'le seuil de tolérance' – the threshold of tolerance – for the presence of immigrants. The phrase suggests that intolerance is somehow justified when some unspecified 'threshold' is crossed. Actually the two words don't belong in the same phrase and such language is imprecise, unfortunate, demagogical or all three. Developed country leaders would do better to speak honestly to their own citizens and help them to understand the facts of life.

The first one they should accept is that most people don't migrate for the fun of it. If they take the plunge, in the vast majority of cases it is because they see it as their only chance. The ones who manage to get into Europe or the US are surely among the more vigorous and forward-looking members of their own societies. They have that enterprising spirit so beloved of the G-7 leaders except, it seems, when it applies to the free movement of labour towards their own countries.

The second fact of life is that borders are permeable. The US cannot be sealed off from Mexico or the Caribbean and the Mediterranean is, for all practical purposes, a pond. Imagine simply trying to police the entire Italian coastline! The six original EC countries (France, Germany, Italy and the Benelux) are trying through the 'Schengen convention' to develop common policing mechanisms but, in spite of their efforts, by 1 January 1993 most immigrants will be able to move freely throughout Europe.

The third consideration, most powerful of all, is sheer demographics. By the year 2025, the population of the European Community will have shrunk from its present 320 million to 306 million. Meanwhile, the population of Africa will, according to current projections, have skyrocketed from 555 million to 1.6 billion. Many African countries which seem middle-sized today will have shot far beyond the populations of even the largest European countries. By 2025, according to *The Economist*, 'Turkey will have 20 million more people than united Germany, Sudan as many as France, Egypt as many as Spain and Italy combined.' These populations, as everyone knows, will be young, hungry and easily persuaded to try their luck abroad – Europe will appear to them a promised land dripping with milk and honey.[32]

Although we have concentrated here on South–North migrations, East–West movement will accelerate as well as unemployment grows in the formerly state socialist countries of Eastern Europe. They too will want to join the West European workforce at virtually any price.

In other words, pressures on European frontiers cannot help but increase. Even if NATO – that Cold War leftover in search of a mission – finds a new lease on life by turning its sights and its guns southwards, there is no hope of holding back the tide through defence measures. The Fortress will crumble.

There are only two rational ways to deal with the problems of immigration. The first is to promote the well-being of those who have already settled. The French Senate report suggests a financing scheme by which the state could and should help municipalities proportionally to the foreign population under their jurisdiction. At present – and this is doubtless true throughout Europe – the towns with the most dense immigrant populations and the heaviest expenditures to integrate them properly also have the most meagre tax bases.

Since a town of 10,000 people on the periphery of a large city is likely to have a much higher percentage of foreigners than one of comparable size in a rural area, one could take the national average of foreigners in towns of similar size and give extra budgetary aid to towns for every point they scored above that average. (But the Senate also suggests a ceiling, so as not to encourage ghettoisation.) This would create a kind of 'national solidarity' in favour of integration. For purposes of aid calculations, naturalised foreigners could be counted in the totals as well for a period of X years after their naturalisation. Municipal services could also be exempted from the value-added tax on all investments made to serve the needs of immigrant populations. School districts should also receive help proportional to their task of helping foreign children succeed.

The second way to deal with the problem is to make it less necessary for the *forces vives* – the vital elements – of a given population to migrate. Here the first step is to create jobs in the countries concerned, with debt relief and the elimination of recession-creating structural adjustment policies as a prerequisite. At present, it is a joke to talk about 'aid' when even Africa, during the lost decade of the 1980s, became a net *provider* of funds to the creditor countries.

Between 1982 and 1990, net resource flows to Africa – including all bilateral and multilateral development aid, both public and private; investments and new loans, plus export credits – came to $214 billion dollars. Part of these supposed inflows will require outflows in future – for example, interest on new loans. Meanwhile, during the same period, Africa paid out in debt service alone $217 billion. These stark figures require little comment – except to note that debt service payments obviously do not represent total outflows: one should add to the $217 billion figure royalties, capital flight, repatriated profits, etc. It would also be necessary and honest to take into account the drastic drop in raw material prices which has contributed so much to impoverishing the African continent.[33]

The Economist can be counted on for a free-market, comparative advantage solution to every problem, expressed in that crisp, no-backtalk style that always makes it sound so authoritative. In the present case, however, the magazine is entirely sensible in saying that trade can create more jobs than aid (particularly since there isn't any aid, although this detail goes unmentioned by *The Economist*):

the most labour-intensive industries – textiles, metal manufacturing, engineering, food processing – are all ones where rich countries struggle most fiercely to protect their own markets. Absurdly, those industries often survive in richer lands partly by employing cheap immigrant labour. Wise governments will let the jobs go to the countries that can do them most efficiently.[34]

The Economist might have added farming to its list. As we have seen, people who migrate to the North have usually made a first transition from the countryside to the city. If Europe and the United States would stop dumping their food surpluses in the South, thereby ruining the local peasantries, they would simultaneously stop creating one inexhaustible reservoir of future migrants.

For the moment, the sending countries have no interest in stopping emigration because their 'development' partners have made no effort to make it worth their while. One expert who has examined the relationship between development assistance strategies and migration concludes that

Most sending countries showed a marked preference for ... emigration rather than developing cooperative policies aimed at stabilizing the workforce at home. The immediate financial and political benefits accruing from the export of surplus workers and the inflow of remittances outweighed by far the immediate benefits of alternative development strategies.[35]

That is doubtless because there *are* no 'alternative development strategies' on offer. Nothing of the kind has even been tried.

Finally, if Europe wants to halt the alarming – from whatever point of view – increase in the numbers of asylum-seekers, the first step is to stop supporting dictators. Among major nationalities of those seeking asylum in Europe are Malians and Zairois. The Malians got rid of their dictator, but as of this writing the unspeakable Mobutu is still in place (and has enjoyed George Bush's hospitality and praise).

Let us end, as we began, with Auden's timeless 'Refugee Blues':

Walked through a wood, saw the birds in the trees;
They had no politicians and sang at their ease:
They weren't the human race, my dear, they weren't the human race.

The Sixth Boomerang:
Conflict and War

by Dan Smith

The banker making the loan for war,
The expert designing the long range gun
To exterminate everyone under the sun,
Would like to get out, but can only mutter:
'What can I do? It's my bread and butter.'
     WH Auden,*On this Island*, XVIII

Introduction

War and debt have long had an intimate relationship. In its most familiar form, war produces debt. So, of course, do preparations for war. But this relationship takes other forms: in a variety of ways, debt can also be a resource for use in war; in this chapter, the question is whether debt can also be a cause of war.

One obvious way to explore this question would be to see if the incidence of war in the third world changed with the onset of the debt crisis in 1982. Unfortunately and somewhat curiously, the quality of the available data on wars before then do not let us do this. There are various lists of wars, but even the best are useful only for the period since about 1980. Even a few years earlier than that, the data become vague. This is especially true with small wars, a topic to which Western scholars paid little attention until the 1980s.

Despite this lack of data, there are some answers to questions about the influence of debt on war. They have to be approached and treated cautiously, but in the end the pattern is clear. Debt prepares the ground on which the seeds of conflict fall, watering the martial crop as it grows. There is one war in which debt was a more direct cause, and it is one of the largest of recent years – the Gulf War. Here, we first consider the character of current wars, then look at the role of war in causing debt and the use of debt as an instrument of power. We then assess the opposite causation – from debt to war.

War in the Late Twentieth Century

Most images of war in most people's minds are entirely misleading. It is not simply that warfare is a great deal less glorious than Hollywood used to tell us and some politicians still seem to believe. Most popular ideas about war in the era since 1945 are drawn from the Second World War itself, or from films about it, together with a small number of atypical conflicts which get a lot of instant media coverage and, later on, become the subject of Hollywood films. But that coverage and those films themselves embody fixed assumptions, preconceptions to which most actual wars do not conform.

In general, today's wars are little reported. In this sense as well as others, the Gulf War of 1990–1 and the Vietnam War in the 1960s were atypical. For most Westerners, most wars happen in small countries far away about which they know little and care less. Most of them, as Table 6.1 shows, are civil wars. They do not always or even usually begin with a formal declaration. Many have no clear starting date or endpoint. They tend to last a long time – about two-thirds of current wars have lasted over a decade – but they are not fought at the same level of intensity for their whole duration. They splutter into action, subside, kick viciously again, tick over at a relatively low level of mayhem, seem to stop, return to find more victims. It is often extremely difficult to be sure whether combat at a given moment represents a new war or an old one which has flared up again.

In short, wars today generally do not have the clear, dramatic outlines which are familiar from news media and commercial films. For most of the time they are difficult for journalists to report because they continue for years without the sort of decisive moments which, to the news media, constitute news. For the same reason, they are hard to understand. They are unclear and untidy. This untidiness makes the definition of what constitutes war particularly important. There is no universally agreed definition. Our definition, used in compiling Table 6.1, is:

- War consists of open armed conflict in which
- the regular uniformed forces of a state are involved on at least one side,
- there is a degree of central organisation on both sides, and
- there is some continuity between clashes.

This is a deliberately flexible definition which catches in its net far more conflicts than most definitions manage. Trying to fit the messy reality of war into a more rigid definition simply leaves a lot of violent conflict and bloodshed outside the category and introduces fake distinctions. The most common way of defining war includes the number of people killed. Violent conflict between two centrally organised forces may be regarded as war either when more than 1000 people have been killed, or when at least 1000 people are killed each year.[1] Both criteria are wholly arbitrary. There is no ethical or practical basis for choosing one numerical threshold rather any other. Using an annual threshold is especially arbitrary; it means that some conflicts are regarded as war intermittently across decades as the number of casualties fluctuates annually, while others never qualify as war despite causing some thousands of deaths (for example, the Northern Ireland war). Besides, the statistics of war-deaths are so unreliable they can hardly serve as a sensible cornerstone for defining war.

Using the definition of war proposed above, at the beginning of 1991 there were 48 wars in the third world involving 39 countries. Of that total, 46 were civil wars. The two international wars were the Gulf War and Morocco's war in the Western Sahara against the Polisario Front.* In six countries – China, Ethiopia, India, Indonesia, Myanmar and the Philippines – there was more than one civil war. These wars are listed in Table 6.1 which shows 41 countries at war from January 1990 to February 1991 inclusive; it includes the wars in Nicaragua and Lebanon which stopped during 1990, though in either case the cessation may turn out to have been temporary, and in the case of Lebanon it may also have been incomplete.

Victims

There is no reliable information about the number of victims. Estimates are wide-ranging; some are reflected in Table 6.1. On those figures, between 3.5 and 8.5 million deaths had been caused by the 48 wars in the third world which were active in January 1991. Allowing for exaggeration in estimating casualties in the most violent of these wars, a serviceable rounded estimate would be 5 million.

Why are estimates so different? Some of the figures derive in the first place from stories filed by journalists far from the fighting. There they have little chance of producing reliable counts, yet if they were close at hand, the fog of war would give them no better chance. The other major sources are agencies which are *parti pris* – for example, the information offices of governments, or of insurgents, or guerrillas' political representatives abroad or foreign supporters. In other words, most of the data on war deaths are generated by ignorance or bias.

---

* Morocco regards this as a civil war since it claims Western Sahara as its own territory. This is, of course, precisely what the war is about.

The problem is not simply a tendency to produce propaganda rather than reliable information. Part of the difficulty is that nobody is responsible for counting the vast majority of those who die in war. This century has seen a profound change in the pattern of casualties caused by warfare. A common estimate is that in the First World War some 85–90 per cent of war dead were military personnel, the remainder civilians. In the Second World War, counting all theatres of war, some estimates suggest civilians made up about a half of war deaths, including victims of death camps and massacres as well as those killed in the massive bombing raids on cities, while other estimates suggest an even higher civilian proportion – up to two-thirds. In today's wars, some estimates suggest that three-quarters of war dead are civilian, while others indicate that civilians account for as many as 90 per cent of victims including refugees.[2]

Thus war has long ceased to be an affair largely limited to the contending armed forces. In all kinds of war, civilians participate, usually against their will, as victims. As such, civilians often go uncounted. Armed forces, even guerrillas, generally know how many people they start out with and how many they end up with. Allowing for desertions, the difference between the two figures provides an estimate of how many have been killed, even when it is impossible actually to count the bodies. But civilians are a different matter. Outside highly urbanised societies, there may be no reliable count to begin with. If they can flee, they do, which further disturbs the statistical base. They bury their own dead and do not contribute the figures to an overall tally. Occasionally, aid agencies or church missions can provide some reliable information about specific instances of combat, terror or massacre, but rarely does this allow for precise overall data. The result is that figures for those killed in war are regularly rounded, sometimes to the nearest hundred thousand, sometimes to the nearest half million (and look even more suspect when they are not).

So it is probably reasonable to say that about 5 million people have died in the wars active in January 1991, but nobody really knows for sure. In equally approximate terms, deaths by war since 1945 probably number rather in excess of 20 million.*

---

* A range of 15 to 20 million is suggested by Brogan, *World Conflicts*, pp. 567–71; William Eckhardt offers a figure of 21,809,000 (which gives a spurious impression of precision) in Sivard, *World Military and Social Expenditures 1989* (Washington DC, World Priorities Inc, 1989). The latter explicitly employs a more restrictive definition of war than that utilised here, and the former implicitly. But the conflicts they miss are the small ones. Regrettably, at this scale of carnage, a few thousand deaths – even a few hundred thousand, truth to tell – do not affect these necessarily rough estimates either way.

Table 6.1: Third World Countries at War 1990/91

	War Began	Comment	Deaths
SAUDI ARABIA	1991	Against IRAQ after annexation of KUWAIT	N.A.
QATAR	1991	Against IRAQ after annexation of KUWAIT	N.A.
EGYPT	1991	Against IRAQ after annexation of KUWAIT	N.A.
RWANDA	1990	Civil war	N.A.
IRAQ	1990	Invasion and annexation of KUWAIT. 1991: general war vs. US, UK, France, Saudi Arabia, Kuwait, Italy, Qatar, Syria, Egypt. Then civil war: Kurdish & Shiite uprisings	N.A.
KUWAIT	1990	Invasion & annexation by IRAQ	N.A.
LIBERIA	1989	Civil war	>10,000
PAPUA NEW GUINEA	1989	Gov't against Bougainville landowners	<1,000
CHINA	1987	Armed conflict in TIBET; XINJIANG since 1989	<5,000
SURINAME	1986	Civil war. Coup December 1990	<5,000
COLOMBIA	1986	Civil war against guerrillas [largest group – M-19 – stopped 1990] and Drug Barons. US intervention 1990	6-20,000
BOLIVIA	1985	Civil war. Intervention by USA against Drug Barons 1986	<5,000
ZIMBABWE	1984	Intervention in MOZAMBIQUE against MNR (Renamo)	[see below]
SRI LANKA	1983	Civil war: Tamil Tigers secessionists; intervention by India 1987–90; earlier communist JVP war on gov't, 1977–90	<20,000 >5,000
PERU	1980	Civil war	10–15,000
EL SALVADOR	1979	Civil war	>50,000
IRAN	1978	Uprising against Shah, followed by armed conflict of varying intensity with opposition groups including Kurds	17–88,000
AFGHANISTAN	1978	Civil war. Soviet intervention 1978–89	<750,000
SOMALIA	1977	Civil war. Barre government overthrown by guerrilla coalition, January 1991	>60,000
TURKEY	1977	Against KURDS	<5,000
SYRIA	1976	Intervention in LEBANON [+ fighting against IRAQ, 1991]	[see below]
MOZAMBIQUE	1976	Civil war against MNR [Renamo] following war of independence. Intervention by ZIMBABWE since 1984	400–700,000
MOROCCO	1976	Annexation of WESTERN SAHARA	10–16,000
WESTERN SAHARA	1976	Polisario Front resistance to annexation by MOROCCO	[see above]
LEBANON	1975	Civil war: interventions by Syria [since 1976], Israel [1980, 1982.], France & USA [1982–4] (+ Italy & UK)	130–165,000
ANGOLA	1975	Civil war following anti-colonial war. Intervention by Cuba & South Africa on opposite sides 1975–88. Ceasefire talks 1990–1	<350,000

	War Began	Comment	Deaths
BANGLADESH	1975	Civil war in Chittagong region	<5,000
CAMBODIA	1975	Civil war against Khmer Rouge & others after 1970–5 war against USA. 1977 invasion by Vietnam. Withdrew 1989. Ceasefire talks 1990–1	750,000–2 million [high estimate includes famine]
INDONESIA	1975	Multiple civil wars. In EAST TIMOR after annexation and massacres. In 1980s & into 1990s, wars also in IRIAN JAYA and north-west SUMATRA	100–200,000
UGANDA	1971	Civil wars, beginning with Amin terror, continuing through devastation to banditry	35–600,000
NICARAGUA	1970	Sandinistas against Somoza [to 1979] and Somocista Contras [from 1980]. War ended 1990	>30,000
PHILIPPINES	1969	Civil wars against: Communist New People's Army; (now sporadically) Moro forces. Army coup attempted Dec. 1989	35–100,000 40–50,000
GUATEMALA	1968	Civil war	45–140,000
CHAD	1965	Civil war with sporadic French & Libyan intervention	>25,000
SOUTH AFRICA	1964	ANC war against apartheid state (ceasefire declared 1990); ANC/INKATHA conflict since 1987	<5,000 >3,000
ETHIOPIA	1962	Multiple civil wars: Eritrea 1962; Tigray from 1974; Oromo from 1977 General civil war began 1989	95,000–2 million [high est. inc. famine]
SUDAN	1955	Civil war: sporadic; currently intense	400,000–1 million
ISRAEL	1948	More or less continuous war, conflict, terrorism by and against Palestinians	c.20,000
MYANMAR	1948	Multiple civil wars against communists in SHAN (north) (now mostly disbanded), KACHIN (northeast) and KAREN (southeast) nationalists and opium-trading ex-Kuomintang armies	<25,000
PAKISTAN	1947	Serial civil wars since independence. Latest in SIND since 1984	N.A.
INDIA	1947	Multiple civil wars since independence. Wars identifiable in 1990/91 [with start dates]: JAMMU & KASHMIR [1947, upsurge 1990]; UTTAR PRADESH [1962]; Naxalites in ANDHRA PRADESH and BIHAR [1969]; PUNJAB [1981]; TAMIL NADU [1987]; TRIPURA[1988]; ASSAM [1990 – latest resurgence]	c.20,000?

Sources: C. Ahlström, *Casualties of Conflict* [Uppsala University, Department of Peace & Conflict Research, 1991]; P. Brogan, *World Conflicts* [London, Bloomsbury, 1989]; J.F. Dunnigan & A. Bay, *A Quick & Dirty Guide to War* [New York, Wm Morrow, 1985]; G.C. Kohn, *Dictionary of Wars* [New York, Doubleday, 1987]; J. Laffin, *The World In Conflict 1990: War Annual 4* [London, Brassey's, 1990]; R.L. Sivard, *World Military & Social Expenditures,* successive years [Washington DC, World Priorities Inc, annual]; *Strategic Survey,* successive years [London, International Institute for Strategic Studies,

annual]; *World Armaments & Disarmament: SIPRI Yearbook* 1989 and 1990 editions [Oxford University Press, 1989 & 1990]; P. Wallensteen [ed] *States in Armed Conflict 1988* [Uppsala University, July 1989]; *The Europa World Yearbook*, successive years [London, Europa Publications, annual]; *Keesing's Register of World Events* [Harlow, Longman's, annual]; *Amnesty International Report*, successive years [London, Amnesty International, annual]; C. Humana, *World Human Rights Guide*, 2nd edn [London, Pan, 1987]; Minority Rights Group, *World Directory of Minorities* [Harlow, Longman, n.d. (1989/90)]; Africa Watch, *Somalia: A Government at War With Its Own People*, January 1990; Africa Watch, *Sudan: A Human Rights Disaster*, March 1990; C. Clapham, 'The political economy of conflict in the Horn of Africa', *Survival*, Sept/Oct 1990; The Panos Institute, *Beyond Law Enforcement: Narcotics and Development*, February 1990; W.S. Turley, 'The Khmer war: Cambodia after Paris', *Survival*, Sept/Oct 1990; H.W. Degenhardt, *Revolutionary and Dissident Movements, An International Guide* [Harlow, Longman, 1988]; C. Hobday, *Communist and Marxist Parties of the World* [London, Longman, 1986]; R.F. Starr [ed.], *Yearbook on International Communist Affairs* [Stanford, Hoover Institution, 1987]; *Pacific Research* [quarterly journal of the Peace Research Centre, Australian National University, Canberra] various issues; press reports.
Note: War is defined as open armed conflict in which there are: regular armed forces of the state on at least one side, some degree of continuity between clashes and some degree of central organisation on both sides. This is a much wider definition than often used, and therefore catches more conflicts than others which limit themselves by, for example, arbitrary numerical criteria [the number of people killed]. Despite its flexibility, there are times when it is not flexible enough; the ANC/Inkatha war in South Africa has been included even though it does not appear to involve regular armed forces. Included in this list are countries in which there were wars from January 1990 to January 1991 inclusive, even if they stopped during that time [e.g., Nicaragua, the ANC war against the South African government].
N.A: Information not available

In each of several wars since 1945, more than 1 million people have died. For the 1950–3 war in Korea, estimates of war-deaths range from 1.5 to 3 million. They go as high as 2 million for China from 1946 to 1950, Vietnam from 1960 to 1975, Nigeria from 1967 to 1970 and two countries where wars continue – Ethiopia and Cambodia. Even when the figures are not so horrifying, smaller wars can be just as sickening. From the war in Mozambique comes an account of guerrillas cutting off a boy's fingers one by one until he accepted their order to shoot his father, after which they forced him to join them.[3] From Nicaragua, a journalist reports that she learned from children about their dead parents' faces being peeled off by Contra guerrillas.[4] These accounts are not untypical.

The victims of war, of course, are not only those it kills. Table 6.2 shows that in 1989, before the Gulf War, there were more than 35 million refugees worldwide. More than half were refugees in their own countries and were therefore excluded from official reckonings of the refugee total. The largest producer of refugees today is the war in Afghanistan, although Africa has more refugees in it than any other continent, while the Middle East and Central America both produce large numbers of refugees relative to their overall population. In 1989 almost 30 million people were refugees in or from war-torn countries, and about 26 million could be regarded as refugees from war itself. Table 6.3 shows the major 'producers' of refugees. Figures for 1990 and 1991 will show big increases in the number of refugees, registering the effects of war in the Middle East, and of the combination of war and famine in six African countries – Angola, Ethiopia, Liberia, Mozambique, Somalia and Sudan.

Table 6.2; Refugees, 1989: World and Regional Totals

	External	Internal	Total
AFRICA (16 countries)	4,455,000	10,795,000	15, 250,000
ASIA (11)	6,855,000	3,165,000	10,020,000
MIDDLE EAST (5)	3,795,000	2,870,000	6,665,000
CENTRAL AMERICA (6)	1,415,000	980,000	2,395,000
SOUTH AMERICA (3)	13,000	80,000	93,000
EUROPE (3 inc. USSR)	250,000	765,000	1,015,000
WORLD (44 countries)	16,785,000	18,655,000	35,440,000

Table 6.3: Refugees: The Top 25 Countries of Origin, 1989

Country of Origin	External	Internal	Total	Per Cent of World Total
1 AFGHANISTAN	6,000,000	2,000,000	8,000,000	23
2 ISRAEL	2,970,000	870,000*	3,840,000	11
3 SOUTH AFRICA	25,000	3,570,000	3,595,000	11
4 MOZAMBIQUE	1,355,000	1,700,000	3,055,000	9
5 SUDAN	435,000	2,600,000	3,035,000	9
6 ETHIOPIA	1,000,000	1,100,000	2,100,000	6
7 ANGOLA	440,000	900,000	1,340,000	4
8 IRAQ	500,000	750,000	1,250,000	4
9 HAITI	1,200,000	–	1,200,000	3
10 SOMALIA	390,000	400,000	790,000	2
11 IRAN	270,000	500,000	770,000	2
13 LEBANON	–	750,000	750,000	2
14 SRI LANKA	100,000	500,000	600,000	2
15 USSR	–	500,000	500,000	1
16 NICARAGUA	90,000	390,000	480,000	1
17 PHILIPPINES	–	450,000	450,000	1
18 GUATEMALA	60,000	300,000	360,000	1
19 CAMBODIA	335,000	–	335,000	1
20 EL SALVADOR	60,000	270,000	330,000	1
21 UGANDA	15,000	300,000	315,000	1
22 CYPRUS	–	265,000	265,000	1
23 CHAD	35,000	225,000	260,000	1
24 BULGARIA	250,000	–	250,000	1
25 RWANDA	235,000	–	235,000	1

Tables 2&3
Source: Derived from *World Refugee Survey – 1989 In Review* [Washington DC, US Committee for Refugees, 1990].
Note: The statistics of refugees are another minefield of misinformation because of the politics of acknowledging displaced people as refugees. In officialese, the category of refugee includes only those who have fled their country (not just their home) and who receive official aid. It does not recognise those who are forcibly relocated, driven off their land or defined as economic migrants. The figures above include all those categories. All figures are rounded, virtually all are estimates, most are disputed and in many cases the differences between high and low estimates are several hundred thousand. In those cases, the table gives the average of two widely divergent figures.
NB: 'External' refugees have crossed an international border, 'internal' refugees remain within their country of origin.
* West Bank and Gaza Strip treated here as within Israel.

Beyond the dead and the displaced, there are uncounted millions of people physically and psychologically injured in war, both those who have engaged in combat and those who have only been its victims. Among the many who are or have been both participant and victim, are the child soldiers. Worldwide, there are reported to be approximately 200,000 of them under the age of fifteen.[5] Like so many figures in this business, the status of this estimate is unclear. It cannot have been reached on the basis of detailed counting; it is, in effect, shorthand for 'an awful lot and, by any civilised standards, far too many'.

From War to Debt

In sixteenth century England under Elizabeth I and Spain under Philip II, up to 75 per cent of government spending was devoted to meeting the current costs of war or repaying the debt incurred in previous wars.[6] War is capable of producing so much debt that victory is not always a protection against the potentially ruinous consequences of too much borrowing. The debt incurred during France's successful war of 1778–83 against England – the intervention in the American War of Independence – put such strain upon the *ancien régime*'s finances that it became a contributory cause of the French Revolution of 1789.[7] Britain was on the winning side in two World Wars this century, and ended up broke. Of the loan from the USA which Britain was forced to seek in 1945, *The Economist* magazine remarked, with a bitterness no less striking for being understated, 'It is rather aggravating to find that the reward for losing a quarter of our national wealth in the common cause is to pay tribute for half a century to those who have been enriched by the war.'[8] That resentment was widespread; public and political opinion in Britain held that the money should have been granted outright by the US. It may, however, seem a little over-wrought to anybody familiar with the terms of external debt today, for the interest rate was a mere 2 per cent, and the interest payments were to be waived if they exceeded 2 per cent of British export earnings in any year.[9]

The capacity to manage debt is an important asset in war. In the great rivalry between England and France through the eighteenth and into the nineteenth century, one of England's decisive advantages lay in its superior system of public credit. That is, it won wars because it could finance them better, and it could do that because it could borrow and repay more efficiently. Dutch financiers were an especially reliable source of war loans.[10] Of course, this was by no means England's only advantage: a superior naval strategy provided control of the seas and allowed it to blockade its continental enemies, aid its allies and expand its trade with every successful war.[11] Still, there can be no doubt that the capacity to incur debt was a major attribute of the successful warring state.

In the twentieth century, Britain still had its strategically important capacity to borrow, but it was unfortunate enough to lose the ability to pay debts back. Perhaps the Bush administration has understood that debt produced by war can humble even the mightiest. In the Gulf War, rather than borrowing, it has partly financed its campaign by getting others – notably Saudi Arabia, Kuwait, Japan and Germany – to contribute about $55 billion towards its costs.[12]

This means of financing war, however, is not open to all. A government that wants or needs to prosecute a war will usually have to meet the often enormous expense by borrowing from its own citizens and from bankers at home or abroad. War not only leads to debt; it may well reduce the ability to repay. Especially when conducted on home territory, war destroys economic assets, consumes foreign exchange (for importing arms, ammunition and other supplies) and hinders economic activity. So output falls, which reduces the capacity to pay off the debt.

There is little mystery about this form of the debt–war relationship, which continues to thrive. Table 6.4 ranks third world states by gross debt and by debt service ratio (the ratio of interest payments to export earnings). Of the 25 third world states with the biggest debts, 12 were at war in 1990 or early 1991. Of states with the highest debt service ratios, 12 of the top 27 were involved in war, and four of the top five.

Table 6.5 looks at the same issue from the other side: rather than showing which big debtors are at war, it shows which governments at war also carry heavy debt burdens. It uses both indicators from Table

6.4 and adds a third, showing which states have had to turn to the IMF or World Bank for the special loans. These loans are sought only by states having difficulty repaying debts and always come with strings attached. Of the 41 states involved in war in 1990 or 1991, data on debt are available for 38, of which 25 – about two-thirds of

Table 6.4: Debtors At War

Ranking Of Third World States by Gross Debt (US$bn)			War, 1990–1	Ranking Of Third World States By Debt Service Ratio		(%)	War, 1990–1
1	BRAZIL	(113)	–	1	NICARAGUA	96	YES
2	MEXICO	(113)	–	2	SOMALIA	81	YES
3	ARGENTINA	(65)	–	3	MOZAMBIQUE	72	YES
4	INDIA	(61)	YES	4	MADAGASCAR	64	–
5	EGYPT	(54)	YES	5	GUATEMALA	63	YES
6	INDONESIA	(54)	YES	6	ALGERIA	62	–
7	CHINA	(45)	YES	7	COTE D'IVOIRE	61	–
8	SOUTH KOREA	(44)	–	8	GHANA	59	–
9	TURKEY	(37)	YES	9	UGANDA	53	YES
10	NIGERIA	(32)	–	10	MEXICO	53	–
11	VENEZUELA	(30)	–	11	MYANMAR	52	YES
12	PHILIPPINES	(28)	YES	12	NIGER	51	–
13	ALGERIA	(28)	–	13	BOLIVIA	46	YES
14	THAILAND	(25)	–	14	CONGO	46	–
15	ISRAEL	(24)	YES	15	BRAZIL	44	–
16	CHILE	(22)	–	16	HONDURAS	42	–
17	PERU	(21)	YES	17	JAMAICA	42	–
18	MOROCCO	(21)	YES	18	COLOMBIA	41	YES
19	MALAYSIA	(20)	–	19	URUGUAY	41	–
20	PAKISTAN	(18)	YES	20	ARGENTINA	40	–
21	COLOMBIA	(17)	YES	21	INDONESIA	39	YES
22	IRAQ	(15)	YES	22	KENYA	37	–
23	COTE D'IVOIRE	(15)	–	23	VENEZUELA	37	–
24	ECUADOR	(13)	–	24	ETHIOPIA	36	YES
25	VIETNAM	(12)	–	25	PHILIPPINES	35	YES
					TURKEY	35	YES
					NIGERIA	35	–

Sources: OECD, *Financing and External Debt of Developing Countries: 1989 Survey* [Paris, OECD, 1990]; *World Bank, World Debt Tables 1989-90* [Washington DC, World Bank, 1989].
Note:
(1) Debt data are from 1988.
(2) Debt Service Ratio is the cost of servicing debt as a proportion of earnings from the export of goods and services. Thus, interest payments take up 96% of what Nicaragua earns from exports.
(3) Taiwan and the oil-rich Arab states of Saudi Arabia and the United Arab Emirates have been left out of the list of major debtors measured by gross debt.

Table 6.5: Debt Status Of Third World Countries At War, 1990-1

	War Began	Among Top 25 Debtors Measured by:		IMF/world Bank Special Arrangements 1980–90
		Gross Debt	Debt Service Ratio	
EGYPT	1991	–	–	YES
SAUDI ARABIA	1991	–	–	–
QATAR	1991	–	–	–
RWANDA	1990	–	–	–
IRAQ	1990	YES	N.A.	–
KUWAIT	1990	–	–	–
LIBERIA	1989	–	–	YES
PAPUA NEW GUINEA	1989	–	–	YES
CHINA	1987	–	–	–
SURINAME	1986	–	N.A.	–
COLOMBIA	1986	YES	YES	–
BOLIVIA	1985	–	YES	YES
ZIMBABWE	1984	–	–	–
SRI LANKA	1983	–	–	YES
PERU	1980	YES	–	YES
EL SALVADOR	1979	–	–	YES
IRAN	1978	–	N.A.	–
AFGHANISTAN	1978	–	N.A.	–
SOMALIA	1977	–	YES	YES
TURKEY	1977	YES	YES	YES
SYRIA	1976	–	–	–
MOZAMBIQUE	1976	–	YES	–
MOROCCO	1976	YES	–	YES
WESTERN SAHARA	1976	N.A.		
LEBANON	1975	–	N.A.	–
ANGOLA	1975	–	N.A.	–
BANGLADESH	1975	–	–	YES
CAMBODIA	1975	N.A.	N.A.	–
INDONESIA	1975	YES	YES	–
UGANDA	1971	–	YES	YES
NICARAGUA	1970	–	YES	–
PHILIPPINES	1969	YES	YES	YES
GUATEMALA	1968	–	YES	YES
CHAD	1965	–	–	–
SOUTH AFRICA	1964	N.A	–	–
ETHIOPIA	1962	–	YES	–
SUDAN	1955	–	–	YES
ISRAEL	1948	YES	N.A.	–
MYANMAR	1948	–	YES	–
PAKISTAN	1947	YES	–	YES
INDIA	1947	YES	–	YES

See next page for source.

Sources: On war, as for Table 6.1; on gross debt and debt service ratio, as for Table 6.4; on IMF and World Bank special arrangements, the International Monetary Fund, *Annual Report*, various years and the World Bank, *Annual Report*, various years.
Note: 'Special arrangements' include Structural Adjustment and stand-by loans, extended fund facilities, etc.
N.A. = Not applicable

---

the total – have heavy debt burdens. Long wars are even more closely associated with debt; of 27 states involved in war for more than a decade, data on debt are available for 24, of which 18 – exactly three-quarters – have heavy debt burdens.

There are, however, many cases in which the accumulation of debt results from several factors, not war alone. War has been a major cause of heavy debt in 12 states: El Salvador, Ethiopia, Guatemala, Israel, Mozambique, Morocco, Myanmar, Nicaragua, Somalia, Sri Lanka, Sudan and Uganda. Some other countries – such as Angola where war ended in 1991, and Laos and Vietnam whose several decades of war ended in 1988 – are not among the most heavily indebted but carry debts which are a serious burden on their impoverished societies. In other cases, like Egypt, India, Pakistan and Turkey, it is not so much war as high military spending – preparations for war – which constitutes the military factor in the build-up of debt.

Preparations for War

The most indebted state in the world is the US. Its national debt is in excess of 3 trillion dollars (including both domestic and external debt). That total represents the accumulation of deficits in successive annual budgets because, when budgets show a deficit, the government borrows. Chart 6.1 shows that during the Reagan presidency of 1981–8, annual deficits rose way past the levels associated with the Vietnam War, largely because the administration did not raise enough revenue through taxation to fund the boom in military spending from 1981 to 1985. Though US military spending stabilised in the years after 1985, because Congress refused to provide the funds on the bloated scale the military continued to demand, and despite some minor trimming as the Cold War ended, annual expenditure still runs to about $290 billion, not far short of $800 million daily. That figure excludes the effects of the Gulf War which was initially estimated to be costing the US somewhere between $500 million and $1 billion a day.[13]

The boom in military spending actually began in 1980, the last year of Carter's presidency but Reagan accelerated it. By then, the scale of the deficit was already increasing, reflecting longer term structural problems in US federal budgeting. These problems express themselves as a political stalemate between the Republican Party, which promises low taxes, and the Democrats who successfully defend spending on social programmes. Taken as a whole, the US body politic has consistently refused to raise enough revenues to fund the level of government spending it has decided on.[14] This political stalemate remains one cause of large deficits. The problem has been exacerbated by the policies of both the Reagan and Bush administrations. Having begun to fall at the end of the Reagan period, as Chart 6.1 shows, the annual federal deficit has now shot up again, largely because of the costs of clearing up the mess after the collapse of the savings and loans associations.

Chart 6.1: The US Federal Deficit 1940–88

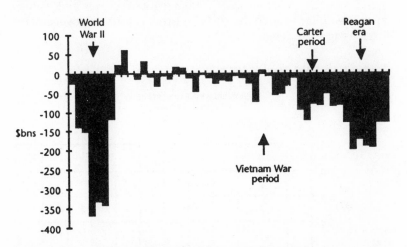

Source: *Historical Tables, Budget of the US Government, Fiscal Year 1990* [Washington DC, US Government Printing Office, 1989] Table 1.3.
Note: Constant dollars, Fiscal Year 1982 values. The transitional quarter between Fiscal Years 1976 and 1977, when the dates for the fiscal year were changed to run from 1 October to 30 September, has been omitted for convenience. The omission has no effect on the trends.

Thus, it would be wrong to attribute the scale of the federal deficit or the size of the national debt at the start of the 1990s *wholly* to military spending. There are other factors at work. But military spending is *substantially* responsible. Even after military spending was reined in during the second half of the 1980s, it accounted for about a quarter of total US federal government spending, and some 60 per cent of that part of the total government budget (only one quarter of it) which can be affected relatively easily by Congress and administration.[15]

Noteworthy, and perhaps even astonishing, is that, though the Reagan era deficits were smaller than those necessary to pay for the Second World War, they created a much larger relative long-term burden. Chart 6.2 shows that interest payments in the 1980s were taking a larger share of Gross National Product over a longer period than in the late 1940s and early 1950s. This reflects, in part, the greater cost of servicing large debt. It also reflects the Reagan administration's awesome propensity to borrow.

The loans the administration needed in the early 1980s in order to cover the budget deficits attracted foreign investors – especially British, Dutch and Japanese banks – because US interest rates were high. The loans had to be made in US currency so the dollar's value rose. These two developments – higher interest rates and a more expensive dollar – raised the costs for other countries' governments of servicing their debts.

Chart 6.2: US Debt Service 1940–88

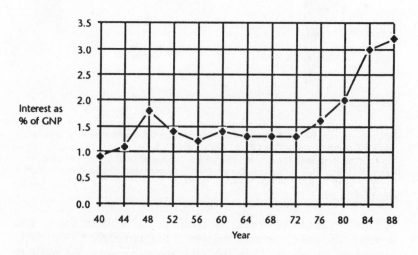

Federal Interest Payments as %
of GNP, 1940–88

Source: *Historical Tables, Budget of the US Government, Fiscal Year1990* [Washington, DC, US Government Printing Office, 1989] Table 6.2.
Note: As in Chart 6.1, the transitional quarter between FY1976 and FY1977 has been omitted.

Thus the Reagan boom in military spending increased the national debt burden not only in the US but further afield. Indeed, the rise in US interest rates triggered the debt crisis in 1982. In this sense, when one considers the deaths attributable to the debt crisis, the US's preparations for war in the early 1980s killed people in the third world without a shot being fired.

Military spending was not the sole cause of the growth of third world debts up to 1982, but it was a major factor. Third world governments – especially those categorised as upper- and-middle income developing countries, but also some low-income countries – borrowed heavily to pay for imports of advanced weaponry. Initially, the main purchasers were oil-exporting states in the Middle East whose wealth grew dramatically after the oil price rises of 1974. But others also imported more, and most financed their purchases, at least in part, through loans. According to one estimate, between 1960 and 1987 third world governments borrowed close to $400 billion to fund arms imports from advanced industrial states.[16]

Chart 6.3: Third World Arms Imports 1970–89

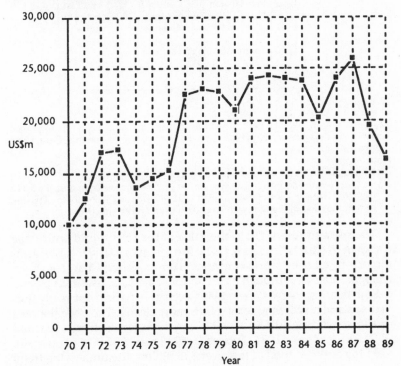

Chart 6.4: Third World Arms Imports by Region 1970–87

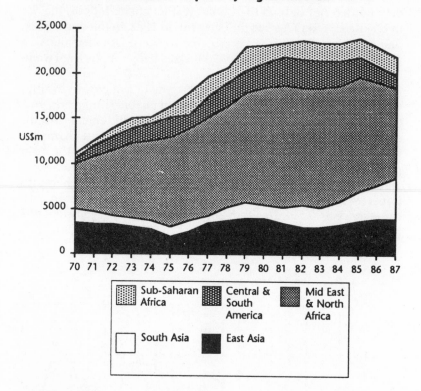

Charts 6.3 & 6.4
Source of: I. Anthony & H. Wulf, 'The trade in major conventional weapons', *World Armaments & Disarmament: SIPRI Yearbook 1990* [Oxford, Oxford University Press, 1990] (Appendix 7A).
Note:
(1) Figures are in US$m at constant 1985 prices.
(2) In Chart 6.4, the figures for each year are five-year moving averages; thus, the figure for 1980 is the average of the figures of 1978–82 inclusive. Using these eliminates odd jumps and dips and reveals long-term trends more effectively.

The rise and recent fall in the value of the third world arms trade is shown in Charts 6.3 and 6.4. The former gives yearly totals in arms imports by all third world countries taken together; Chart 6.4 shows regional totals and, though based on the same data, uses a simple statistical technique – five-year moving averages – to iron out yearly fluctuations and reveal long-term trends more clearly. The trade boomed in the second half of the 1970s, began to level off in 1981 and started to decline in 1984. Though in 1986 and 1987 it leapt up again, reaching a record total of just over $26 billion, the underlying trend was downwards; the fall in its value continued in 1988 and 1989. The Middle East has been by far the biggest regional arms importer. But while the value of imports there fell the late 1980s, like the world total, the value in South Asia increased strongly.

This increase is almost entirely due to India which, as Table 6.6 shows, was the largest third world importer of arms in the second half of the 1980s, displacing Iraq. These two states together with Saudi Arabia were responsible for one-third of third world arms imports from 1985 to 1989. The trade is highly concentrated, with the top 15 importers making almost 80 per cent by value of all purchases during that period.

Table 6.6: Top Third World Arms Importers 1985–9

Ranking		State	Arms Imports 1985–89		Ranking by Gross Debt [if in top 25]
In Third World	In Whole World		Value [US$m, 1985 prices]	Share of Third World Total	
1	1	INDIA	17,345	15.7	4th
2	2	IRAQ	11,989	10.9	22nd
3	4	SAUDI ARABIA	8,764	8.0	*
4	5	SYRIA	5,876	5.3	–
5	6	EGYPT	5,795	5.3	5th
6	8	NORTH KOREA	5,275	4.8	–
7	10	TURKEY	4,751	4.3	9th
8	12	AFGHANISTAN	4,610	4.2	–
9	13	ANGOLA	3,719	3.4	–
10	15	LIBYA	3,186	2.9	–
11	19	TAIWAN	2,946	2.7	**
12	20	IRAN	2,940	2.7	–
13	21	PAKISTAN	2,919	2.7	20th
14	22	SOUTH KOREA	2,794	2.6	8th
15	24	ISRAEL	2,687	2.5	15th

Sources: On debt, as for Tables 6.4 and 6.5; on the arms trade, I. Anthony & H. Wulf, 'The trade in major conventional weapons', *World Armaments & Disarmament: SIPRI Yearbook 1990* [Oxford, Oxford University Press, 1990] Table 7.2.
Notes
* Saudi Arabia's gross debt in 1988 was $15 billion, the same as Iraq's, but with its oil revenues this level of debt did not constitute a real problem.
** Taiwan's gross debt in 1988 was $18 billion, the same as Pakistan's, but its strong export industries meant this level of debt was not a problem.

The heavy concentration distorts the overall pattern of the trade as revealed in Chart 6.3. The renewed growth in the trade in 1986 and 1987, following two years of decline, was in some senses artificial.

In 1986, the value of the trade jumped by a little under $3 billion; almost all of this is accounted for by the increased purchases of just two states: $1800 million by India (virtually doubling its imports) and $950 million by Saudi Arabia (a two-thirds increase). In 1987 there was a similar pattern. The increase in the value of the trade in the third world as a whole was $2600 million. Four states, however, increased their purchases by a combined total considerably in excess of that figure; they were India (up by $900 million, increasing its imports by a quarter), Egypt ($680 million, a 40 per cent rise), Iraq ($1800 million, 75 per cent) and Israel ($1180 million, a one-off jump of 265 per cent over the previous year).[17] Had it not been for these large increases by a few states, the value of the arms trade in the third world would have continued the decline it began in 1984. In the event, the fall was renewed in 1988 and 1989.

By the end of the 1980s, the third world arms market's value had fallen back to about the level it was at in the mid-1970s, before the boom, at just over $16 billion. At that point, imports by third world countries were worth just over half the value of the total international arms trade; at their peak in 1987, they had been worth two-thirds of the global total.[18] The reason for the decline was simply that many third world governments could no longer afford imports in such quantities as new loans became harder to find and ever more expensive to service. The sharpest fall was Angola's: imports in 1987 were worth over $1 billion; two years later they were worth $24 million, a fall of 98 per cent. Argentina stopped figuring as a major arms importer (that is, among the top 15) only in 1989. Similarly, Nigeria had been among the big buyers until 1986.[19]

The boom is over but the debts remain. Argentina is the third largest third world debtor and Nigeria the tenth largest. Of the top 15 third world arms importers from 1985 to 1989, the data show that nine of them carry heavy debts.

From Debt to War

The Gulf War

From war to debt, the connection is well established and, as we have seen, flourishing today. The connection the other way round, from debt to war, is less clearly established in the aggregate but, among recent wars, there is one very clear case of the causality working in that direction – the Gulf War. In fact, there are so many debt-war links that one wonders if this war did not inaugurate a new era in the relationship between debt and conflict.

The origins of the Gulf War owe much, though not all, to debt. During the 1980–8 war against Iran, Iraq was financed by other Gulf states. Nominally the money was borrowed, but Saddam Hussein believed or pretended to believe the loans would never be called in. In Iraq, the war is officially known as the 'Qadisiyyat Saddam', named after the great Arab victory over the Persians in Qadissiyah in southern Iraq in AD 636. Saddam argued that Iran was the old Persian enemy, against whom Iraq was fighting on behalf of the Arab nation. Other Arab states, he held, were duty bound to fund him. Kuwait saw things differently and after the war insisted it should be repaid sums which were variously reported at $10 or $12 billion.[20] So doing, it courted disaster.

Naturally, Iraq did not invade Kuwait solely because of the debt. Saddam's Ba'athist regime also made territorial claims on a state he said had no right to exist, its borders having been 'artificially' drawn up by the British (as were Iraq's own, but no matter). When Kuwait became independent in 1961, its annexation by Iraq was forestalled only by an airlift of British troops.[21] Saddam made a second, more limited claim for two virtual mudflats – Warbah and Bubiyan Islands – to gain egress to the Gulf. Perhaps more pertinent in the short term, Iraq also had economic and financial complaints against Kuwait, in addition to the debt issue. Saddam accused Kuwait of over-fulfilling its quota for oil production agreed by the Organisation of Petroleum Exporting Countries. The result was that oil prices were driven down, hurting Iraq whose economy was 95 per cent dependent on oil revenues. It needed higher prices so it could recover from eight and a half years of war. The accusation was valid, though Kuwait was not OPEC's only quota-breaker. Saddam also accused Kuwait of stealing oil from the Iraqi part of the Rumaila oilfield which sits on both sides of the border.

On top of this list of claims and grievances, there were further unstated motives. One was greed, for by annexing Kuwait, Iraq doubled its oil reserves and got hold of some $8 billion in the Kuwaiti treasury. Another was Saddam's ambition to make Iraq the major power in the Gulf region. And his shift to an aggressive posture towards Kuwait during 1990 may also have been shaped by domestic considerations. The Iraqi people wanted and were not getting an economic pay-off after the privation during the long war with Iran. By annexing Kuwait, Saddam may have sought both to distract the people and to take a short cut towards meeting at least some of their material needs.

The reasons for Iraq's invasion of Kuwait, then, were by no means confined to debt. Not unusually, one finds a complex set of motives lying behind an act of aggression. But debt figured strongly among them. Even after a month of US and allied bombing, when Saddam first acknowledged the possibility of withdrawing from Kuwait, sorting out Iraq's debts remained a prominent goal. In its statement, the Iraq Revolutionary Command Council insisted that, 'All debts owed to aggressor Gulf and foreign countries by Iraq ... should be forgiven.'[22]

Debt also played an important role in other states' participation in the Gulf War. Though the full story is not available as we go to press, it is already clear that, in the lead-up to the war, the US exploited the power of debt and found in it an asset as valuable as strategic raw materials.

In September 1990, the US announced it would forgive $7 billion worth of Egyptian debt.[23] Egypt had incurred the debt to purchase American military equipment, some of which, presumably, was with its forces deployed in Saudi Arabia as part of the US-led coalition against Iraq. For the US, there is a process here of feedback which is not just positive but creative. Egypt's pro-American policy led it to purchase US weapons and thus get into debt to the US. That debt provided an incentive to Egypt to be a very significant member of the US coalition against Iraq, and gave the US administration a way of rewarding its client for loyalty by eliminating that same debt. Further rewards came when Egypt's Arab creditors, mainly Saudi Arabia and the government-in-exile of Kuwait, agreed to forgive a further $6.5 billion of debt and give the Cairo government $2 billion in direct grants, while between $5 billion and $10 billion of foreign debt, owed to governments of major industrial countries, were also wiped out.[24] In sum, Egypt's agreement to participate in the grand coalition earned it between $20 billion and $25 billion, mostly in written-off debt.

Why was Egypt's participation worth so much? Though it bears repeating that the full story is not yet known, enough has come out to have a sense of the crucial role Egypt's President Mubarak played. He appears to have made a key change of policy at a critical point, early in the Gulf crisis, in the two days following the Iraqi invasion of Kuwait. According to accounts which have surfaced from Jordanian sources, several Arab states – including Saudi Arabia, Jordan and Egypt – believed that Saddam meant only to give Kuwait's rulers a quick, hard warning.[25] The idea was an incursion, swiftly followed by withdrawal, and then a return to negotiations, which had hitherto proved fruitless, to discuss Iraq's various claims upon Kuwait. In this belief, King Fahd of Saudi Arabia, King Hussein of Jordan and President Mubarak agreed to avoid public condemnation of the invasion, since that would make withdrawal politically difficult if not impossible. At the last moment, Mubarak backed out of this agreement and publicly condemned the invasion. Explaining himself to King Hussein of Jordan, he reportedly said he was 'under tremendous pressure'.

If there was pressure on Mubarak to change policy and ensure there could be no easy settlement (if such a settlement were possible – a thought which became anathema to the whole Western news media), there is only one possible source for it. And if this account is reliable, at least as far as the views and statements of the Arab leaders are concerned, regardless of whether they interpreted Iraq's aims accurately,* then it would seem that 'pressure' is a new euphemism for bribery.

This does not mean the Bush administration intended war against Iraq from the very first. There is no clear evidence about when the decision was taken not to rely on sanctions but to use force to compel Iraq's withdrawal from Kuwait. One account of the Bush administration's policy-making suggests the decision took shape in October 1990.[26] But the decision to force a confrontation, where it may not have been wholly necessary, seems to have been taken immediately after the invasion.

One of the rewards Egypt received came with strings attached. Of the three rounds of debt-forgiveness, the third – for $5–10 billion – was dependent on Egypt's accepting the familiar package of financial and economic policies consistently favoured by the IMF. For two years, the Mubarak government had been refusing to agree to this programme, arguing it needed more time to implement it than the IMF was willing to allow, so as to avoid short-term economic damage. It seems that Egypt's support for US policy against Iraq led the IMF to be more sympathetic to this worry. It agreed to modify the programme's timing. But it remains fundamentally the same programme; even if the immediate price is lower, the long-term cost will be the same as in other cases – sacrifices by the people and restricted independence for the government.

On the other hand, many governments might well envy this 40–50 per cent debt reduction. The economic effects of the Gulf War have been serious and widespread, despite the US stating it intended to help heavily indebted governments whose problems were exacerbated by higher oil prices.[27] In the catastrophic economic consequences of the war, we find a further debt-war link; this time, war

* The Iraqi invasion of Kuwait was on 2 August 1990; on 8 August came the announcement that Kuwait was annexed. Though short, this delay is consistent with the view that Saddam's initial intention did not go as far as annexation. It is possible he decided upon it only because public condemnation made withdrawal politically impossible.

exacerbates debt problems, even (or perhaps especially) for non-combatant states.

For the Philippines, for example, the cost of the Gulf crisis by the end of 1990 was already half a billion dollars: the increased cost of oil was responsible for $400 million, while the value of lost remittances from workers in Iraq and Kuwait amounted to over $100 million.[28] Though oil prices fell when war began, returning to their levels before the August invasion, another period of high prices could still exact a heavy toll: the direct cost to Brazil if oil were to be priced at $30 a barrel for a year, for example, was estimated to be $3 billion.[29] Oil exporting debtors such as Mexico, Nigeria and Venezuela would benefit from higher prices, of course. Overall, however, early reckonings of the economic effect of the war reveal a terrible toll. At least 40 countries have lost more than 1 per cent of Gross National Product (GNP), which is the established benchmark for defining a 'natural disaster'.[30] Bangladesh has lost about $1.5 billion, Yemen has lost $1 billion, and $1 billion has been lost by 14 sub-Saharan African countries which were already in dire straits.[31] Perhaps worst hit of all was Jordan: it lost one-quarter of its GNP and the proportion of its population living below the poverty line increased from 20 to 30 per cent between August 1990 and March 1991.[32]

If Egypt was rewarded for supporting the US, the case of Jordan reveals the the other side of the coin. The US's announcement that Egypt's debt would be forgiven coincided with a warning to King Hussein that he could not expect economic aid if he did not toe the anti-Iraq line.[33] The policy is based, not very subtly but nonetheless effectively, on a classic carrot-and-stick approach. Egypt's government-to-government debt allowed for a particularly direct reward for supporting US policy. In other cases, the US can use its influence within the IMF and the World Bank to secure the same outcome, offering rewards and threatening punishment as appropriate.

Desperate Choices

The Gulf War is not typical of modern warfare. It was unusual not only in its intensity and brevity but also because it was a war between states. The vast majority of today's wars are fought between states and their citizens. They are symptomatic of the failure of a model of development these countries have implemented. The economic and social conditions it has created form a breeding ground for violence. As the development prospects of third world countries come increasingly to be determined by the debt crisis, so the terms and management of debt must be identified among the underlying causes of violence and conflict.

When the ordinary conditions of life are a violence, a violent attempt to change them is only to be expected. That reactive violence may be individualistic or collective; that is, it may mean criminal or political activity. If collective, it may be more or less disorganised, as in rioting, or highly organised and disciplined as in war or terrorism. The character of the violence will be decided by many things – personal psychology, familial circumstance, social pressures and inhibitions, national history and political opportunities among them. Neither debt nor any other economic indicator is likely to do much to explain why one individual does or does not choose to join the guerrillas. What it may do, however, is set the context of desperation within which desperate choices are made.

Table 6.7: Political Violence 1987–91

ARGENTINA	late 1980s/1990	Riots, terrorism, attempted military coups, recent history of military dictatorship
BRAZIL	late 1980s, 1990	Terrorism, death squads killing street children & political activists, recent history of military dictatorship
CAMEROON	1990	Anti-government riots
CÔTE D'IVOIRE	1990	Anti-government riots
GABON	1990	Anti-government riots
HAITI	1991	Attempted military coup, recent history of dictatorship & violent repression including 'disappearances'
JORDAN	1989	Anti-government riots
KENYA	1990	Anti-government riots; government repression includes extra-legal executions
MALI	1991	Anti-government riots
MEXICO	1989/90	Government use of troops & violent policing to suppress strikes & general political unrest; government repression includes extra-legal executions
NEPAL	1990	Democracy uprising despite killings by government forces
NIGER	1990	Ethnic conflict including massacre of Tuaregs
TRINIDAD & TOBAGO	1990	Anti-government riots
VENEZUELA	1989	Anti-government riots: over 300 dead
ZAMBIA	1990	Anti-government riots at time of attempted overthrow of president

Sources: Press reports

Table 6.7 shows 15 third world countries in which, during the late 1980s and the very early 1990s, there was major violence which did not amount to war. In every case, large numbers of people were or are involved; the ensuing deaths numbered from a handful to several hundred, together with many injuries. Every one of these countries has a serious debt problem; all have had to turn to the IMF or World Bank for the special agreements and attached conditions which are the fate of the heavy debtors. In all, though to varying degrees, the economic conditions which grow from indebtedness are important factors in conflict. To summarise:

- Argentina's high inflation and poor economic performance, combined with the reduced government spending demanded by the IMF and World Bank, have spoiled the hopes raised by democratisation in 1983, creating conditions in which some turn to terrorism while others, against their interests, long for a return to military rule.
- Similar causes in Brazil have strengthened movements for radical change. In violent response, workers' and Indian leaders have been murdered. Death squads are flourishing. Made up of off-duty police and military personnel, the death squads have also mounted a campaign of murdering street children.
- In Cameroon, like Côte d'Ivoire and Gabon, long-term political stability was upturned in 1990 as masses of people rioted in protest against their government's austere economic policies and authoritarianism.
- In Haiti, the latest round of violence in January 1991 was a mass mobilisation to protect democracy from the reassembling wolves of the old Duvalier dictatorship. It is a simple matter of the poor desperately needing democracy while the privileged would accept a return to dictatorship.
- In Jordan, price rises sparked an uprising which demanded democracy and led to the election of a national assembly of limited powers.
- In Kenya, pressure for democracy creates periodic violence as, once again, an elite which has done well out of dictatorship by first Kenyatta and now Arap Moi is threatened by the mobilisation of the masses.
- In Mali, 100 to 200 people were killed in demonstrations for democracy and against a corrupt, authoritarian regime and its economic failures.
- In Mexico, the debt burden has both intensified the struggles of workers' movements and, because it has eroded support for the

one-party state's government, escalated the violence of the government's response.

- In Nepal, the impoverished and powerless joined the street protests demanding democracy. They got the promise of it.
- In Niger, the social tensions and ethnic conflicts which attend a development process going nowhere erupted into a government massacre of Tuaregs, the ethnic minority, following protests at living conditions.
- In Trinidad and Tobago, a Muslim uprising led to large-scale looting. The rebels seemed to have little support for their solutions to the country's problems, but general agreement – even within the government – on the diagnosis of economic mismanagement and inequality.
- In Venezuela, price rises and economic austerity were greeted by riots, to which government forces responded with extraordinary violence.
- News of the overthrow of Zambia's President Kaunda was followed by celebrations in the street amid anger at the way a country which ten years ago seemed to have relatively good economic prospects had since been ground down. The coup against Kaunda, however, had failed.

Table 6.8 records similar kinds of violence in 21 third world countries from 1976 to 1986, all in response to austerity measures. It adds skeleton comments on later salient events. To summarise:

- In six countries, wars were active at the time (El Salvador, Guatemala, Morocco, the Philippines, Sudan and Turkey); in all six, the wars continue.
- In Bolivia and Peru, violence later escalated into war.
- In Jamaica violence surfaces every election time.
- In Turkey, there was a military coup during the disturbances, ousting the more or less democratic government.
- The dictators in eight countries were later overthrown:

  - in Argentina, Brazil and Chile, democracy was restored, but in Argentina and Brazil, violence has remained chronic; in all three countries the forces which supported dictatorship remain powerful;
  - in Haiti and the Philippines, democracy was restored but is still threatened;
  - in Panama, the dictator was voted out but stayed in power until US forces invaded, took him away and occupied the country;

- in Sudan, one dictator replaced another; later the war escalated;
- likewise in Liberia, one dictator ousted another, producing a vicious tyranny which ended in 1990 after an atrociously bloody civil war.

Table 6.8: Political Violence and Economic Austerity, 1976–86

State	Dates	Later Events
Argentina	1982–5	Democratisation, 1983; economic catastrophe; endemic violence; occasional attempted coups
Bolivia	1983–5	War began 1986
Brazil	1983	Democratisation, 1985; endemic violence; death squads
Chile	1983–5	Democratisation, 1989
Dominican Republic	1984–5	
Ecuador	1982–3	
Egypt	1977	President Sadat assassinated, 1981
El Salvador	1985–6	War continued
Ghana	1978	Coups 1979 and 1981
Guatemala	1985	War continued
Haiti	1985	Coups 1986 & 1988; democratisation 1990–1; attempted coup 1991
Jamaica	1979 & 1985	Repeated political violence
Liberia	1979	Coup 1980; uprising, civil war & massacre 1985; civil war 1989–91
Morocco	1981 & 1984	War in Western Sahara continued
Panama	1983	US invasion December 1989
Peru	1976–85	Guerrilla war began 1980
Philippines*	?	Marcos overthrown; anti-Aquino coup attempted; war continued
Sudan	1982 & 1985	Coup 1985; war escalated late 1980s
Tunisia	1984	Rise of Islamic fundamentalism
Turkey	1980	Coup 1980; war with Kurds continued
Zaire	1980	

Sources: D. Sulmont, Deuda y Trabajadores: un reto para la solidaridad [Lima, ADEC-ATC, 1988] pp. 64–73; various sources as for Table 6.1 including press reports
Note
* Sulmont gives no date for the incidents in the Philippines. The description he gives, however, suggests they were before the overthrow of the Marcos dictatorship in 1986.

By no means all the countries where there is serious violence ascend the ladder of conflict to full-scale war. But there is a widespread pattern of violence begetting violence, to which many third world governments seem to have no response except more violence. A major reason for this is the pressure of debt.

Table 6.9: The Proportion of Total Government Spending Allocated to Military Spending and Debt Service

	External Debt Service, % of Total Gov't Spending	Military Spending, % Total Gov't Spending	% of Total Gov't Spending
	(1)	*(2)*	*(1 + 2)*
EL SALVADOR	41	26	67
BOLIVIA	52	14	66
COLOMBIA [1987 Figures]	51	14	65
PHiLIPPINES	44	12	56
INDONESIA	48	8	56
TURKEY	45	10	55
PAKISTAN	23	30	53
UGANDA	25	26	51
ISRAEL	20	27	47
MEXICO	40	1	41
VENEZUELA	35	6	41
KENYA	30	9	39
PERU	16	20	36
ARGENTINA	27	7	34
SRI LANKA	23	10	33
INDIA	13	19	32
BRAZIL	21	4	25
NEPAL	6	6	12

Sources: OECD, Financing and External Debt of Developing Countries: *1989 Survey* [Paris, OECD, 1990]; *World Bank, World Development Report 1990* [Oxford, Oxford University Press, 1990]; S. Sen, 'Debt, financial flows and international security', World Armament & Disarmament: SIPRI Yearbook 1990 [Oxford, Oxford University Press, 1990].
Note
This table lists states where there was civil war in 1990/1, or violent conflict short of war in the late 1980s and early 1990s, and for which data are available.

Debt is squeezing the hope out of societies whose governments have borrowed too heavily. It also directly squeezes government resources. Table 6.9 shows the proportions of government spending taken by servicing debt and by military spending, for those countries which were at war in 1990/1 or where there was serious violence from 1987 to 1991 (that is, the countries in Tables 6.1 and 6.7), where data are available. The percentages in the right hand column in Table 6.9 can be regarded as being comparable with the figure given earlier in this chapter, that 75 per cent of English and Spanish government spending in the late sixteenth century was for current or previous wars. No government shown in Table 6.9 quite scales those Tudor heights, though a few are not far behind. But 400 years ago, much less was expected of central government for the welfare of the people. Major health and education programmes were things of the future. Heavy spending on urban infrastructure and an effective road system were not known. There were no price subsidies to protect people from the vagaries of a global market which did not exist. When modern expectations of government are taken into account, it might be fair to regard 40 per cent as a threshold. If more than that proportion of government spending is allocated to debt service and to the military, the result is a serious squeeze on government resources. Regardless of what governments would like to do, whatever their preferred policies would be, they are unable to fund the programmes which could ease the lot of the mass of people in the short term, and lay the foundations for more widespread prosperity in the long term. Even where debt is not the initial cause of problems, it blights solutions.

There are many governments that would probably not develop solutions which would improve the conditions of the majority of the people, even if they had the resources. In Myanmar, for example, an enlightened government could seek to break through the logjam of hate and warfare with a classic programme of policies from which the mass of ordinary people could benefit in real, material, immediate ways. No such thing could be expected from the current regime. But even if the government were different, it would find such programmes difficult to finance because of the debt burden. Like the Aquino government in the Philippines, it would face a choice between servicing the debt and financing programmes to aid the poor. When the Aquino government chose to service the debt, it guaranteed that the war it inherited from the Marcos regime would continue. And should it win the war, unless it chooses then to sacrifice the debt for the poor instead of the other way round, it will guarantee the ground will remain fertile for violent conflict. In Bolivia and Peru, the warfare of the 1980s is, in part, simply a symptom of the failure of development, in the same way as reliance on cocaine exports. Debt has not caused the wars; it has, however, made it harder to prevent them, and harder now to stop them.

From War to War

We tend to think about war the way we were told to by Carl von Clausewitz, nineteenth-century Prussian general and military philosopher. He defined it as 'an act of force to compel our enemy to do our will' and, more famously, as 'the continuation of policy by other means'.[34] The latter statement is also worded as 'a continuation of political activity by other means'. It summarises the conclusion of an argument about the relationship between means and ends which Clausewitz stated more fully as: 'Policy, then, will permeate all military operations, and, in so far as their violent nature will admit, it will have a continuous influence on them.' He regarded this as the most important of his insights. It is as much prescriptive as descriptive: 'He insists and reiterates that war is always *an instrument of policy* because he knew, and we know today, that the usual practice is rather to let war take over national policy.'[35]

Clausewitz's rational, ordered emphasis on the link between war and policy is all very well if we seek to understand the causes and course of a conflict such as the Gulf War. It can be difficult to identify exactly what policy either side intended the war to serve, but that is because official propaganda obscures the full story, or because the policy may seem ill-judged. But at bottom we do not doubt that both sides had war aims.

Some wars, however, get to a point when it is legitimate to wonder whether there are any aims of real salience to the conflict. War is always terrible, but it can deteriorate. It can cease to be a means and become an end in itself. The armed groups begin to focus on ensuring their own survival, and on doing whatever is necessary for that, in the name of a long-term goal. Over a period, grisly experience cauterises sensibilities and suffocates idealism. More and more, the long-term goal receives only a ritual genuflection; it becomes detached from the real business of the war. As one writer on guerrilla war put it, 'Once the banner of rebellion has been raised and blood has been shed, it is no easy matter to give up. The rebels begin to fight for whatever reason: they continue because they must.'[36] The Clausewitzian link between war and policy is broken and the result is violence virtually for its own sake.

It does not happen with all wars, but it makes a common pattern in South America, Africa, South Asia and Southeast Asia. For example:

- In Colombia in 1990 and 1991, the largest and most effective guerrilla groups abandoned war; the smaller, less effective ones fight on.
- In Liberia, the defeat and death of the tyrant Doe in 1990, and in Somalia the defeat and flight of the tyrant Barre in 1991, have been followed by fighting among those who overthrew them.
- In Uganda, rational war aims have been a contradiction in terms for a decade; war has become banditry.
- In India, the long guerrilla campaigns of the Naxalites in Andhra Pradesh and Bihar are fought mainly to keep the Naxalites in existence; in other provinces, war has descended into banditry.

- In Myanmar (formerly Burma), some of the anti-government armies started out as opium gangs – notably, the ex-Kuomintang irregulars who arrived in Burma after losing to the Communists in China in 1949; other insurgent armies came to the opium trade as a convenient source of revenue only after years of fighting.
- In Malaysia, the guerrilla war which was at its height in the 1950s – the 'Emergency' – finally ended in December 1989, a year after joint Thai-Malaysian air strikes against the Communists' camps in southern Thailand. What war aims the guerrillas could reasonably have had during the intervening three decades is a mystery.

In part, what we see in these cases is the self-reproduction of violence, the habit of war. But to say that is not enough. Consider the many long guerrilla wars. While few forces can claim the longevity of those in Myanmar, or of the Malayan Communists before they surrendered, a decade is by no means unusually long, as Table 6.1 shows. Yet to fight for even a few years, a guerrilla force must renew itself. It must gain new recruits to replace those who are killed, or wounded too seriously to return as combatants, or who desert, or die of disease.

Where does it find those new recruits? Some guerrillas terrorise peasants into joining them. Some draw on political idealists. But almost all of them also recruit from the impoverished, the miserable, the starving, the people with no other prospects, with no hope and no reason for hope.

Debt is neither the only nor the original cause of privation in the third world. But through it, much of the third world is held in conditions of desperation. It is the oxygen of the fire of war.

Conclusion

From country to country, the details inevitably differ. Yet at a general level, it is the same dreary story. We witness the failure of a development model still enthusiastically endorsed by the IMF and the World Bank, the main managers of the debt system. It is a slow failure. It wounds and it tortures before it kills. In its current stage, the key element is the way debt drains countries of their material and spiritual resources. It is a violence; in response, for some, violence seems the only or at least the best option. Sometimes that violence is in the form of a riot, sometimes a new war, sometimes an old one.

Most wars today are messy, long-running, civil wars. They happen in places of which most people in the richer countries know little and care less. Occasionally, there is a movement of generosity towards the victims; the combination of war and famine in Cambodia in the late 1970s, in Ethiopia in the mid-1980s and in Mozambique a year or two later touched consciences and fellow-feeling. But for most of the time, for most of the wars, that does not happen.

Wars in the third world are far away and it is only human to feel they ought to – and are likely to – stay that way. But for a long time, it has seemed probable to those who follow these things closely that some conflicts at least would not remain so remote. From the Middle East, the export of terrorism has shown one way in which wars could chase after the populations of the richer countries. The explosion of a dispute between two Arab states into a major war involving the most large-scale use yet seen of the most destructive conventional military technology has shown another way.

It is, of course, easier to sense a general risk than to predict its future specific source. It may not be the Middle East. In 1990, there was a surge of violent conflicts short of war in Africa. It affected the ex-colonies of both the British and French empires, reflecting the general failure of post-colonial development. No predictions – but full-blown wars may start there and thence may come new exports of terrorism. India and Pakistan are riven by conflicts, some at the level of war, others not. Those conflicts could easily flow over into Europe at some point. The crisis in Latin America is acute, and involves several wars as well as the terrorism of death squads. Already the export of cocaine to the US has added new dimensions to its social problems and violence. Will the export of war follow?

To do nothing to remove the conditions which create war and brutality in the third world is, very simply, to risk waking up to find that war and brutality have, like all boomerangs, come home.

Conclusion

The personnel of the World Bank and the IMF, of our national aid bureaucracies and government agencies refer to themselves as 'professionals'. Ask them, for instance, how many people there are in their department and they reply – carefully distinguishing themselves from their 'support staff' – 'X or Y professionals'. Their view of themselves is similar to that held by a doctor or a lawyer and they believe this view is justified since they generally possess several diplomas and considerable field experience.

But in one crucial respect, people working in the field of 'development' are wholly disqualified from claiming 'professional' status. Unlike other, genuine, professionals, they are accountable to no one (except in the ordinary hierarchical way). If they make a mess of a development project, they will not be there to see it and they can walk away from their victims, towards the next disaster. In the realm of their professional conduct, they are not even accountable to themselves or to their fellow members of the corporation because they are not held to any particular ethical norms.

Doctors are: they swear the Hippocratic oath and can be excluded from their profession (or sued for malpractice by their patients); shady, dishonest lawyers can be disbarred; overtly sinful priests unfrocked. Scientists and professors understand their duty to publish only what they believe conforms to the data and to the truth, so far as they can know it. Professional standards may not always be perfectly upheld by all members of all professions, but they are, on the whole, recognised and maintained. Above all, they exist. We know – society knows – at least in a general way what the rules for professional people are and how they are supposed to behave.

Yet when it comes to determining the economic destiny of entire nations and disrupting, ruining or terminating the livelihoods – indeed the lives – of millions, no similar standards apply. In the development domain, no universally accepted measures, no acknowledged methods exist for distinguishing fact from dogma, truth from falsehood, success from failure, myth from reality. As a consequence, the practice of these 'professionals' can proceed forever with no reality check ever intervening. The fact that most of them, and the agencies they work for, are totally beyond the reach of any sort of political accountability as well only serves to make matters worse.

The myth of 'development' has been functioning virtually undisturbed for decades now; everywhere sowing chaos and destruction. Our civilisation – such as it is – cannot seem to recognise, much less confront, the irrational beliefs underlying the whole notion of development. Nor do we seem to grasp that the current doctrine, the one that affirms that somehow, left to itself, the market will provide everything for everyone, is inherently crazy. Our inability to see the naked emperors parading all around us is perhaps due to the widespread belief that ours is a rational society run by people who know what they are doing. But if our society is purely rational, technocratic, bureaucratic, scientific and all the rest of it, then it is the first one in the history of the world to function that way, without myths. Somehow, this seems unlikely.*

If the myths upon which the official theory and practice of 'development' or 'structural adjustment' rest were merely quaint and harmless, all would be well. Unfortunately, this is not the case. The tribal gods of the development professionals and the structural adjusters are demanding more sacrifices every day. Since I began working more or less full time on *The Debt Boomerang*, about 300,000 third world kids have died as a direct result of the debt crisis – I use UNICEF's figures as a basis for this calculation. In the North, as I hope this book has amply demonstrated, we have continued to lose our jobs, our savings, and part of the quality of life in our cities – as we wait for the climate to deteriorate to the point where even the president of the United States will have to admit the possibility of the greenhouse effect.

Many of those who consider themselves 'professionals' are simply innocents, whatever their advanced university degrees. They function quite happily within the confines of the mythical structures. Some do not question because they are well paid not to; others are the true believers, the priesthood. For them, the debt crisis is being rationally dealt with; the remedies of the Bank, the Fund and the US Treasury will put everything right if we just keep applying them vigorously enough, and long enough. Meanwhile, it doesn't really matter how many poor people get hurt – such people are generally in the way anyhow.

---

* For proof that it is not only unlikely but impossible, see Gilbert Rist and Fabrizio Sabelli, *Il était une fois le développement* ... ('Once upon a time, development') Editions d'en Bas, Lausanne, Switzerland 1986; and Rist, Sabelli and Dominique Perrot, *Les Dieux sont Tombés sur la Terre*, Presses Universitaires de France, Paris 1992, forthcoming.

At an entirely different level of responsibility are those who profit from the power of the myth and who spend their lives entrenching its hegemony. They are a tiny minority and their 'natural opponents' constitute most of humanity. In the South, the victims of the debt crisis do not need a book like this one to tell them that they are victimised: they feel it in their bellies and they see it in the hollow eyes of their children.

For the moment, in the North, the effects are less obvious, but they will become increasingly poignant as it finally dawns on people, in the most disagreeable way, that there are literally billions of potential workers out there prepared to accept virtually any wage; that a few people in our own countries are delighted that this should be so. The debt crisis helps to put us in direct competition with the desperate and the destitute. It is not an exaggeration to affirm that the way we solve this crisis, or don't, will determine our own living standards for generations to come. Advantages painfully won can disappear almost overnight.

The task of research, and of the researcher, is to uncover what is hidden, to make transparent what is opaque and to reveal links, and meaning, where one might least suspect them. I hope, and believe, that we who have contributed to this book have practised our craft honourably. But one should have no illusions that merely exposing those links, making this meaning more manifest can, in and of itself, dislodge or defeat the interests that profit from present arrangements and from the smokescreen that habitually surrounds them.

For this to happen, we must first think for ourselves and recognise the modern mythology that prevents us from acting; then act. This book shows some obvious directions to take to help the 'natural majority' – now suffering to one degree or another from the debt crisis – to become effective. Trade unionists and other workers, farmers, NGOs and solidarity groups, 'greens', immigrants and people working for immigrant rights, parents and municipal authorities worried about drugs, taxpayers have to get together, talk, strategise among themselves and make common cause against the common danger.

As we said at the outset, we do not want to prescribe a programme but to state some principles:

- Those who borrowed were rarely elected by their peoples. They squandered much of the money, spent it on arms, or used it to further entrench their own power and privilege, counting on their poorer compatriots to make the sacrifices to pay back the loans when they came due. Democratically elected governments should not be expected to assume the debt burdens of dictatorial predecessors.

- Those who loaned were either irresponsible or intentionally attempting to make the debtors subservient to their interests. The creditors have been richly rewarded and they are in no danger if the debt is markedly reduced, cancelled or converted to provide for genuine development. They should play by normal rules and not expect the public to pay for their costly mistakes.
- The debt has already been largely or entirely paid. The North is, in fact, substantially in debt to the South since it has received, since 1982, the cheapest raw materials on record and the equivalent of the value of six Marshall Plans, net, from the indebted countries.
- Cancellation and other debt reduction measures must not be used as an excuse or a pretext to further cut the debtor countries out of the benefits of the world economy.
- Debt can be used to help save the environment – rural or urban – and to empower the people who live in it. Various practical proposals to that end (including one by the present author) have been made. It is time to take them seriously. The guiding precepts should, as always, be *popular participation in decision making at every level, social equity,* and *ecological prudence.*

Here we have described the several boomerangs that the unprecedented misery of the South has sent flying back towards the North. We do not pretend to have treated these broad subjects exhaustively, but the debt connections and their impact have been as convincingly argued as our scholarship and our commitment to justice can make them. What happens now is largely up to you.

THE DEBT BOOMERANG PROJECT

If you, or your organisation, wish to endorse the afore-mentioned principles; if you wish to devote time to stopping the boomerang, and to building coalitions among the 'natural opposition' to debt, kindly photocopy and fill in the following form and send it to Agnès Bertrand, The Debt Boomerang Project,

> c/o the Transnational Institute,
> Paulus Potterstraat 20,
> 1071 DA Amsterdam,
> the Netherlands.
> The fax number is (+31-20) 675 71 76.

NAME:

PROFESSION or NAME OF ORGANISATION:

ADRRESS, Tel/Fax:

I wish to add my name (the name of my organisation) to the list of those endorsing the Debt Boomerang Principles and a solution to the debt crisis based on popular participation in decision-making, social equity and ecological prudence.

(Please sign)

I would like to participate in the work of coalition-building among the 'natural opposition' in order to change debt-management strategies. Kindly let me know if you can help to put me in touch with others in my area.

(Please sign)

Notes and References

Chapter 1: The Environment

We express our thanks to Karen Baker and Diana Española, IPS interns; Tony Juniper, Friends of the Earth, London; and Peter Madden, Christian Aid Research Unit, London for help with documentation. We also salute 20 years of prophetic, thorough and tireless documentation and advocacy on environmental issues supplied by *The Ecologist*, founded and first edited by Edward Goldsmith, now edited jointly by Goldsmith with Nicholas Hildyard. Anyone wanting more information on problems under discussion in this chapter – and many others – should look to *The Ecologist*.

All calculations relative to third world debt rely on the OECD volume *Financing and External Debt of Developing Countries, 1989 Survey*, Organisation for Economic Cooperation and Development, Paris 1990. Figures in the introduction have been updated to include data from the *1990 Survey*.

1. Robert Repetto, 'Deforestation in the Tropics', *Scientific American*, Vol. 262 no. 4, April 1990, p. 36).
2. The best comprehensive sources on the existence, causes and consequences of the greenhouse effect are Jeremy Leggett (ed.), *Global Warming: The Greenpeace Report*, and World Resources Institute, *World Resources 1990–91*, both published in 1990 by Oxford University Press, Oxford and New York. See also the various reports released in 1990 by the Intergovernmental Panel on Climate Change (IPCC) covened by the United Nations. A more popular and extremely readable account of environmental processes including such phenomena as the greenhouse effect and the destruction of the ozone layer is Jonathan Weiner, *The Next One Hundred Years*, Bantam Books, New York, London, 1990.
3. Intergovernmental Panel on Climate Change (IPCC), 'Report to IPCC from Working Group 1: Policymaker's Summary of the Scientific Assessment of Climate Change', June 1990.
4. IPCC as above, cited in Jeremy Leggett's summary for Part I of the Greenpeace Report, cf. note 2. Leggett's introduction and conclusion

to the Greenpeace Report stress the feedback issue as does Weiner, see note 2.

5. Professor David Schimel, 'Biogeochemical Feedbacks in the Earth System', Chapter 3 in Jeremy Leggett (ed.), *Greenpeace Report*.

6. Norman Myers: *Deforestation Rates in Tropical Forests and their Climatic Implications*, Friends of the Earth, London 1989. This is the exhaustive version, based on 400 references. A shortened version will be found in 'Tropical Forests', Myers' chapter in the *Greenpeace Report*, as above, note 2. These quotes are from this chapter, pp. 395–6. We also recommend Peter Bunyard, 'World Climate and Tropical Forest Destruction', *The Ecologist*, Vol. 15, no. 3, 1985, which summarises the proceedings of a major United Nations University Conference on 'Climatic, Biotic and Human Interactions in the Humid Tropics, with Particular Emphasis on Vegetation and Climate Interactions in Amazonia'.

7. Christopher Flavin, 'Slowing Global Warming', Chapter 2 of *State of the World 1990*, Worldwatch Institute, Washington DC; W.W. Norton, New York and London 1990, p. 17.

8. Richard Houghton, 'Emissions of Greenhouse Gases', Part 4 of the Myers Friends of the Earth (FOE) Report, cf. note 5, pp. 54–5.

9. Myers chapter in *Greenpeace Report*, pp. 395–6.

10. Myers in FOE, see also copious references to this phenomenon in Myers' notes 48 and 70 to Myers' chapter in the Greenpeace Report.

11. World Resources Institute as in note 2, pp. 101–2.

12. Rates of change from Myers, *Friends of the Earth Report*, Table 2, p. 49, cf. note 5.

13. Proportions of present forest cover calculated from Myers and current annual rates of destruction given directly by him, Table 15.1 in *Greenpeace Report, Global Warming*.

14. Myers, *Greenpeace Report*, p. 377

15. Population figures used to calculate debt per capita from UN Development Programme, *Human Development Report 1990*, Table 20: 'Demographic Balance Sheet'; GNP per capita in World Bank, *World Development Report 1990*, Table 1: 'Basic Indicators'.

16. Rainforest Action Network, February 1991 ('Action Alert', no. 57).

17. James Painter, 'Unpaid Debts to Nature' and box 'The Rape of the Forest', *South*, August 1989.

18. Debt service ratios are calculated from OECD, *Financing and External Debt of Developing Countries 1989 Survey*, OECD, Paris 1990 using individual country tables for debt service effectively disbursed in 1988, and World Bank, *World Debt Tables, 1989–90*, Washington DC 1989, for export values of goods and services, figures also for 1988.

19. International Monetary Fund, *Annual Reports*, 1989, 1990.

20. See World Bank, *Annual Report 1982* (under Loans to Transportation, p. 113). Fires burning near Bank-financed highway from Graham

Hancock, *Lords of Poverty*, Macmillan, London 1989. Other valuable sources on the Banks' activities in Brazil are Cheryl Payer, *The World Bank, A Critical Analysis*; José Lutzenerger, 'The World Bank's Polonoreste Project', *The Ecologist*, Vol. 15, no. 1/2, 1985. Since 1985, *The Ecologist* has frequently published articles describing in detail the ecological depradations of the Bank.

21. Paul Crutzen is quoted in Richard Monastersky, 'Biomass Burning Ignites Concern', *Science News*, 31 March 1990; see also Monastersky, 'Amazon Forest Unlikely to Rise from Ashes', *Science News*, 17 March 1990.

22. Myers in *Greenpeace Report*, plus copious references to 'shifted cultivator' phenomcnon

23. Myers in *Friends of the Earth Report*, p. 67.

24. José Lutzenberger, 'Who is destroying the Amazon Rainforest?', *The Ecologist*, Vol. 17, no. 4–5 1987, p. 155ff.

25. Robert Repetto, 'Deforestation in the Tropics', note 1.

26. Anne Erlich, 'Agricultural Contributions to Global Warming' in the *Greenpeace Report*, p. 404 and *passim*.

27. On the myriad possibilities for alternative products from the rainforest which could make logging economically unneccesary, see, for example, Fred Pearce, 'Brazil, where the Ice Cream Comes from', *New Scientist*, 7 July 1990 and Ghillean Prance, 'Fruits of the Rainforest', *New Scientist*, 13 January 1990. In the US, Ben and Jerry's ice cream already offers a flavour called 'Rainforest Crunch' made with nuts from Brazilian Amazonia. There is, however, considerable debate about whether the traditional culture of Indians would not be destroyed by any exposure to the culture of the marketplace.

28. Khor Kok Pen, 'Roots of Rainforest Destruction', *Third World Resurgence* (published by Third World Network in Malaysia), no. 4, December 1990.

29. Richard Houghton, 'Emissions of Greenhouse Gases', note 8; see also Jonathan Weiner, *The Next One Hundred Years*, note 2, p. 48ff.

30. This section on bio-diversity uses Nigel Stork and Kevin Gaston, 'Counting Species One by One', *New Scientist*, 11 August 1990 (concerning animals, especially arthropods). The most often quoted estimate of rainforest arthropods is Terry Erwin's, putting forward a figure of 30 million. The *New Scientist* authors cite other evidence which would allow for the 5–80 million estimate. Also Ghillean Prance, 'Fruits of the Rainforest', note 27 (for rainforest vegetable, especially tree, diversity); the excellent 'Worldwatch Paper' by Edwin C. Wolf, *On the Brink of Extinction: Conserving the Diversity of Life*, Worldwatch Institute Paper no. 78, Washington DC, June 1987, Table 1 on 'Known and Estimated Diversity of Life on Earth'; Jonathan Weiner, *The Next One Hundred Years*, note 2.

31. On the island effect, Peter Bunyard (note 6) describes the work of botanist Judy Rankin and others; Thomas Lovejoy, now with the Smithsonian Institution, has devoted much of his scientific work to this phenomenon; the quotes on pests and parasites are from Weiner (note 2) in his chapter called 'Lovejoy's Islands', p. 181; see also Wolf (*On the Brink of Extinction*, note 30, p. 11ff and his notes). The expression 'ecosystem decay' is Lovejoy's.

32. Wolf, *On the Brink of Extinction*, citing work by Daniel Simberloff, p. 12, Table 2.

33. Linda Fallows, 'Botany Breaks into the Candy Store' (the subtitle is more descriptive: 'Plants are turning up trumps with an assortment of small, sugar-shaped molecules that may help not only to treat cancer and AIDS but also to control insect pests'), *New Scientist*, 26 August 1989.

34. Vandana Shiva, 'Biodiversity, Biotechnology and Profit', *The Ecologist*, Vol. 20, no. 2, March/April 1990.

35. John Maxwell Hamilton, *Entangling Alliances: How the Third World Shapes our Lives*, Seven Locks Press, Cabin John, MD/ Washington DC 1990, pp. 78–9.

36. Calculated as in note 15.

37. Hamilton, as in note 35.

38. OECD table on Costa Rica.

39. Omar Sattaur, 'The Shrinking Gene Pool', *New Scientist*, 29 July 1989 and Hamilton, *Entangling Alliances*, p. 82.

40. Jack R. Kloppenburg, Jr, *First the Seed: the Political Economy of Plant Biotechnology 1492–2000*, Cambridge University Press 1988, pp. 175–89.

41. Edith Hamilton, *Mythology*, Little Brown, Boston 1940, p. 43.

42. Weiner, *The Next One Hundred Years*, (note 2) p. 188.

43. Figures from OECD 1990, table on Mexico.

44. Sandy Tolan, 'The Border Boom: Hope and Heartbreak', *New York Times Magazine*, 1 July 1990, p. 19.

45. The Maquiladora Industry in Mexico, Sacramento, Office of California-Mexico Affairs, 1988, p. 10.

46. Mark A. Anderson, international economist, American Federation of Labor and Congress of Industrial Organisations, *Statement* before the Subcommittee on Trade, Committee on Ways and Means, US House of Representatives, on US–Mexico economic relations, 28 June 1990.

47. The Mexico-California environmental problems are described by Katrina Burgess and and Abraham Lowenthal, 'Mexico's Impact on California', *California Policy Choices*, Fall 1990. Other information, including the quote from the *San Francisco Examiner* from Leslie Kochan, 'Maquiladoras: The Hidden Costs of Production South of the Border', American Federation of Labor-Congress of Industrial Organisations Publication no. 186, February 1989.

48. Quoted in Kochan, ibid.
49. Mark A. Anderson, *Statement*, note 46.
50. Peter Bunyard, 'Guardians of the Amazon', *New Scientist*, 16 December 1989, acknowledging Dr Martin von Hildebrand, head of Indigenous Affairs in Colombia and a major instigator of the policy.
51. For more information on TFAP see Susan George, 'Managing the Global House' in *Greenpeace Report*, note 2, pp. 450ff and notes.
52. Sandra Postel and Lori Heise, *Reforesting the Earth*, Worldwatch Paper no. 83, Worldwatch Institute, Washington DC, April 1988.

Chapter 2: Drugs

1. A 1989 *CBS-New York Times* poll cited in Corine Lesnes, 'Le raid déstructif du "crack" sur New York', *Le Monde*, 3 October 1989.
2. *United States Anti-Narcotics Activities in the Andean Region*, Thirty-eighth Report by the Committee on Government Operations, United States Congress, USGPO, Washington DC, 30 November 1990, p. 1, hereafter cited as *Committee*.
3. See *Committee*, idem, p. 2 and Joseph B. Treaster, 'Tide of Cocaine in US may be Ebbing', *International Herald Tribune (New York Times)*, 2 July 1990; 'L.A. Police Chief Urges Shooting Casual Users', *IHT*, 7 September 1990 (citing Senator Joseph Biden on increase of hard-core addicts; Corine Lesnes in *Le Monde*, 3 October 1989; Peter Andreas, Eva Bertram and John Cavanagh, *Intricate Web: Drugs and the Economic Crisis*, General Board of Global Ministries, United Methodist Church, 1990 (this section relies mostly on data from NIDA).
4. Andreas, et al., *Intricate Web*, citing the *Philadelphia Inquirer* of 30 March 1990; and Tracy Thompson, 'Drug Cases Overload Courts', IHT, *(Washington Post)*, 26 December 1990.
5. Andreas et al., *Intricate Web*, citing local press sources.
6. Andreas et al., ibid., citing Barbara Ehrenreich, *Fear of Falling*, Pantheon 1989; Bluestone and Harrison, 'America's Great U-Turn', *New Perspectives Quarterly*, Fall 1989; for Omaha, Jane Mayer, 'In the War on Drugs, Toughest Foe may be Alienated Youth', *Wall Street Journal*, 8 September 1989.
7. See the comprehensive volume by Guy Delbrel et al., *Géopolitique de la Drogue*, La Découverte/Campagne Européenne d'Information sur la Drogue, Paris 1991. Some other sources on European cocaine use are 'The Coming Cocaine Plague in Europe', *US New and World Report*, 20 February 1989; Alan Riding, 'Colombian Cocaine Dealers Tap European Market', *New York Times*, 29 April 1989; Karen Wolman, 'Europe's Cocaine Boom Confounds Antidrug War', *Christian Science Monitor*, 19 June 1989; Tom Mashberg, 'Drugs in

Europe: Signs of a Spreading Plague', *New York Times*, 18 November 1990 and *Wall Street Journal*, 'Europe's Cocaine Epidemic', 16 November 1990. An earlier account is to be found in Alain Delpirou and Alain Labrousse, *Coca Coke*, Editions La Découverte, Paris 1986, Chapter 19. They estimated, for the mid-1980s, the numbers of cocaine users in Spain between 100,000 and 250,000 and France 50,000–150,000. The Bogota, Colombia, *El Tiempo* article on Europe as a larger cocaine market than the US is cited in an AP dispatch ('Europe Passes US as Top Drug Market') *Atlanta Constitution*, 27 August 1990.

8. OECD, *Financing and External Debt of Developing Countries 1989 Survey*, Paris 1990, tables for Bolivia, Colombia and Peru; for GNP and exports of goods and services used to calculate debt service ratios: World Bank.

9. Basic data on Bolivia from United Nations Development Programme, *Human Development Report 1990*, various tables.

10. 'The Cocaine Economies', *The Economist*, 8 October 1988, p. 22.

11. Machicado is cited in Jo Ann Kawell, 'The Addict Economies', *Report on the Americas*, NACLA, Vol. XXII, no. 6, March 1989, p. 37, and in *Committee*, note 2, p. 68.

12. Humberto Campodonico, research report using a wide variety of official and non-official, independent Latin American sources. Many of Campodonico's conclusions have been published in his 'La Política del Avestruz' ('The Ostrich Policy') in Diego García Soyan (ed.), *Coca, Cocaína y Narcotráfico*, Comisión Andina de Juristas, Lima 1989.

13. Campodonico, research report.

14. Samuel Doria Medina, testifying before the (US) Senate Committee on the Judiciary and Senate Caucus on International Narcotics Control, 27 March 1990.

15. Kevin Healy, 'The Boom within the Crisis: Some Recent Effects of Foreign Cocaine Markets on Bolivian Rural Society and Economy', in D. Pacini and C. Franquemont (eds), *Coca and Cocaine, Effects on People and Policy in Latin America*, Cultural Survival, Inc., Cambridge, Mass. 1985.

16. R.T. Naylor, *Hot Money and the Politics of Debt*, Simon and Schuster, New York 1987, p. 168. For general patterns of the uses of borrowed money, from which Bolivia's do not depart, the reader may want to consult Susan George, *A Fate Worse than Debt*, Chapter 1.

17. See *Committee*, and Andreas et al., *Intricate Web*.

18. Jeffrey Sachs, 'The Bolivian Hyperinflation and Stabilization', *American Economic Review*, Vol. 77 no. 2, May 1987

19. Eduardo Gamarra, *Testimony* before the House Subcomittee on Western Hemisphere Affairs, 6 June 1990.

20. From the EEC 'Introductory paper for the Proceedings of the Meeting of European Community Countries' Youth Organisations on North–South Interdependence', 20–5 November 1989, VIII/1020/89-EN. Authors names not given but the views are 'the authors' own; in no way may they be taken as representing the views of the Commission of the European Communities'. Other figures from Robert Jordan Pando, 'Coca, cocaína y narcotráfico', *Presencia*, La Paz, 14–15 March 1986.
21. Cited in Sam Zuckerman, 'Banking on More than Tin and Coca', *Euromoney*, June 1987.
22. Antonio Aranibar Quiroga, Presentation at the Seminar organised by the Washington Office on Latin America, 18 May 1990.
23. *IMF Survey*, 11 December 1989 p. 370.
24. Quotes of the Ambassador and of director of the Central Bank both from articles by Michael Isikoff in the *Washington Post*, cited in *Committee*, cf. note 2, p. 71.
25. *The Economist*, 8 October 1988, note 12 and Campodonico, research report, note 14.
26. Campodonico, research report and Committee, note 2.
27. Oscar Aliaga-Abanto, 'Coca and the Drug Trade in Peru', in *Peru Solidarity Forum*, Vol. I, no. 1, May 1990 published by Fr Raphael P. Keyes, San Juan Bautista Parish, Lima 14.
28. See Peter Andreas, 'Peru's Addiction to Coca Dollars', *The Nation*, 16 April 1990.
29. GATT, *Le Commerce International 1987–88*, Geneva 1988, Vol. II, Table AA6, 'Merchandise Trade of 15 Indebted Countries and OECD, Financing and External Debt*, 1990, Table on Peru p. 172.
30. InterAmerican Development Bank, *Economic and Social Progress in Latin America*, Washington DC, 1989, section on Peru, pp. 410–17.
31. On 'Fujishock', 'Inflation Unbeaten', *The Economist*, 3 November 1990, p. 52; Sally Bowen, 'Fujimori's Austerity Drive Backfires', *Financial Times*, 25 September 1990; Eugene Robinson, ' 'Fujishock Pulls Peru Up Short', *Washington Post*, 26 September 1990; on illnesses, Professor Denis Sulmont, personal communication.
32. Nicole Bonnet, 'Le Pérou a réintégré la communauté financière internationale', *Le Monde*, 2 October 1990.
33. Campodonico, research report.
34. Quoted in Peter Andreas, 'Peru's Addiction to Coca Dollars', note 28.
35. Oscar Aliaga Abanto, 'Coca and the Drug Trade in Peru', note 29.
36. Jo Ann Kawell, 'The Addict Economies', note 13, and Campodonico.
37. *The Economist*, 8 October 188, note 12
38. Andreas, 'Peru's Addiction to Coca Dollars', Draft, and *Committee*, note 2, p. 81.
39. Naylor, *Hot Money and the Politics of Debt*, p.177

40.   Eduardo Sarmiento, *La Economía del Narcotráfico*, Centro de Estudios sobre el Desarrollo Económico, Universidad de Los Andes, Bogota, Colombia, March 1990, p. 69.

41.   Marc J. Dourojeanni, Head Professor, National Agrarian University, Lima, 'The Environmental Impact of Coca Cultivation and Cocaine Production in the Peruvian Amazon Basin', mimeo, Lima, 1988.

42.   Douglas Farah, 'Cocaine Chemicals Foul Amazon Basin', *Washington Post*, 20 November 1990 and James Brooke, 'Peruvian Farmers Razing Rain Forest to Sow Drug Crops', *New York Times*, 13 August 1989.

43.   Peter Andreas, *Testimony* before the Committee on Commerce, Science and Transportation, Subcommittee on Foreign Commerce and Tourism, US Senate, Hearings concerning Chemical Diversion and Trafficking, 1 August 1990.

44.   Douglas Jehl, 'US Solvents Helped Fuel Colombia Cocaine Trade', *Los Angeles Times*, 7 February 1990.

45.   Andreas, *Testimony,* note 43.

46.   *Hearings, Operation Snowcap: Past Present and Future*, House Committee on Foreign Affairs, 23 May 1990, p. 27.

47.   The rest of this discussion is drawn from the Committee's November 1990 Report, particularly the introduction. The Peruvian colonel is cited on p. 41. See note 2.

48.   James Brooke, 'US Anti-drug Pilots in Peru in Fierce Battle with Rebels', (*New York Times*), *International Herald Tribune*, 13 April 1990.

49.   James Brooke, 'Peru Gets US Military Aid in Drug War', (*New York Times*) *International Herald Tribune*, 23 April 1990 and on *Sendero*'s control, Aliaga-Abanto, 'Coca and the Drug Trade in Peru', p. 9. Also very helpful on background is Michael Klare, 'Fighting Drugs with the Military', *The Nation*, 1 January 1990. The Grupo de Trabajo de la Coordinadora Nacional de Derechos Humanos regularly publishes a *Boletín* with the tallies of victims of guerrilla violence in Peru: Capac Yupanqui no. 2151, Oficina 204, Lince, Lima 14. These figures are from the *Boletín no. 10*, December 1990.

50.   Marc. W. Chernick, 'The Drug War', *Report on the Americas* NACLA, Vol. XXIII, no. 6, April 1990, p. 32. Most of this issue of the NACLA *Report* is concerned with the strife in Colombia.

Chapter 3: Banks

In this chapter, unless otherwise noted, data on commercial bank claims on the third world, and the definition of the SIMICs, SILICs, MIMICs and MILICs are from World Bank, *Quarterly Review; Financial Flows to Developing Countries*, March 1991, several tables.

1. These questions are treated in detail in Stephany Griffith-Jones, 'European Banking Regulations and Third World Debt: The Technical, Political and Institutional Issues', Institute of Development Studies, Sussex, 1989; and in Michel Henry Bouchet, 'International Banks and External Indebtedness of Developing Countries: A Review of Regulatory Regimes and their Impact on Debt Restructuring Transactions', copyright Owen Stanley Financial, November 1990. Bouchet was previously a consultant to the World Bank on matters pertaining to the tax treatment of sovereign debt.

2. Michel Henry Bouchet, *International Banks and External Indebtedness of Developing Countries: A Review of Regulatory Regimes and their Impact on Debt Restructuring Transactions*, Appendix C, copyright Owen Stanley Financial, November 1990. Desktop-type report; intention or existence of publication in another format not indicated.

3. IBCA, 'US banks Holding Companies: Statistics', IBCA 1989; Andrew Froman, 'Still Exposed After All These Years', *Latin Finance*, no. 20, September 1990.

4. Griffiths-Jones, 'European Banking Regulations', basing her suggestion on an earlier study co-authored for the World Bank by Michel Henry Bouchet.

5. Greg Root, President of BankWatch, quoted in Froman, 'Still Exposed', note 3.

6. 'Creditor Review', *Latin Finance*, no. 20, September 1990, pp. 65–71.

7. Ibid.

8. Bouchet, 'International Banks', p. 53.

9. Brian Quinn, Address to the Association of British Consortium Banks, London, 1 November 1989, cited in Bouchet, pp. 42–3 whose description of the Matrix system we have also used.

10. IBCA, *Rewriting the Matrix*, February 1990.

11. See IBCA, *Rewriting the Matrix*, and Mitchell Hogg, partner Deloitte Haskins & Sells, 'New Moves on Provisioning Requirements for Banks and Tax Treatment for Bad Debt Provisions', photocopy, n.d. (early 1990).

12. Aside from World Bank figures and Bouchet, used consistently, we quote from IBCA, 'Capital without Tears: Inclusion of LDC Reserves in French Banks' Basle Ratios', May 1991.

13. We are grateful to Roy Culpeper of the Canadian North South Institute, Ottawa, for personal communication on the Canadian banking situation and thanks to him we have also used Standing Committee on External Affairs and International Trade, *Securing our Global Future: Canada's Stake in the Unfinished Business of Third World Debt*, House of Commons, Canada, June 1990.

14. GDP and ODA figures, all for 1987, from UNDP, *Human Development Report*, 1990 Tables 22 and 19; UNICEF's 1990 budget was $721 million; in 1990 the average after-tax income for the lowest 20 per

cent of Americans was $6975: see UNICEF's *Annual Report 1990* and Bread for the World Institute on Hunger and Development, *Hunger 1990: a Report on the State of World Hunger*, Washington 1990, citing a report by Citizens for Tax Justice, pp. 89–90.

15. IBCA, 'Rewriting the Matrix', February 1990 p. 3.

16. The figures are from OECD 1990, Tables V.1 and V.2. Debt owed to banks (V.1) is based on OECD categories 'Financial markets: Banks', plus 'Short term debt: (1) Banks (2) Export credits'. Practically all short-term export credits are due to banks rather than to governments. In any event these credits never represent more than 18–19 per cent of all short-term debt during the period 1982–9. The OECD categories 'Bonds' and 'Other private' are excluded. Debt service paid to banks (Table V.2) is based on 'Long-term debt service payments: Financial markets', plus 'Interest, short-term debt' which again is mostly owed to banks. It excludes payments on 'export credits' because in this table on payments these are listed only under 'long-term debt service payments' and are thus probably mostly owed to public sources. It is regrettable that the two tables are not wholly compatible with each other. Nor can one make them compatible with World Bank tables. The OECD is, however, probably preferable as a source for this table because it depends on creditor reporting systems whereas the World Bank relies on the debtors who might be tempted to exaggerate the levels of their reimbursements. For other differences in reporting systems between OECD and Bank, see OECD, *Financing and External Debt of Developing Countries* (1990), *Technical Notes*, pp. 75ff.

     'New bank lending' is from OECD, Table III.1

17. Hobart Rowen, 'Soon a New Boss at a Changed Bank', *Washington Post* in the *International Herald Tribune*, 20 March 1991.

18. Jeffrey D. Sachs, Professor, Department of Economics, Harvard University, *Testimony* to the Subcommittee on International Finance, Trade, and Monetary Policy of the House Banking Committee, 13 July 1988.

19. Manuel Pastor, Jr., *Capital Flight and the Latin American Debt Crisis*, Economic Policy Institute, Washington DC 1989.

20. OECD, *Financing and External Debt of Developing Countries, 1988 Survey*, OECD 1989, Table III.1.

21. Donald Lessard and John Williamson, *Capital Flight and the Third World*, Institute for International Economics, Washington DC 1987.

Chapter 4: Lost Jobs and Markets

1. 'Non-Fuel Commodity Prices Fell in 1990' (and chart), *IMF Survey*, 4 February 1991, p. 42.

2. 'Expansion of Global Output and Trade Continued in 1990, According to GATT', *IMF Survey*, 10 December 1990, pp. 376–8 and charts, emphasis added.

3. This and subsequent quotes from Sanjay Dhar, 'US Trade with Latin America: Consequences of Financing Constraints', Federal Reserve Bank of New York, *Quarterly Review*, Autumn 1983.

4. The figures are from Dhar's Tables 3 and 4; he also explains that 'In addition to the depressing effects of merchandise trade, reduced service receipts from Latin America have also retarded growth in the United States. Although total US service receipts from Latin America in 1982 remained steady, this was entirely due to the continued growth of "Other Private Receipts" – mainly interest receipts by US banks – to over $25 billion in 1982', ibid., p. 18.

5. Statement of Stuart K. Tucker before the Subcommittee on Economic Stabilization of the House Committee on Banking, Finance and Urban Affairs, Washington DC, 25 July 1985.

6. Stuart K. Tucker, *Update: Costs to the United States of the Recession in Developing Countries*, Working Paper no. 10, Overseas Development Council, Washington DC, January 1986.

7. Ibid.

8. Calculated from export data in *Foreign Agricultural Trade of the United States* (*FATUS*), US Department of Agriculture, various Calendar Years, except 1990 which is based on Fiscal Year (1 September–31 August) data.

9. The figures, drawn from *FATUS*, are commented on in *The Impact of the Latin American Debt Crisis on the US Economy*, a Staff Study prepared for the use of the Joint Economic Committee, Congress of the United States, 10 May 1986.

10. Ibid., pp. 13–14.

11. Alfred J. Watkins, *Till Debt do us Part*, Roosevelt Center for American Policy Studies, University Press of America, New York/London 1986, pp. 12–13.

12. Staff Study, *The Impact of the Latin American Debt Crisis*, pp. 14–15.

13. Stuart K. Tucker, 'The Debt–Trade Linkage in US-Latin American trade', *Statement* before the Subcommittee on International Economic Policy and Trade, Committee on Foreign Affairs, US House of Representatives, 29 September 1988 and Stuart K. Tucker, 'Impact of the debt overhang', *Statement* before the Subcommittee on International Debt of the Committee on Finance, US Senate, 2 March 1990.

14. Tucker, *Statement*, 1990, pp. 2–3.

15. Hyman Minsky, Professor of Economics, Washington Univeristy, a 1984 conference paper cited in Watkins, *Till Debt do us Part*, note 11, p. 14.

16. See Kevin Phillips, *The Politics of Rich and Poor: Wealth and the American Electorate in the Reagan Aftermath*, Random House, New York 1990, p. 122 and *passim*.

17. The Democratic staff of the Joint Economic Committee, US Congress, *Trade Deficits, Foreign Debt and Sagging Growth: An Analysis of the Cause and Effects of America's Trade Problem*, September 1986, pp. 37–8. More documentation to be found on these points in Staff Study, *The Impact of the Latin American Debt Crisis*, note 9.

18. US Department of Commerce, International Trade Administration, 'Contribution of Exports to US Employment 1980–7', n.d., Table 4.

19. Dr Indra Wahab used the export figures as presented in current dollars in the United Nations *International Trade Yearbook* (various issues) and calculated *export unit values* from the International Monetary Fund *Yearbook of International Financial Statistics* (various issues). Dr Wahab indicates in his methodological notes that 'By correcting the export flows in current dollars against the export unit values (1985 = 100), the export flows are expressed in constant 1985 dollars.' Thanks and acknowledgements to Jon Henley who translated the whole of Wahab's Dutch original.

20. Brendan Martin, 'Privatisation and the Developing World', paper prepared for the PSI (Public Services International) Conference on Privatisation, Geneva, 25–7 March 1991.

21. Ibid.

22. Jeff Faux, 'The Impact of Privatisation on the Range and Quality of Public Services: Recent Experience in the United States', paper presented at the PSI Conference on Privatisation as above, 25 March 1991.

23. From *Financial Weekly*, 9 October 1981, cited in Public Services International, *Privatisation: A Trade Union Response*, PSI, Ferney-Voltaire, France 1989, p. 17

24. Ibid., p. 10.

Chapter 5: Immigration

1. Franz Nuscheler, 'Refugees Flooding Islands of Affluence', UN *Development Forum*, Vol. 19: 3, May–June 1991.

2. Seth Mydans, 'Poverty and Plenty: Cultures Clash as Aliens Cross into San Diego Area', *International Herald Tribune* (*New York Times*) 27 March 1990.

3. Various French press reports, especially around 28–9 March 1990.

4. *La Repubblica*, 6 March 1990, reprinted in COSV, Centro di Documentazione, *Razzismo 3: I Dati dell'Immigrazione*, Milan and Rome, October 1990.

5. Richard Reeves, 'Our World on the Move: A Succinctly Illustrated History', *International Herald Tribune*, 14 February 1991, reporting on the Ellis Island museum opened in September 1990.

6. Sylvia Ann Hewlett, 'Coping with Illegal Immigrants', *Foreign Affairs*, Winter 1981–2. Many of the same points are made in the well documented article by Michael S. Teitelbaum, 'Right versus Right: Immigration and Refugee Policy in the United States', *Foreign Affairs*, Fall 1980 on which Hewlett's article is partially based.

7. 'The New Americans', *The Economist*, 11 May 1991.

8. Hewlett, 'Coping with Illegal Immigrants', p. 360.

9. Christopher Hitchens, 'Minority Report', *The Nation*, 3 June 1991.

10. As elsewhere in this book, we use country figures from OECD, *Financing and External Debt of Developing Countries 1989 Survey*, Paris 1990 (population figures allowing for calculation of per capita debt are from World Bank, *World Development Report 1991*, Basic Indicators). 'Other West Indies' includes Anguilla, Antigua, Cayman Islands, Dominica, Grenada, Montserrat, St Kitts-Nevis, St Lucia, St Vincent, Turks and Caicos Islands, and Virgin Islands.

11. I rely here and for subsequent quotes on the Caribbean on Kathy McAfee's excellent series of articles under the general title 'Hurricane: IMF, World Bank, US Aid in the Caribbean', NACLA *Report on the Americas*, Vol. XXIII no. 5, February 1990. Officials cited were usually interviewed by McAfee herself.

12. World Bank, *Country Paper, Haiti* (Review Draft), 20 May 1983, p. 16.

13. Calculated from Immigration and Naturalization Service (INS), *Annual Report 1988*, US Government Printing Office, Washington DC 1988, Tables concerning 'Immigrants Admitted by Country or Region of Birth, Fiscal Years 1970–1988'.

14. Alejandro Portes and Ruben G. Rumbaut, *Immigrant America: A Portrait*, University of California Press, Berkeley 1990, Figures 1 and 2 and Table 1.

15. Larry Rohter, 'Soft Underbelly: Sneaking Mexicans (and Others) into US is Big Business, *New York Times*, 20 June 1989.

16. Alicia was interviewed by David Pedersen, research associate at the Institute for Policy Studies, in Washington in late 1990.

17. Quoted in Sylvia Anne Hewlett, 'Coping with Illegal Immigrants', note 6.

18. Conseil de l'Europe, *L'Evolution démographique récente dans les Etats fembre su Conseil de l'Europe*, Strasbourg 1990.

19. French Senate, *Rapport d'Information* (au nom de la mission d'information chargée d'étudier les problèmes posés par l'immigration en France et de proposer les éléments d'une politique d'intégration). Jacques Thyraud, Rapporteur, no. 101, Première session ordinaire de 1990–1991, Tome I, pp. 30–1. This report is the Bible for those

who want exhaustive and up-to-date information on immigration in France; it also gives shorter case studies on the US, Germany, Italy, Japan and Canada, as well as intra-third world migrations.

20. Ibid., p. 125.
21. Ibid., p. 135.
22. SOPEMI 1989 (Système d'observation permanente des migrations), OECD, Direction des Affaires Sociales, de la Main d'Oeuvre et de l'Education; Paris 1990, Table 1. (NB: The figures for some countries receiving small numbers of request for asylum – Greece, Italy, Portugal, Spain – were not available for 1988 and 1989 in this table. I have therefore added the same numbers as for 1987 to the available totals for 1989. If these countries followed their own post-1983 trend and the trend in the rest of Europe, requests for asylum were greater in 1989 than in 1987, so the per cent increase is also higher than 56 per cent.)
23. Michel Poulain, *Populations étrangères et mouvements migratoires dans les pays membres du Conseil de l'Europe*, Document for the 11th meeting of the Comité Européen sur la Population, Strasbourg 12 July 1990 (no. FCDP010-90), pp. 20–1 and Table VII. Also SOPEMI 1989, p. 15.
24. The table is adapted from Poulain, ibid., p. 11.
25. SOPEMI 1989, p. 17.
26. Poulain, *Populations étrangères*, p. 12.
27. Alan Riding, 'Europe Confronts its Ghettos', *International Herald Tribune* (New York Times Service) 25 March 1991.
28. See for examples three articles in *Le Monde* of 25 May 1991: Robert Solé, 'Réfugiés ou immigrés', Erich Inciyan, 'La police face à la crise des banlieus' and 'La violence des bandes en région parisienne'.
29. Figures from the Italian Ministry of Justice and Pardons, reproduced and presented in COSV, note 4.
30. SOPEMI 1989, tables B6.1 through B6.6. From these tables one cannot get an idea of the total remittances, because (1) they are expressed in the national currencies of selected European countries and (2) the countries to which remittances are made are not consistent. It is clear, however, that billions of dollars are involved in these transactions.
31. Oumar Sy, General Secretary of the SOE, a Senegalese Non-Governmental Organisation, remarks at the 'Journées d'Etude' on the occasion of the 50th anniversary of the CIMADE (a French Protestant solidarity organisation), cited in *CIMADE Information*, no. 6/90, June 1990, p. 10.
32. These population projections are cited in French Senate, *Rapport d'Information*, note 19, p. 49 and in 'Poor Men at the Gate', *The Economist*, 16 March 1991, p. 11–12.

33. See OECD, 1990 Survey (1991), note 10 (same series), tables III. 5 ('Net resource flows to total Africa') and V.10 ('Total annual debt service of total African countries during 1982–90 by source and terms of lending').
34. *The Economist,* 6 March 1991.
35. Georges P. Tapinos, 'Development Assistance Strategies and Emigration Pressure in Europe and Africa', Commission for the Study of International Migration and Cooperative Economic Development, Working Papers, no. 56, July 1990, p. 10.

Chapter 6: Conflict and War

1. The criterion of 1000 is used, for example, in P. Wallensteen (ed.), *States in Armed Conflict 1988,* Uppsala University, July 1989, and his chapters in *World Armaments & Disarmament: SIPRI Yearbook* 1989 and 1990 editions, Oxford University Press, 1989 and 1990. The criterion of 1000 *annually* is used by William Eckhardt whose data appear in R.L. Sivard, *World Military & Social Expenditures,* World Priorities Inc, Washington DC, annual. No explicit definition is given in two very useful works: P. Brogan, *World Conflicts,* Bloomsbury, London 1989 and G.C. Kohn, *Dictionary of Wars,* Doubleday, New York 1987.
2. C. Ahlström, *Casualties of Conflict,* Uppsala University, Sweden, Department of Peace & Conflict Research, 1991, pp. 8, 19; Sivard, *World Military & Social Expenditures 1985,* pp. 10–11.
3. Ahlström, *Casualties of Conflict,* p. 19.
4. L. Cockburn, *Out of Control,* Bloomsbury, London 1988, p. 8.
5. 'Child Warriors', *Time,* 18 June 1990.
6. P. Kennedy, *The Rise and Fall of the Great Powers,* Random House, New York 1987, p. 71.
7. W. Doyle, *The Oxford History of the French Revolution,* Oxford University Press, Oxford 1989, pp. 65–9.
8. *The Economist,* 15 December 1945, cited in D. Dimbleby and D. Reynolds, *An Ocean Apart,* Hodder & Stoughton, London 1988, pp. 166–7.
9. M. Faber, 'Conciliatory Debt Reduction: Why it Must Come and How it Could Come', Fifth Dudley Seers Memorial Lecture, Free University of Berlin, 25 September 1988, text available from Institute of Development Studies, University of Sussex.
10. Kennedy, *The Rise and Fall of the Great Powers,* pp. 78–83.
11. A.T. Mahan, *The Influence of Sea Power upon History 1660–1783,* Hill & Wang, New York 1957 [First edition 1890].
12. 'Bush's Backers', *Guardian,* 16 February 1991.
13. 'Making 'em Pay', *The Economist,* 26 January 1991.

14. See H. Smith, *The Power Game,* Collins, London 1988.
15. Figures on the relatively uncontrollable element of US government spending are provided annually in *Historical Tables, Budget of the US Government,* US Government Printing Office, Washington DC, annual. It is made up of prior obligations, such as civilian and military contracts signed but not yet paid for, mandatory payments such as those involved in social programmes, and interest on the national debt.
16. Sivard, *World Military and Social Expenditures 1989* , p. 21.
17. I. Anthony and H. Wulf, 'The Trade in Major Conventional Weapons', *World Armaments & Disarmament: SIPRI Yearbook 1990,* Oxford University Press, Oxford 1990, Table 7.2.
18. Ibid.
19. See successive editions of *World Armaments & Disarmament: SIPRI Yearbook,* Oxford University Press, Oxford, annual and specifically the annual chapters 'The trade in major conventional weapons' by various authors: Table 17.7 in the 1986 edition, 7.7 in 1987 and 6.3 in 1989.
20. 'Saddam's Gulf of Threats', *The Economist,* 21 July 1990.
21. F. Halliday, *Arabia Without Sultans,* Penguin, Harmondsworth 1974, p. 433.
22. 'Communiqué Lists Demands', *Guardian,* 16 February 1991.
23. 'Bush to Forgive Egypt's Arms Debt', *International Herald Tribune,* 3 September 1990.
24. 'Egypt's Debt Burden Eased by Nearly $14bn', *Financial Times,* 24 January 1991.
25. M. Viorst, 'A Reporter at Large: The House of Hashem', *The New Yorker,* 7 January 1991.
26. M. Massing, 'The Way to War', *The New York Review,* 28 March 1991.
27. 'IMF Backs Plan To Aid Nations Hurt by Gulf', *International Herald Tribune,* 25 September 1990.
28. 'Sorry, Just Kidding', *The Economist,* 15 December 1990 and Philippine Resource Centre, London, *Briefing,* 30 November 1990.
29. 'Third Time Lucky', *The Economist,* 11 August 1990.
30. '"Disaster" for Third World Economies', *Guardian,* 4 March 1991.
31. 'La guerre perdue des pays pauvres', *Le Monde,* 21 March 1991.
32. '"Disaster" for Third World Economies', and 'Jordan's Fate in Hands of Others', *Guardian,* 4 March 1991.
33. *International Herald Tribune,* 3 September 1990.
34. Carl von Clausewitz, *On War,* ed. & trans. by M. Howard and P. Paret, Princeton University Press, Princeton, NJ 1976, pp. 75, 87.
35. B. Brodie, 'A Guide to the Reading of *On War*' in ibid, pp. 645–6.
36. R Taber, *The War of the Flea,* Paladin, St Albans 1970, p. 45.

Index

Note: The Notes to the text are not indexed.
LDCs refer to Less Developed Countries

Afghanistan:
  arms imports, Table 6.6
  civil war, Table 6.1
  debt and war, Table 6.5
  refugees from, 142, Table 6.3
Africa:
  emigration from, 132
  loans by French banks, 80
  net resource flows, 134
  projected population figures, 133
  refugees in, 142, Table 6.2
  sub-Saharan, cost of Gulf War
    to, 158
agriculture:
  cash crops, 3
  food exports, 99–100
  and genetic material, 23
  loss of markets and jobs, 93
Algeria:
  debt and war, Table 6.4
  migrant labour from, 123
Angola:
  arms imports, 154, Table 6.6
  civil war, Table 6.1
  debt and war, 148, Table 6.5
  refugees, Table 6.3
Argentina:
  agricultural exports, 99, 100
  arms imports, 154, Table 6.9
  debt and war, Table 6.4, Table
    6.9
  debt-for-equity swaps, 75, 76
  malnutrition, 100
  political violence, 160, 161,
    Table 6.7, Table 6.8
  secondary market loan prices,
    Table 3.1
  US loan loss reserve
    requirement, 74

arms trade:
  third world, 151–4, Chart 6.3,
    Chart 6.4, Table 6.6
  see also military spending
Asia, refugees in, Table 6.2
austerity measures, violent pro-
    test against, 161, Table 6.8
Austria, tax relief on LDC debt,
    82

Baker, James, Baker Plan, 89
Bangladesh:
  civil war, Table 6.1
  cost of Gulf War to, 158
  debt and war, Table 6.5
  deforestation, 9
Bankers Trust, debt-for-equity
    swaps, 76
banks:
  benefit from foreign earnings of
    debtor countries, 95, 97
  regulators and tax relief on LDC
    debt, 65–6
  restricted information from,
    64–5, 69–72
  return on invested capital
    (USA), 97–8, Table 4.2
banks, commercial:
  debt trading in US, 74, 75
  debt transferred to public sector,
    86–90
  exposure to LDC debt, Table
    3.2, Table 3.3
  losses on third world loans, 84
  returns on third world loans,
    85–6, Table 3.5
  tax relief for, 65–7
Belgium:
  birth rate, 128–9, Table 5.3

migrant labour in, 123
requests for political asylum, 126
tax relief on LDC debt, 82
biological diversity, 20–4
birth rates, in Europe, 128–9
Bolivia:
  austerity programme, 14, 44
  civil war, Table 6.1
  coca economy, 44–5
  debt figures, 40, Table 2.1, Table
    2.2
  debt and military spending,
    164, Table 6.9
  debt service ratio, Table 1.5
  debt and war, Table 6.4, Table
    6.5
  deforestation, 13–14, Table 1.1,
    Table 1.4
  drug production in, 38, 39, 40–6
  drugs war and USA
    intervention, 60
  economic problems, 42–4
  political violence, 161, Table
    6.8
  pollution by coca production,
    55–6
  secondary market loan prices,
    Table 3.1
borders, international, and
    immigration, 133
Brady, Nicholas, Brady Plan, 89–90
Brazil:
  agricultural exports, 99, 100
  debt and military spending,
    Table 6.9
  debt service ratio, Table 1.5
  debt and war, Table 6.4
  debt-for-equity swaps, 75
  deforestation, 9–13, 14, Table
    1.1, Table 1.2
  economy and deforestation,
    16–19
  effect of oil prices on, 158
  forest products, 19
  high-condition EFF, 15
  malnutrition, 100
  political violence, 160, 161,
    Table 6.7, Table 6.8
  secondary market loan prices,
    Table 3.1
  US loan loss reserve
    requirement, 74

Brundtland Commission *see* World
    Commission on
    Environment and
    Development
Bulgaria, refugees, Table 6.3
Burma *see* Myanmar
Bush, President George:
  denial of global warming, 5n
  war on drugs, 34

Cambodia:
  civil war, 142, 167, Table 6.1
  debt and war, Table 6.5
  refugees, Table 6.3
Cameroon:
  debt service ratio, Table 1.5
  deforestation, 9, 12, 13, Table
    1.1, Table 1.4
  political violence, 160, Table 6.7
Canada:
  commercial bank exposure to
    LDC debt, 81–2, Table 3.2
  debt reduction, 81–2
  immigrants to USA, Table 5.2
  tax relief, 81, Table 3.4
capital, dominance of finance
    capital, 93
capital flight, 90–1
Cargill grain trading company,
    100
Caribbean:
  debt and debt service, 116–17,
    Table 5.1
  migrants to USA, 116, 118–19,
    Table 5.2
Caribbean Group for Cooperation
    in Economic Development
    (CGCED), 117
Catholic Church, role in
    immigration, 130
cattle ranching, in Amazon, 18–19
Cayman Islands, tax shelter for
    Japanese banks, 76–7
Central America:
  deforestation, 11, Table 1.1,
    Table 1.2, Table 1.3
  refugees in, 142, Table 6.2
  see also Costa Rica; El Salvador;
    Guatemala; Honduras;
    Nicaragua
Chad:
  civil war, Table 6.1

debt and war, Table 6.5
refugees, Table 6.3
Chicago School of economists, privatisation theory, 106
child labour laws, 28
Chile:
    debt and war, Table 6.4
    debt-for-equity swaps, 75, 76
    deforestation, 9
    free-market restructuring of economy, 106
    political violence, 161, Table 6.8
    secondary market loan prices, Table 3.1
China:
    civil wars in, 138, 142
    debt and war, Table 6.4, Table 6.5
    immigrants to USA, 121, Table 5.2
    war in Tibet, Table 6.1
Citicorp Bank:
    debt reduction, 75
    debt-for-equity swap, 75
Clausewitz, Carl von, 164–5
coca production:
    in Bolivia, 44–5
    and deforestation, 54–5
    in Peru, 46–7
    see also cocaine production
cocaine:
    in Europe, 37, 38
    in USA, 35
cocaine production:
    in Colombia, 52–3
    and debt, 39–40
    and pollution, 54, 55–6
    see also coca production
coffee, collapse of international agreement, 53
Colombia:
    civil war, Table 6.1
    cocaine production, 39, 52–3, 56
    continued violence, 165
    debt figures, 40, Table 2.1, Table 2.2
    debt service ratio, Table 1.5
    debt and war, Table 6.4, Table 6.5, Table 6.9
    deforestation, 12, 13, Table 1.1, Table 1.2
    drug traffickers from, 38
    economy, 53–4

forest management model, 28–9
immigrants to USA, Table 5.2
secondary market loan prices, Table 3.1
US drugs war in, 61
commodity prices, fall in, 94
Congo, debt and war, Table 6.4
conservation, underfunded, 4
Costa Rica:
    biological diversity in, 22–3
    debt burden, 22
    deforestation, 9
    high-condition EFF, 16
    secondary market loan prices, Table 3.1
Côte d'Ivoire (Ivory Coast):
    debt service ratio, Table 1.5
    debt and war, Table 6.4
    deforestation, 11, 12, Table 1.1, Table 1.2, Table 1.3
    high-condition EFF, 15
    political violence, 160, Table 6.7
    secondary market loan prices, Table 3.1
    US loan loss reserve requirement, 74
crack (cocaine derivative):
    in Europe, 37–8
    in USA, 35, 37
creditor countries, choice between interest and exports, 94
criminal violence, drug-related (in USA), 35
Cuba, immigrants to USA, 121, Table 5.2
Cyprus, refugees, Table 6.3

dams, financed by World Bank (Brazil), 16
debt:
    burden shifted to public sector, 85, 86–90
    as cause of deforestation, 8–14, Tables 1.1–4
    connection with migration, 110–11, 118–19
    and Gulf War, 155, 156–7, 158
    increase, xvi
    increased service payments, 85, 86, Table 3.5
    and military spending, 163–4, Table 6.9

new loans to service old, 88
relationship with war, 136,
    144–5, 158
debt crisis:
    caused by US interest rates, 151
    effect of, 169–70
debt figures, total South-to-North,
    xiv, xv–xvi
debt management policy, need to
    change, 28–9
debt managers, international:
    lack of accountability, xvi,
        168–9
    see also International Monetary
        Fund; World Bank
debt reduction:
    Canada, 81–2
    by Japanese banks, 77
    need for, 171
    suggestions for, 30
debt service ratio (DSR), 14, Table
    1.5
debt trading, 67–9, Table 3.1
    by US banks, 74, 75
debt-for-equity swaps, xviii
    privatisation by, 106
    by US banks, 75–6
debt-for-nature swaps, 30–1
debtor countries:
    class inequality, xvii–xviii
    lack of unity, xvii
    structural trade surpluses, 94
deforestation:
    and agriculture, 4, 18–19
    and coca production, 54–5
    correlation with debt, 8–14,
        Tables 1.1–4
    and debt service ratio (DSR), 14,
        Table 1.5
    release of greenhouse gases, 4,
        6–8
    and species extinction, 20–1
    see also forests
democracy:
    importance of, 171
    political violence demanding,
        160–1
development model:
    export-led growth, xix, 2–3,
        27–8
    flawed, xix, 28, 166
    proposed new, xx

development, myth of, 169
development plans: to stem flow of
    emigrants, 135
dictators, Northern support for,
    135
displaced people *see* shifted
    cultivators
Dominican Republic:
    immigrants to USA, 119, 120–1,
        Table 5.2
    political violence, Table 6.8
Drug Enforcement Administration
    (USA), 38
drug trade, 61–2
    in Europe, 37–8
    in USA, 34–7
    see also coca; cocaine; crack
drugs war, 57–61
    corruption in, 59–60

Eastern Europe:
    migration to West, 133
    and privatisation, 106–7
ecological destruction, 1
    as cause of migration, 112
    need for prudence, 171
    see also deforestation; pollution
Ecuador:
    debt service ratio, Table 1.5
    debt and war, Table 6.4
    political violence, Table 6.8
    secondary market loan prices,
        Table 3.1
    US loan loss reserve
        requirement, 74
education, effect of drug problem
    on (USA), 37
Egypt:
    arms imports, 154, Table 6.6
    debt and war, 148, 156 7, Table
        6.4, Table 6.5
    Gulf War, 131, 156–7, Table 6.1
    political violence, Table 6.8
    projected population figures, 133
El Salvador:
    civil war, Table 6.1
    debt and war, 148, Table 6.5,
        Table 6.9
    immigrants in USA, 116, 120,
        Table 5.2
    political violence, 161, Table 6.8
    refugees, Table 6.3

Ethiopia:
civil wars, 138, 142, 167, Table
6.1
debt and war, 148, Table 6.4,
Table 6.5
refugees, Table 6.3
war and famine, 167
Europe:
drug problem in, 37–8
exports to LDCs, 102–3, Table
4.3, Table 4.4
immigrant labour, 123, 129
and immigration, 113, 123–9
immigration and borders, 133
immigration statistics, 124, 129
refugees in, Table 6.2
and threat of war, 167
trade surplus, 101
European Community, exports to
LDCs, 105, Table 4.6
export trade:
effect of debt crisis (simulation),
104–5, Table 4.5
to LDCs declines, 102–4, Table
4.3, Table 4.4
export-led growth model, xix, 2–3,
27–8
Extended Fund Facilities (EFF)
(IMF), 15

famine, 167
farm banks, failure of, 100
farms:
failure of, 100
see also agriculture
Finland, migrant labour from, 123
forests:
management model, 28–9
products of, 19
reforestation, 21, 29–30
see also deforestation
France:
commercial bank exposure to
LDC debt, 80–1, Table 3.2,
Table 3.3
illegal immigrants in, 124
immigrant integration, 125,
133–4
immigration, 113, 123, 125, 131
immigration statistics, 123, 129
requests for political asylum,
126–7

tax relief regulations, 80–1
free trade, disadvantages of, 31
Fujimori, Alberto, President of
Peru, 50

Gabon:
deforestation, 12, 13
high-condition EFF, 15
political violence, 160, Table 6.7
Galán, Luis Carlos, Colombian
presidential candidate, 54, 61
García, Alan, President of Peru,
48–50
GATT (General Agreement on
Tariffs and Trade), 31
world trade figures, 94–5
genetic material, stocks of, 23
Germany:
commercial bank exposure to
LDC debt, 79–80, Table
3.2, Table 3.3
Gulf War finance, 147
and immigration, 123, 125, 129
increased debt exposure, 79
requests for political asylum,
127
tax relief system, 80, Table 3.4
Ghana:
debt and war, Table 6.4
political violence, Table 6.8
ghetto phenomenon, of
immigrants, 130
global warming:
climatic models, 5–6
and species extinction, 20–1
see also greenhouse gases
Great Britain *see* United Kingdom
Greece:
illegal immigrants in, 124, 128
migrant labour from, 123
greenhouse gases:
carbon dioxide, 6, 7, 17, 19
and cattle ranching, 18
CFCs (chlorofluorocarbons), 7
and deforestation, 4, 6–8,
16–17
emissions by industrial
countries, 32
methane, 6, 7, 17, 18, 19–20
nitrous oxide, 6, 7
Guatemala:
civil war, Table 6.1

debt and war, 148, Table 6.4,
    Table 6.5
political violence, 161, Table 6.8
refugees, Table 6.3
Gulf War, 138
caused by debt, 154–8

Haiti:
immigrants to USA, 119, 120,
    Table 5.2
political violence, 160, 161,
    Table 6.7, Table 6.8
refugees, Table 6.3
rural-urban migrants in, 118
health and safety regulations, 28,
    31
heroin, in Europe, 37
Hispanic migrants in USA, 112–13,
    115
Holland *see* Netherlands
Honduras:
debt and war, Table 6.4
high-condition EFF, 15
Hungary, privatisation in, 106–7

ICERC (InterAgency Exposure
    Review Committee) (USA),
    73–4
illegal immigration, 121–2
into Europe, 128
immigrants:
birth rates in Europe, 129, Table
    5.3
concentration of, 130
definition of, 124
family regrouping, 131–2
integration of, 125
and political asylum, 126–7
treatment of, 112–13, 133–5
see also migration; refugees
India:
arms imports, 153, 154, Table
    6.6
civil wars, 138, Table 6.1
continued violence, 165
debt and military spending,
    Table 6.9
debt service ratio, Table 1.5
debt and war, 148, Table 6.4,
    Table 6.5
deforestation, 9, 10, 12, 13,
    Table 1.1, Table 1.2, Table 1.3

high-condition EFF, 15
immigrants to USA, 121, Table
    5.2
Indonesia:
civil wars, 138, Table 6.1
debt and military spending,
    Table 6.9
debt service ratio, Table 1.5
debt and war, Table 6.4, Table 6.5
deforestation, 9, 10, 12, 13,
    Table 1.1, Table 1.2
variety of flora in, 22
industry:
loss of markets and jobs, 93
return on foreign capital
    investment (USA), 97, 98,
    Table 4.2
International Labour Organisation
    (ILO): refugee estimates, 112
International Monetary Fund, xiv
and Bolivia, 45–6
and capital flight, 90
and Caribbean, 117–18, 119
and Egypt, 157
Extended Fund Facilities (EFF),
    15
index of raw materials prices, 94
lack of accountability, 168–9
and Mexico, 25
and Peru, 48, 50–1, 52
policies and drug economy,
    45–6, 56–7
privatisation policy, 105
proportion of LDC debt
    holding, 86, 87
Stand-by Arrangements, 15
Iran:
arms imports, Table 6.6
debt and war, Table 6.1, Table 6.5
immigrants to USA, 120, Table
    5.2
refugees, Table 6.3
Iran–Iraq war, 155
Iraq:
arms imports, 153, 154, Table 6.6
debt and war, Table 6.1, Table
    6.4, Table 6.5
Gulf War, xx, 155, Table 6.1
refugees, Table 6.3
Ireland, migrant labour from, 123
island effect, and species
    extinction, 21

Israel:
    arms imports, 154, Table 6.6
    debt and war, 148, Table 6.4,
        Table 6.5, Table 6.9
    refugees, Table 6.3
    war with Palestinians, Table 6.1
Italy:
    commercial bank exposure to
        LDC debt, 81, Table 3.2,
        Table 3.3
    illegal immigrants in, 124, 128
    immigrants, 113, 131
    limited tax relief, 81, Table 3.4
    migrant labour from, 123
Ivory Coast *see* Côte d'Ivoire

J.P. Morgan bank, debt reduction,
    75
Jamaica:
    debt and war, Table 6.4
    immigrants to USA, 119, Table
        5.2
    political violence, 161, Table 6.8
    secondary market loan prices,
        Table 3.1
Japan:
    commercial bank exposure to
        LDC debt, 76–7, Table 3.2,
        Table 3.3
    exports to LDCs, 102, 104, Table
        4.3, Table 4.4
    Gulf War finance, 145
    and SE Asian deforestation, 19
    tax relief, 76–7, Table 3.4
    trade surplus, 101
    and USA trade policy, 101
job losses *see* unemployment
Jordan:
    and Gulf War, 156–7, 158
    political violence, 160, Table 6.7

Kenya:
    debt and war, Table 6.4, Table
        6.9
    political violence, 160, Table 6.7
Korea:
    immigrants to USA, 121, Table
        5.2
    war deaths, 142
Kuwait:
    debt and war, Table 6.5
    Gulf War, 147, Table 6.1

land reform, 29
Laos:
    debt and war, 148
    immigrants to USA, Table 5.2
Latin America:
    capital flight from, 90
    threat of war, 167
    US exports to, 95–6, 99, Table 4.1
law courts, drug-related offences in
    (USA), 35–6
Lebanon:
    debt and war, 138, Table 6.1,
        Table 6.5
    refugees, Table 6.3
Liberia:
    civil war, 165, Table 6.1
    debt and war, Table 6.5
    political violence, 162, Table 6.8
    US loan loss reserve
        requirement, 74
Libya, arms imports, Table 6.6
loan-loss reserve ('provision'), 65
    see also tax relief
Lutzenberger, José, Brazilian
    Environment Minister, 18
Luxembourg, migrant labour in,
    123

Madagascar:
    debt service ratio, Table 1.5
    debt and war, Table 6.4
    deforestation, 13, Table 1.1,
        Table 1.3, Table 1.4
Madagascar periwinkle: alkaloids
    from, 22
Malawi, Mozambican refugees in,
    130
Malaysia:
    continued violence, 166
    debt and war, Table 6.4
    deforestation, 12, 13, Table 1.1,
        Table 1.2
Mali, political violence, 160, Table
    6.7
malnutrition, in debtor countries,
    100
manufacturers, return on foreign
    capital investment (USA), 97,
    98, Table 4.2
maquiladora, Mexican-American
    border zone, 25–8
Marshall Plan, xv–xvi

Medellín cocaine syndicate, 52
medicines, from tropical plants,
    21–2, 24
Mexico:
    debt burden, 24–5, Table 1.5
    debt and war, Table 6.4, Table
        6.9
    debt-for-equity swaps, 75, 76
    deforestation, 10, 12, 13, Table
        1.1, Table 1.2, Table 1.3
    effect of oil prices on, 158
    high-condition EFF, 15
    immigration to USA, 120,
        121–2, Table 5.2
    political violence, 160–1, Table
        6.7
    pollution from border area, 26–7
    secondary market loan prices,
        Table 3.1
    and USA border, 24–8, 121–2
Middle East:
    arms imports, 151, 153
    refugees in, 142, Table 6.2
    wars in, 167
migrant workers, importance of
        remittances home, 131, 132
migration:
    causes of, 111–12, 132, 133
    East-West, 133
    rural-to-urban, 111, 118
    South-North, 111, 112
    see also immigrants; refugees
MILICs (Moderately Indebted Low-
        Income Countries), 71, 72
military spending:
    and debt, 163–4, Table 6.9
    see also arms trade
MIMICs (Moderately Indebted
        Middle-Income Countries),
        71, 72
minimum wage laws, 28, 31
Mitterrand, François, President of
        France, and immigrants, 132
Money Center banks (US), 75
Morocco:
    debt and war, 148, Table 6.4,
        Table 6.5
    migrant labour from, 123, 131
    political violence, 161, Table
        6.8
    secondary market loan prices,
        Table 3.1

war in Western Sahara, 138,
        Table 6.1
Mozambique:
    civil war, 142, 167, Table 6.1
    debt and war, 148, Table 6.4,
        Table 6.5
    refugees, Table 6.3
Myanmar (Burma):
    civil wars, 138, 166, Table 6.1
    debt service ratio, Table 1.5
    debt and war, 148, 164, Table
        6.4, Table 6.5
    deforestation, 9, 12, 13, Table
        1.1, Table 1.4

National Drug Control Strategy
        (USA), 34
National Institute of Drug Abuse
        (NIDA) (USA), 34–5
natural resources, exhaustion of,
        3–4
Nepal:
    debt and military spending,
        Table 6.9
    political violence, 161, Table 6.7
Netherlands:
    immigration, 123, 124, 129
    tax relief on LDC debt, 82
Nicaragua:
    civil war, 138, 142, Table 6.1
    debt service ratio, Table 1.5
    debt and war, 148, Table 6.4,
        Table 6.5
    refugees, Table 6.3
    US loan loss reserve
        requirement, 74
Niger:
    debt and war, Table 6.4
    political violence, 161, Table
        6.7
Nigeria:
    arms imports, 154
    debt service ratio, Table 1.5
    debt and war, Table 6.4
    deforestation, 10, 12, Table 1.1,
        Table 1.2
    effect of oil prices on, 158
    secondary market loan prices,
        Table 3.1
    war deaths, 142
Non-OPEC (NOPEC) countries, and
        export trade, 104, Table 4.6

North America:
  exports to LDCs, 102, 103–4,
      Table 4.3, Table 4.4
  see also USA
North Korea: arms imports, Table
      6.6

OECD:
  Permanent Observation System
      of Migrations (SOPEMI),
      127
  survey of public sector role, 108
oil:
  dependence on, 32
  prices and effect on trade, 104,
      158
OPEC countries, share of export
      trade, 104, Table 4.4, Table 4.6

Pakistan:
  Afghan refugees in, 130
  arms imports, Table 6.6
  debt and military spending,
      Table 6.9
  debt and war, 148, Table 6.1,
      Table 6.4, Table 6.5
Panama, political violence, 161,
      Table 6.8
Papua New Guinea:
  debt service ratio, Table 1.5
  debt and war, Table 6.1, Table
      6.5
  deforestation, 12, 13, Table 1.1,
      Table 1.4
Paraguay, deforestation, 13, Table
      1.1, Table 1.4
Peru:
  coca economy in, 39, 46–7,
      51–2, 55
  collapse of economy, 49–50
  collapse of public health system,
      50
  debt figures, 40, Table 2.1, Table
      2.2
  debt problems, 16, 47–9, Table
      2.3
  debt and war, 164, Table 6.1,
      Table 6.4, Table 6.5, Table 6.9
  deforestation, 12, 13, 55, Table
      1.1, Table 1.2
  secondary market loan prices,
      Table 3.1

  US drugs war in, 59, 60
  US loan loss reserve
      requirement, 74
pesticides, from tropical plants,
      21–2
Philippines:
  civil wars, 138, Table 6.1
  cost of Gulf War to, 131, 158
  debt service ratio, 14, Table 1.5
  debt and war, 164, Table 6.4,
      Table 6.5, Table 6.9
  deforestation, 9, 11, 13, Table
      1.1, Table 1.2, Table 1.3
  government spending priorities,
      4
  high-condition EFF, 15
  immigrants to USA, Table 5.2
  political violence, 161, Table
      6.8
  refugees, Table 6.3
  secondary market loan prices,
      Table 3.1
political asylum, 125–7, 135
political violence, 159–62, Table
      6.7, Table 6.8
pollution:
  and coca production, 54, 55–6
  from Tijuana-San Diego area,
      26–7
population growth:
  and migration, 133
  in tropical forest countries, 8
Portugal:
  illegal immigrants in, 124, 128
  migrant labour from, 123
poverty:
  as cause of migration, 112
  and drugs in USA, 36–7
  and ecology, 3
privatisation, 105–6, 109
  effects of, 108
  of transport systems, 107
'provision' (loan-loss reserve) *see*
      tax relief
public sector role, OECD survey,
      108

Qatar, debt and war, Table 6.1,
      Table 6.5

reforestation *see* deforestation;
      forests

refugees:
  from wars, 142–3, Table 6.2,
    Table 6.3
  proportion in Europe, 130
  statistics, 112, Table 6.2, Table
    6.3
  see also immigrants; migration
roads, financed by World Bank
  (Brazil), 16, 17
rubber tappers, Brazil, 29
Rwanda:
  debt and war, Table 6.1, Table
    6.5
  refugees, Table 6.3

Saddam Hussein, motives for
  invading Kuwait, 155
Saudi Arabia:
  arms imports, 153, 154, Table 6.6
  debt and war, Table 6.5
  Gulf War, 147, Table 6.1
schools, role in immigrant
  integration, 130–1
secondary markets in loans *see* debt
  trading
Senegal, groundnut scheme, 3
Seoul, World Bank-IMF meeting
  (1985), 89
shifted cultivators, 16, 17–18
Shining Path (*Sendero Luminoso*)
  guerrillas in Peru, 60
SILICs (Severely Indebted Low-
  Income Countries), 71, 72
SIMICs (Severely Indebted Middle-
  Income Countries), 71, 72
  German bank exposure to, 80
  Japanese bank exposure to, 76
smuggling, of people, 121–2
social equity, need for, 29, 171
Somalia:
  civil war, 165, Table 6.1
  debt and war, 148, Table 6.4,
    Table 6.5
  refugees, Table 6.3
South Africa:
  debt and war, Table 6.1, Table 6.5
  refugees, Table 6.3
South America, refugees in, Table
  6.2
South Korea:
  arms imports, Table 6.6
  debt and war, Table 6.4

Southeast Asia, Japanese
  deforestation of, 19
sovereign loans, 67, 83–4
soybeans, in Brazil, 16
Spain:
  birth rate, 128
  illegal immigrants in, 124, 128
  migrant labour from, 123
  tax relief on LDC debt, 82
species destruction, 4, 20–1
Sri Lanka:
  civil war, Table 6.1
  debt and war, 148, Table 6.5,
    Table 6.9
  effect of Gulf War, 131
  immigrants to Europe, 125
  refugees, Table 6.3
Stand-by Arrangements (IMF), 15
structural adjustment programmes
  (IMF), 2–3
Sudan:
  civil war, Table 6.1
  debt service ratio, Table 1.5
  debt and war, 148, Table 6.5
  high-condition EFF, 15
  political violence, 162, Table 6.8
  projected population figures, 133
  refugees, Table 6.3
  US loan loss reserve
    requirement, 74
Suriname:
  civil war, Table 6.1
  debt and war, Table 6.5
Sweden, migrant labour in, 123
Switzerland:
  commercial bank exposure to
    LDC debt, 81, Table 3.2,
    Table 3.3
  immigrant birth rate, 129
  migrant labour in, 123
  requests for political asylum, 126
  and USA trade policy, 101
Syria:
  arms imports, Table 6.6
  debt and war, Table 6.1, Table
    6.5

Taiwan:
  arms imports, Table 6.6
  immigrants to USA, Table 5.2
tax, not payable on non-resident
  income, 91

tax relief:
    for commercial banks, 65–7
    limits of, 70
    by secondary markets in loans,
        67–9
    sums involved in, 83
    US mechanisms for, 73–5
taxpayers:
    cost of tax relief to, 83, 84, 91–2
    funding third world debt, 63–4
telephone companies, acquired in
    debt-for-equity swaps, 75
Thailand:
    debt and war, Table 6.4
    deforestation, 9, 13, Table 1.1,
        Table 1.2, Table 1.3
Thatcher, Margaret, privatisation
    policy, 105–6
Tijuana-San Diego metropolitan
    area, 26–7
tin mining, collapse of market, 43–4
Toronto summit (1988), 88
toxic waste *see* pollution
trade reforms, proposed, 134–5
trade, world: uneven expansion in,
    94–5
transnational corporations, 18, 31
transport systems, privatisation of,
    107
Trinidad and Tobago, political
    violence, 161, Table 6.7
Tropical Forestry Action Plan
    (TFAP), 29
Tunisia, political violence, Table 6.8
Turkey:
    arms imports, Table 6.6
    debt and military spending,
        Table 6.9
    debt and war, 148, Table 6.4,
        Table 6.5
    Kurdish refugees in, 130
    migrant labour from, 123, 131
    political violence, 161, Table 6.8
    projected population figures, 133
    war against Kurds, Table 6.1

Uganda:
    civil wars, 165, Table 6.1
    debt and military spending,
        Table 6.9
    debt and war, 148, Table 6.4,
        Table 6.5

    refugees, Table 6.3
unemployment:
    and drugs in USA, 36
    job losses in USA, 96, 101, Table
        4.1
United Kingdom:
    commercial bank exposure to
        LDC debt, Table 3.2, Table
        3.3
    debt and war, 147
    immigrants to USA, Table 5.2
    immigration, 123, 125, 128
    Matrix debt rating system, 77–8
    migrant labour in, 123
    tax relief on LDC debt, 77–9,
        Table 3.4
United Nations Environment
    Programme (UNEP): refugee
    estimates, 112
Uruguay:
    debt and war, Table 6.4
    secondary market loan prices,
        Table 3.1
USA:
    agricultural exports, 99–100
    banks favoured over jobs and
        trade, 101–2
    banks' return on foreign
        investment, 96, 97–8,
        Table 4.1, Table 4.2
    and Bolivia, 46
    commercial bank exposure to
        LDC debt, 72–6, Table 3.2,
        Table 3.3
    debt factor in Gulf War, 156,
        157–8
    debt service, 150, Chart 6.2
    debt and war, 147
    drug problem in, 34–7
    drugs war in S America, 38, 46,
        53, 57–61
    federal deficit, 148, Chart 6.1
    immigration debate, 114–15
    immigration from Caribbean,
        116, 118–19
    immigration from Mexico, 121–2
    immigration statistics, 119–20,
        122–3, Table 5.2
    job losses, 96–7, 101–2
    manufacturers' return on
        foreign investment, 97,
        98, Table 4.2

and Mexico, 26–7, 121–2
military aid to Colombia, 53
military intervention, 115–16,
    Table 6.1
military spending, 148, 149–50
pollution from Mexican border,
    26–7
tax relief, 73, Table 3.4
trade deficit, 101–2
trade with Latin America, 95–6,
    Table 4.1
trade policies, 31, 38, 101–2
USAID, and migration, 119
USSR/Soviet Union, refugees, Table
    6.3

Vavilov centres, gene banks, 23
Venezuela:
    debt service ratio, Table 1.5
    debt and war, Table 6.4, Table 6.9
    debt-for-equity swaps, 75
    deforestation, 12, 13, Table 1.1,
        Table 1.2
    effect of oil prices on, 158
    high-condition EFF, 15
    political violence, 161, Table 6.7
    secondary market loan prices,
        Table 3.1
Vietnam:
    debt and war, 148, Table 6.4
    deforestation, 9, Table 1.1, Table
        1.2, Table 1.3
    immigrants in USA, 116, 121,
        Table 5.2
    war deaths, 142
violence, political *see* political
    violence

war:
    casualties of, 138–9, 142, 144,
        Table 6.1
    as cause of migration, 112
    civil, 138

Clausewitz's link with policy,
    164–5
and continued violence,
    165–6
definition of, 137–8
international, 138
number of, 138, Table 6.1
relationship with debt, 136,
    144–5, 158, Table 6.4,
    Table 6.5
Wells Fargo bank, debt reduction,
    75
Western Sahara, debt and war, 138,
    Table 6.1, Table 6.5
World Bank, xiv
    bondholder losses, 89
    and Caribbean, 117–18, 119
    categories of indebted countries,
        72
    lack of accountability, 168–9
    privatisation policy, 105, 106
    proportion of LDC debt
        holding, 86, 87
World Commission on
    Environment and
    Development (Bruntland
    Commission), 24

Yemen, cost of Gulf War, 158
Yugoslavia, migrant labour from,
    123

Zaire:
    deforestation, 12, 13, Table
        1.1
    high-condition EFF, 15
    political violence, Table 6.8
    US loan loss reserve
        requirement, 74
Zambia, political violence, 161,
    Table 6.7
Zimbabwe, debt and war, Table
    6.1, Table 6.5